SOUL
RESCUERS

SOUL RESCUERS

A 21st Century Guide to the Spirit World

TERRY & NATALIA O'SULLIVAN

Thorsons

CONTENTS

Thorsons
An Imprint of HarperCollins*Publishers*
77–85 Fulham Palace Road
Hammersmith, London W6 8JB

The Thorsons website address is: www.thorsons.com

Published in hardback by Thorsons 1999
This paperback edition 2000

10 9 8 7 6 5 4 3 2 1

Illustrations by Josephine Sumner

Some names and places have been changed

A catalogue record for this book
is available from the British Library

ISBN 0 7225 4041 8

Printed in Great Britain by
The Bath Press, Bath

To Kadamba Simmons
for her love, beauty, sense of adventure and freedom

ACKNOWLEDGEMENTS

A special thanks to Nicola Graydon, our co-author, for her tireless and industrious contribution; the interviews, stories, research and editorial inspiration. Without her determined efforts this book would not be such a powerful read.

Thanks to our ancestors and spirit helpers who have guided us for keeping the heart of the soul rescuers intact. A big 'thank you' to all our family and friends who have already moved into the spirit world for their encouragement and visions of the afterlife; and to our children, Sequoia, Ossian and Bede, for their patience and love as we spent so much time completing the manuscript.

Thank you to our publishers and editorial staff including Michelle Pilley for commissioning us and Lizzie Hutchins for her precise attention to minute detail, patience and tolerance. Without their help this book would not have been born. Thanks also to Dave O'Sullivan from *Spirit* magazine for his unconditional generosity in encouraging our writing talents in his magazine.

We were gifted with the experience and vision from practitioners, shamans, healers and spiritual leaders from many world traditions. Denise Linn, Malidoma Patrice Somé, Credo Mutwa, Emma Restall Orr, Bishop Simon Barrington Ward, Father Edward, Canon Andrew Harvey, Lillian Too, Lama Khemsar Rinpoche and Sister Jemini of Brahma Kumari all spoke to us about the journey of the soul and the craft of soul rescue. Words of wisdom came too from those who help the dying to move through the gateway of death, including hospice workers, nurses, midwives, bereavement and palliative care experts and undertakers. Special thanks to Clare Proust, formerly of The Voyager Trust, Dame Cicely Saunders, Julia Riley, Soizic Aureli, Margaret McGovern, Gillian Lewis, Ali Woozley, Susan Bowes, the paediatricians of Great Ormond

Street Children's Hospital, Roger Gillman Funeral Services, Aggie Richards, Janet Cox, Yvette Tamara, Steven Upton.

And thank you to all our family, friends and clients who sent in stories, experiences and anecdotes to add to the heart of the book: my mother Purita Kovacs, Genie Leiras, Christina Afentakis, Janine Clements, Liz Whiston, Victoria Harvey, Sue Thoday, Diana Scrimgeour, Frank Ozak, Jessie Gabriel, Jack Pleasant, Eileen Quirke, Taryn Hill, Anna Castana, Michelle Bayliss, Nikkita and Joey Rae, Sheila Simpson, Colin Fry, Jenny Waite, Tina Laurent, Connie Beigler, Caro Ness, Bobbie Spargo, Tai and Viv Long.

Generosity of spirit to: Kadamba Simmons' family, John, Kumari and Linda, to Robin Bailie, Patrick Riley, Kathy and Amy Eldon, George Barker of Flying Rhino, Anita Overland, Emma Westcott, Amina Ricciardi, Mary Summers, Ken and Zina Wiwa, Colleen and Philippa Johnson, Jo Lal, Lara Burgess and Isobel for sharing their moving, powerful stories about their loved ones who have died. Although many stories could not be included, the final text is enriched by their love, compassion and courage.

Extra thanks to Marco Wilson for his inspirational contribution and to Mick Brown and Barbara Erskine.

The following extracts are reprinted with grateful acknowledgement:
Rudyard Kipling, *Wee Willie Winkie and Other Stories*, published by permission of A.P. Watt Ltd on behalf of The National Trust for Places of Historic Interest or Natural Beauty.
Timothy Leary, *Design for Dying*, published by permission of Thorsons.
C.S. Lewis, *The Last Battle*, published by permission of HarperCollins*Publishers* Ltd.
Caitlín Matthews, *Singing the Soul Back Home*, published by permission of Element Books Limited, Shaftesbury.

PREFACE

Not long after beginning to write this book a great friend and our children's favourite babysitter was murdered by her boyfriend. She had been preparing to come and stay with us for a retreat which we hold during the summer solstice, but instead we got a call telling us that she was dead. The great shock was followed by deep sadness that this young woman who had so much to live for and who gave so much to life could be killed in this senseless way.

Kadamba, whose name means 'The Flower of Enlightenment', had a beauty and wild charisma which meant that she was seen at all the right parties. She dated Prince Naseem Hamed and Liam Gallagher among other high profile boyfriends while modelling and waiting for her big break into the movies. Called the 'star's star' by the Icelandic pop star Björk, Kadamba had an indefinable quality which the rich and famous hungered for. Portia, her best friend, described being with her as 'like taking off in a plane. It wasn't necessarily smooth, because she was such a ball of energy, but she made things happen and she always took you with her. She was always so generous with people.'

Two years prior to her death, Kadamba had turned away from her party lifestyle and begun to seek some spiritual meaning to her life. She took a sabbatical from modelling and acting, withdrew completely from her high profile friends and became interested first in Buddhism and then shamanism. Many were surprised by her commitment to developing the spiritual side of her life. So was she. She said to us once, 'Why am I doing all this spiritual stuff now, when I am so young? Maybe I should wait until I am older.' But she kept coming, bringing a dancing energy to our workshops and a spiritual maturity which was older than her 24 years.

When she first came to join our shamanic retreats in Somerset she was totally inner city London, dressed in black, tramping over the Quantocks carrying a little red umbrella and complaining about the mud. By the third time she had fallen in love with nature. On one of her last retreats she came back from the woods ecstatically happy. She said that whatever or whoever God was she had felt it. She had found herself merging with the nature around her and seen and felt how alive everything was. 'Spirit is everywhere,' she said. 'It's incredible!'

Soon afterwards she escaped to India, the place where she felt most at home. No one there knew about her high profile life in London, so she was free to just be herself. Portia, who joined her for what would be their last adventure together, had never seen her more beautiful or more at peace.

Some months later she returned to Britain full of plans for the future, although in hindsight it seems as though some part of her knew that she was going to die. She went to see many of her old friends whom she had not seen for ages and, less than a week before she was killed in a flat in London, she said to Portia, 'You know, I've got a feeling that I have really bad karma on this planet. But when I die I'm going to go home and I'm not coming back here.'

After her death, several members of her family and close friends spoke about feeling or seeing her spirit either coming to talk to them as a shadow in the background or as an atmosphere of laughter which was very much her personality. She visited us in dreams. In the first she was trapped and unable to leave the flat that she had died in. I tried to speak to her but she couldn't talk in words and she would not let me touch her. She looked like a corpse, her face was white and her hair long, unkempt. I remember trying to show her the way out of the flat. Eventually she let me take her hand and lead her out.

Two weeks later I dreamt that we went to a high cliff overlooking the sea to Wales, where her mother had come from. She held on to an orange cord in my solar plexus and pulled herself forward to fly in the air. The pain in my solar plexus was excruciating, as it seemed as if she was using my living, grounded energy to help her. As she flew into the air she released dark unhappy women from under her skirts. It occurred to us that with this action she was freeing herself from the ancestral ties that bound her and that she was releasing these women so that they too could find freedom.

Some weeks later we met again, only this time she was surrounded by a halo of light, holding the hand of a tall angelic spirit and looking light and liberated from the trauma of her death. She told me then that she would attend her funeral and go to the world of spirit immediately afterwards. For proof of her presence she said we would see a cloud of butterflies. She had always loved butterflies.

Her visits to us and others were frequent up until her funeral. For friends and family this was a deeply painful time as their grieving process was constantly interrupted by the police and the press and they had to wait three weeks for the funeral. This was a strange limbo time. Kadamba's mother was only allowed to see her daughter's body behind glass. All she wanted to do was to brush her hair, but she could not. The family was not even allowed a priest to anoint the body.

In Tibetan culture rituals continue for 49 days after any death, but with a violent death the anniversary is celebrated every week, for it is said that the soul will return to the death experience each week until the memory is extinguished by the process of purification. In the aftermath of Kadamba's death we followed the Tibetan prescription, lighting candles and saying special prayers on the weekly anniversaries. Everything seemed more agitated on those days and our grief was closer to the surface. It seemed that Kadamba was indeed returning to the moment of her death, but each week it became less intense. As with the dreams, there seemed to be a process whereby she was becoming lighter.

For our summer solstice workshop which she should have attended we prepared a shrine for her with a photograph, some candles and red roses, her favourite flowers. We continued to light candles and say special prayers for her.

The night before her funeral her body was laid out in the funeral parlour and friends and family sat with her. Many were crying as they sang and chanted. They were finally able to release some of the grief which they had contained since she had died. Portia recalls, 'Everyone was putting things in her coffin. Rings, flowers, letters, mementos – all went in. There was hardly any room for her!'

At the funeral Portia remembered Kadamba's words just before she died and at one small moment when a stream of sunlight came through the stained-glass windows her heart lifted as she said to her friend, 'Go, girl. Fly. Fly as high and as fast as you can. Go home.'

The cortège made its way to the cemetery and streams of people walked to the small hill where Kadamba was to be buried flanked by a Celtic cross and an angel. As we gathered in the brilliant sunshine of midsummer a cloud of pink and black butterflies flew up behind the grave. It was just as Kadamba had told us. Butterflies are a powerful symbol of immortality and despite our grief we felt that Kadamba had gone to the spirit world and that she was safe. Occasionally we feel her presence on the beach looking across to Wales and we know that she watches over her beloved sister Kumari.

Kadamba's grave has become a place of pilgrimage for family and friends who need to be close to her. During the late summer following her death it looked like a pirate ship – the wooden plinth was laden with pots of flowers, candles, tiny statues and a dolphin wind chime. As summer turned to autumn it continued to grow as more and more people brought gifts and a notebook with a pencil was put in a plastic case for messages, poems and prayers. There were spices from all corners of the world, tiny cars, crystals, paintings, bindies, locks of hair and jewellery. At Christmas Kadamba had two Christmas trees, a full nativity play at the front of the grave and crystals, stars and Christmas cards on the holly bush behind.

'Her grave is not dead, it is alive,' Portia laughs as she describes the seasonal transformations of her friend's grave. 'It grows. I think she would be really happy with it. It reflects all of her. It is spiritual, wacky, kitsch and stylish all at the same time. She even has a lipstick there. There is an energy at the grave which is so alive. Everyone has put so much thought and love into it. No one has forgotten her and in essence she is still here.'

At the reception after the funeral, as everyone gently tried to celebrate in the sunshine despite their sadness, our older son Ossian came running over to us. He grabbed our hands and pulled us around the house to the other side. 'Look, look,' he said and pointed into the sky. 'There's Kadamba!' We looked up and sure enough there she was in the form of a beautiful white cloud in the shape of an angel with the biggest wings you've ever seen.

INTRODUCTION

WHAT IS A SOUL RESCUER?

A soul rescuer is known as a psychic, healer, shaman, priest, mystic, visionary, pagan, Spiritualist, channel and exorcist. This is a person who is able to walk between the world of the physical and the dimensions of the spirit. As a 'walker between worlds' they must be initiated into the techniques and rituals used in the physical world to rescue trapped spirits, heal the sick and mend the wounds of the soul.

This gift may require a person to help the dying, to bury the dead and pray for the release of the soul into the otherworld. Some soul rescuers rescue the spirits of the dead who are wandering ghosts or earthbound entities; these are not usually evil, but trapped or lost.

Some soul rescuers – the shamans, priests and mystics – seek to cure the sickness in a person's soul. This is exorcism in the traditional Christian sense: they deliver evil from a place or person. They communicate with the spirits and understand the rules of co-existence with the otherworld. They have learnt to walk the dangerous path of death and rebirth, surviving initiations involving all kinds of natural and supernatural phenomena while remaining faithful to their beliefs. We ourselves have followed this path.

THE INNOCENT GHOST HUNTER

As I recall I had just left school at the tender age of 15. At my first job in a shoe factory, making ladies' high-heeled shoes and the winkle pickers that were very popular during the 1960s, I made friends with Gordon Landles, an older boy around 19 years old. At the time he was a devout Christian, a member of the local Baptist church. I was a more rebellious character, interested in pop music and motorbikes. But we still hit it off.

During the breaks at work, Gordon and I began deep discussions exploring belief in God, life after death and any topic surrounding the Holy Ghost. Gordon would use any method he could to try and convert me to the Baptist Church, as if he were one of Jesus' great crusaders. Unfortunately for Gordon it went over my head and I would only use his arguments as ammunition in our discussions.

One day we strayed into the unusual territory of the paranormal and whether we believed in ghosts, as there had been the sighting of a ghost at the factory. It had taken place in the basement, where the shoes were stored and dispatched. The ghost had actually been seen and heard by several staff over the years. When the machinery was switched off and silence fell on the shop floor, shuffling noises would be followed by a clunking sound and then a dragging, scraping noise would echo across the stone floor, causing many of the grown men in the factory to run away or stop stone dead in their tracks. The ghost was nicknamed 'Stumpy'; he appeared to be an old sailor with a wooden leg. It was believed he was a seaman who had died in tragic circumstances and as a result was unable to rest in peace.

This inspired Gordon and I to go on a ghost hunt, although neither of us had seen Stumpy, even though we had spent the night in the basement awaiting a ghostly encounter with him. We decided to go to a haunted graveyard, at night, just to prove the existence of ghosts. The haunting of factories, burial grounds, hospitals, pubs and castles was well documented in many books. I suspect Gordon had some romantic notion of catching sight of a guardian angel, just like St Paul had seen on the road to Damascus, and I had always had a fascination for the supernatural.

It was a cold winter's evening – 1963 was particularly cold. Having chosen a Saxon church with a derelict churchyard, we packed a snack and prepared ourselves for a night vigil. Gordon negotiated the iced dirt track on his motorbike with me riding pillion. We arrived safely and began to search around the grounds. The church dated from around AD 800 and lay in open ground. It had a wooden perimeter fence and gate, and the surrounding land was farmed with scrub and heath, reaching out like a hand into the bitterly cold North Sea.

Gordon left the motorbike at the gate and left the main beam shining at the privet hedge around the fence, so we could see. There were no streetlights and the moon was not yet full. We made our way separately across the graveyard, trying our best to avoid standing on the old gravestones, which mainly lay sunken in the sandy soil, eroded by time and the elements.

After a short time Gordon began to get edgy and to complain about the cold wind shaking the old church and causing creaking noises to join in the symphony of squeaking trees. But I was unwilling to give up our ghost hunt.

Then I lost sight of Gordon for a while. He disappeared as if swallowed up by the ground. When he did reappear his face was ashen white, as if reflecting a full moon on a still lake. He had seen 'something' in the courtyard of the church. He wanted to leave immediately, but I insisted that he took me back to the place. As we walked around the front of the church there was an apparition – tall, still and ethereal.

Terrified, we left the church and skidded across the ice on the motorbike until, miraculously, we reached town in one piece.

Though what we had seen could have been a shadow of one of the trees against the light of the motorbike, I always wanted to believe that it really had been an apparition and this was the beginning of my interest in haunted places. At that time I had no idea that in the future I would see ghosts and apparitions as real as the physical body and experience poltergeists and malevolent ghosts causing paranormal activity worthy of Hollywood movies.

I had, however, always had an awareness on a psychic level. When you are young you think everyone is the same as you. Then it transpires that you are set apart from others, because of this gift. It is easy to compensate by trying too hard to fit in, to be everyone's friend. In doing so the psychic gift then gradually becomes a curse, as people demand advice and support from you or they begin to see you as weird or eccentric. Some will even accuse you of being evil or of doing the work of the Devil!

MY CHILDHOOD INITIATION

I saw my first ghost when I was very young. I remember being in my cot and seeing a strange-looking person standing before me in a purple robe. He looked quite like the mysterious Dr Fu Manchu, the Chinese character in the books of Sax Rohmer. This spirit was obviously a Mandarin Chinese. He had disappeared by the time I was about seven years old and we had moved to a different house. He appeared to me 20 years later through a psychic channelling medium. He said his name was Ching Ling and that he wished to help guide me through my life. He was my first experience with the spirit world.

I also recall seeing other spirits who used to come and stand by my bed. It never occurred to me to ask who they were or why they were there. After all, we used to say a prayer in school asking 'angels to guard us while we slept', so it seemed only natural that these were the angels of my prayers, even though they looked more like people than angels.

So, by the time I was 13 years old, I had already experienced psychic encounters, as well as religious enlightenment. The religious moment came after my first confession. I was brought up as a Roman Catholic. After the first confession, the initiate is expected to turn up for a full confirmation ceremony and to receive the life of Christ. I stood up and immediately felt ecstatic, immortal, as though anything in life could be achieved or made possible. I had visions of angels. I was probably about eight years old at the time. I talked about how I felt to my peer group at school. We had all had different experiences, but mine seemed quite special. At that time I knew I loved God and Jesus, but I was in love with Mary, I believed her to be the Mother of the World.

However, there is a large gap between the ages of eight and 13, and by this time, though a lot of my original faith had held fast, the injustices of the world seduced me into questioning my relationship with the Church. The 'angels' had long since disappeared and my visions of immortality had been overtaken by my interest in listening to rock 'n' roll on radio's Saturday Club. The chart hits of the day and my growing awareness of girls became central interests in my life.

When I was 13 my maternal grandfather died. Grandfather Cooke was one of those 'salt of the earth' characters who work hard all their lives for little financial reward. Neither did he expect any charity. He was born during the 1880s, when everyone knew their place, whether rich or poor. He would not have called himself a Christian, but he did believe in Jesus. In fact he told me that his brother once saw Jesus walking through the living room, 'as plain as day'. This vision of the Lord was probably enough to lend him the faith to prepare him for the afterlife.

He died on the chimes of midnight on New Year's Eve 1960. Grandmother Cooke moved into our small flat the very next day. In a hurry she had neglected to bring along some essential things, which I was asked to go and collect.

It did not bother me going to the house, I always had a good relationship with my grandparents and I was very happy to help out in any way I could. It was only when I arrived at the front door that I had my doubts about going in. It was not the ghost of my grandfather that worried me, but I had to walk past the cupboard on the landing where the 'bogey man' lived. I had been brought up in this house from my birth until I was seven years old and when I broke the rules I was threatened with the bogey man. Much later in life I learned to understand this fear lay within my imagination, but at 13 the bogey man represented the Devil himself, 'Old Nick'. I stood shaking with fear, a sweaty hand clutching at the key which would unlock the door. I was rooted to the spot for what seemed like an eternity. Time had stood still, life had frozen and I could not move my hand. It was only when a friendly dog barked that I snapped out of this entranced state. Slowly I turned the key and the door slid wide open.

Walking over the threshold of that old Victorian terraced house was like walking into the land of the dead. I had never before encountered anyone close dying or being dead. What struck me was the whole atmosphere of the house. It bore inside me and created a feeling of being wrapped in a blanket of cold sweat. I moved as fast as my jellied legs would carry me. First, I went to the living room and pulled a knife from the drawer. This was not to kill a ghost or assailant, but should I encounter the bogey man in the cupboard, I would be as ready for him as any 13-year-old boy would be when stricken by fear!

The house felt heavy, it heaved with death and even possibly ghosts, but I had no fear of them. As they had never bothered me in the past they were no threat now. I felt safe in my relationship with the otherworld. But still I could not call the angels to drive the bogey man away.

Eventually I passed my test of manhood by confronting the cupboard, my curiosity proving greater than my fear. Very slowly I lifted the latch. The door creaked open and squeaked, as it probably had not been opened since Queen Elizabeth's coronation in 1953. The old cupboard housed a flagpole, still with the Union Jack furled around it. The only other object I saw was an old trumpet gramophone which I had never heard being played. I shut the door, gathered my grandmother's things and walked out of the house. This was the only time I feared a confrontation with a being, imaginary or otherwise. I felt I had passed my first initiation.

It was around this time I experienced vivid dreams, which were frightening, but at the same time very entertaining. I would go to bed awaiting the next instalment. It was much like watching television. The characters, however, seemed real. They were moving through life and death scenarios, always violent, which culminated in the eventual death of the character who appeared to be me. Night after night this hero was killed and the shock always woke me up in a cold sweat, wondering where I was.

After a while, the dreams became an indelible part of my life, haunting me, taking me over. I changed my hairstyle, the clothes I wore and my personal hobbies and interests in line with the dream characters. Then one night the dreams just stopped, as if someone had taken the video cassette out of my mind and put it away so I could never find it again afterwards.

Many years later I would experience a sequence of events which would uncover the mystery attached to those early dreams. At night the world of ghosts embraces our living world through dreams and visions. The spirit world crosses over the subconscious and touches on the magical or the terrifying, until the mind has time to work out the past or the connection with the otherworld.

MY ADOLESCENCE

Grandmother Cooke, who now lived with us, was the daughter of a Romany Gypsy. Although she was a Christian, she was never afraid of being psychic and showing off her gift. She could read tea-leaves, divine meanings from a pack of playing cards and even tell the future from reading the shapes in the froth which formed in a beer glass during or after the drink. She treated it as an everyday occurrence and friends and neighbours used to pop in constantly to ask her advice.

This gave me the confidence not to underestimate my own psychic skills. I have never felt threatened or truly afraid of any encounter that I have had, even when working as a soul rescuer in places of darkness and malevolence. My early experiences of the spirit world taught me patience, how to communicate with the ordinary earthbound spirit and the difference between a ghost and a haunting.

In the fishing town where I was brought up, the conflicts in the streets and clubs were caused by drunken trawler crews hardened by long stints on the high seas. My intuition, or gut feelings, which are the basic instincts of all psychics, served me well during these times. Being psychic enabled me to hear unspoken voices from people and from the souls of earthbound spirits who would come and haunt the drunken sailors and others, taunting the living into violent behaviour or uncontrollable actions. I was usually able to detect trouble by feeling a build up in the atmosphere, though in some cases violence seemed to ooze up from the very grounds of the dance halls and nightclubs in which we gathered. I could hear the spirits' intentions and ill will; I could hear the land and the buildings echo past events, sacred memories to the violation of the human spirit.

For many years I could not place why I had these abilities and as I became more aware of how far apart they set me from others I became oversensitive and insecure. By my early twenties I found myself in a Spiritualist church. It was dark, badly lit and with a rather daunting atmosphere. I met my first medium, a very old lady whose way of communicating with the spirits of the dead inspired me. She was the first to tell me that I had a natural talent. She instructed me to develop my psychic gifts and through her guidance I realized the difference between a psychic and a channel for spirit communication.

It became obvious to me that I needed a larger environment in which to develop, so I moved to London. Almost immediately I was thrown in the deep end as within a month of contacting the local Spiritualist church

I was encouraged to become a probationary healer. I joined a development group and within a short time they realized that my gifts were unusual so moved me on to helping their rescue circle.

Rescue circles help lost souls to be relocated to family and friends. This was my first stage in becoming an apprentice soul rescuer. For two years as this work gathered pace I found myself working six nights a week in soul rescue and spirit communication while holding down a professional job in a large international company. This kept me grounded in the physical world, whilst my spare time was spent in the other world.

There were three crafts I was learning at this time which all demanded different techniques. My healing gift was in its infancy, but as I began developing a channel of light, I felt as though I was in contact with the higher powers. Being a conduit for a power source through the laying on of hands felt as though taps were being turned on and a flood of tingling, pulsating life-force would come out, often leaving a feeling of elevation, as if I was physically standing above the ground.

Then came the rescue of disembodied spirits. This practice is vital to many people who had died, sometimes tragically or in great fear of death, or with no belief in an afterlife. This is where I began to understand earthbound spirits and the conditions in which they remained after death – their world, their emotions and their psychological problems.

The Spiritualist rescue groups which I attended attracted well-meaning psychics who believed in a greater order of souls, angels and gods. Denomination was unimportant, but being psychic was necessary, as was possessing good counselling skills and the ability to use them on an unseen human being!

But after two years of learning psychic, healing and communication skills I began to find the work with the church limiting, particularly as I was in my early twenties while many who ran the organization at that time were in their sixties.

MY FIRST TEACHER

One Wednesday evening I attended a demonstration by a clairvoyant called Joan Bajzert. After the demonstration, Joan came over to me for a chat. As we talked we discovered how many beliefs we had in common.

Joan was not a natural psychic; in fact she had had no intention of working with spirits until she had been involved in a car accident. After a near death experience, during many months of recovery in hospital she started to see spirits, people who were invisible to everyone else. This shocked her, especially when her ability did not leave her even after she left hospital.

Shortly afterwards, whilst at home recuperating, she saw a Native American who introduced himself as 'Blue Feather'. Initially she thought he was dressed for a fancy dress party, only to realize he was a true Native American. She wasn't hallucinating. Her NDE had opened the door to an altered dimension; she was 'seeing' another reality. After this visit Joan and Blue Feather agreed that she would work under his tutelage and assist in the work of rescuing disembodied spirits.

It was the guiding wisdom of Blue Feather which encouraged my own natural and raw power to develop into the skills of a soul rescuer. Joan and I would sit together and Blue Feather would channel through her body to the point where Joan's personality would totally disappear and Blue Feather would transform her features and voice into his own. In these times, he would talk about his life in the spirit world, about his family and wife; he would explain how he had incarnated as a shaman not only in the Americas but also in Africa, and as a result of a friendship made in that life his minder was a powerful African called Chumba.

Slowly I was realizing the various levels within the spirit realms and how they could penetrate the physical. I understood the guidance and spiritual protection needed when rescuing spirits. These soul rescuers from the other side of life are usually referred to as 'guides', as they can guide the earthbound spirits to a suitable place to heal, convalesce and forget who they were and remember who they really are within the spirit realms. Later in my life, I discovered how the support and guidance from the spirit world help considerably in offsetting the physical reaction to soul rescue, and gained the ability to cleanse a home or place of an entity without the need to be so physically attacked.

My first experience as an assistant soul rescuer came one day when I was invited to visit a house with a poltergeist. When we arrived it was a dull and rainy day. Thunder was coming from the direction of Heathrow airport, close by. The owner of the house did not believe in ghosts, but she was at her wit's end. She had had the house blessed by the local priest but the phenomena had not gone away. In fact the presence of the vicar had stirred up the spirit and the phenomena were getting worse.

When we arrived Joan began to recite the Lord's Prayer. This was her method of calling in the spirit and cleansing the space of negative energy. When the poltergeist began its assault, first a glass flew across the room and smashed against the wall. Then it turned its attack on Joan. As she was being protected by her guides, the effect on her was minimal. I was the unprotected sitting duck. Suddenly I felt a wind rush around my feet as if it were trying to knock me over. I stood my ground and then, with no other knowledge to call on, said some prayers. The next moment, I was rocking from side to side, assaulted by an invisible force which began to ride my back. This attack seemed to go on for some time. I attempted to throw the attacker off, but I couldn't do it. Then it slowly dawned on me that the spirit attacking me was stuck in or holding on to my electromagnetic field. He couldn't get out, so, like a fly trapped by a spider, he wriggled and jiggled until eventually all went quiet and I felt him slither to the floor.

Joan stopped praying and peace was restored. The poltergeist, which turned out to be an angry earthbound spirit, was taken away by the guides to a place of correction within the spirit worlds.

I was shocked and battered by my experience. Unable to talk, I collapsed onto the sofa, but after a few minutes, and a glass of cold water, I felt myself again. I had survived my first attack by a spirit and had discovered that I had the power to control the impulse of an entity, however angry.

I had been initiated into soul rescue.

The soul who has passed from a physical state and human consciousness into a parallel world soon leaves behind its relationship with the physical world. The earthbound spirit is one which has not been able to move beyond its habitat, attitudes, environment or status, and so it remains, often disenchanted, angry and even pompous. In many cases this is the reason why the spirit is earthbound in the first place.

There are disembodied spirits who wish only evil to befall the living, who wish to cause them harm or who just become a nuisance. They enjoy cruelty and play psychological games with the minds of the living through haunting and 'riding' the backs of their living descendants. I realized I needed to have more experience and knowledge of how to deal with the more malevolent spirits, including unruly ancestral family entities. My work as a soul rescuer began moving away from the Spiritualists and their concept of life after death to the more universal understanding of shamanism and esoteric teachings.

In the past I have been called a 'ghost therapist', which I have taken as a compliment, as I can see how appropriate this term actually is. The skill of the soul rescuer lies in trying to convince the disembodied visitor of three things: first, that they are physically dead; secondly, that they can choose where to go; thirdly, that safe passage can be arranged to their chosen destiny, either to their ancestors or to other realms within the spirit kingdoms. Once you have helped the spirit to adjust to a spiritual dimension, its dependence on physical attachments soon diminishes.

The soul rescuer is also often referred to as a 'walker between worlds', a person who has one foot in this world and the other in an altered dimension. The soul rescuer's path is to travel beyond time and space into a dimension understood only by those initiated to reach into encounters with their own death. They must be able to meet the demons and horrors which haunt them and learn through these experiences that once the darkness is behind us, all there is is light, God and freedom.

THE INNOCENT PSYCHIC

NATALIA'S STORY

As a child I never believed that the dead were really dead. Even when my father expressed his own reluctance to believe in life after death I knew instinctively that there was an afterlife for the soul.

When I was 13 my belief was strengthened when a schoolfriend of mine was killed by a car. In the weeks before she died we had become especially close, travelling home on the bus together and visiting each other's homes. The night before she died she came to me in a dream to say that she was going and we would not see her again. I did not understand what she meant until it was announced at the school assembly the next day that she had been killed in an accident. For three or four days after her death I felt slightly strange. It was as though I was in a tunnel. Everything was dark around me and I felt slightly depressed. Then on the third day the atmosphere lifted and I felt fine.

This was the first time that I had been on a psychic journey with a soul into the realms of the spirit world. Even then there was a part of me which understood that I was linking into my friend's spirit as it moved through the death state and that when my mood had lifted she had been able finally to move on. I did not know where she had gone, but I knew that she was fine.

After that I would often feel her around. Whenever I passed the place where she had died I would feel her spirit enter my body and she would speak to me of her great joy at being in the spirit world but also of her great concern for her family's welfare. She had been an only child, so the family grief at losing her was terrible.

Soon after this I began to see and feel ghosts and family spirits all around me, especially in my aunt's house in Spain, which was over 300 years old and in the old part of town. Often the faint figure of a woman would stand on the stairs. She would disappear as soon as I looked straight at her, as if she was fearful of confrontation.

It was a turbulent time. My sleep was constantly interrupted by the spirits of the dead wandering in and out of my dream state and then I became very sick with an illness which the doctors could not diagnose but which meant that I had to spend some weeks under observation in hospital. Yet it soon passed as mysteriously as it had arrived.

At this time I coped with my psychic experiences through my Catholicism. My mother's side of the family is Spanish and I have warm memories of following the older women to the local church on a Sunday to light candles and pray. At a young age I already understood the concept of purgatory and the practice of praying for the dead so that they could be relieved of their sins and go to heaven. I knew that the spirits I saw needed my help so every night I would say special prayers for them.

MY FIRST SPIRIT COMMUNICATION

I was 17 years old when I had my next experience with a deceased spirit – not a ghost or an apparition, but a spirit that could speak to me, that I could feel and touch.

A friend called Jenny and I decided to play truant from college and go back to her house as her mother was not at home. It was the first time I had been to her house and on the way back she warned me that it was haunted by the spirit of her grandmother. It was a comfortable middle-class home with nothing strange or unusual about it except that it was cold and there was a feeling of someone watching us. Jenny showed me a picture of her grandmother as a child, pointing out a shadow behind her which, she said, had become bigger since her death.

Nothing happened until we went up to Jenny's bedroom. We were sitting drinking tea and chatting when she suddenly looked behind me. I felt a cold draught entering the room and Jenny whispered that her grandmother had just walked in. I was petrified. I felt this chilly hand stroke my head and all I wanted to do was scream and run away. But then Jenny told me that her grandmother wanted to communicate with me. Speaking through Jenny, she told me that I had 'the gift' and that when I grew up I would be working with spirit. This was hard to believe at that time, as I had set my heart on becoming a psychologist.

MY INITIATION

Often the family went to Spain for holidays. One year we decided instead to go to Portugal. It was while I was there I encountered a mystic, a man who could see my future mapped out before me.

We were staying in a town close to the mountains and during one of my solitary walks away from the family I was approached by an elderly gentleman. He spoke to me first in Portuguese, then, when I did not reply, in English, asking whether I knew him. I was very wary and replied that I did not. He laughed at my resistance and I responded to his peaceful and warm manner. This encounter led to a long guiding relationship.

Once I had permission from my family to meet him every day, we walked for hours through the beautiful wild countryside as he taught me about reincarnation, life after death, angels, guiding spirits and most importantly karma, the cycles of life of the soul. We spent a month together and before I left Portugal, he warned me that I would go through a very dark initiation and that this experience would change my life.

So it did. Just after my 'A' level exams, I was looking forward to a fun summer. With a place lined up at university to study psychology, I felt nothing could go wrong. Then at the end of the summer I met a 'wizard'. He was a powerful man with a magnetic charm and was seeking young people to initiate. He used his music business contacts to entice us. Our youthful yearning for fame and power made us vulnerable and he was able to manipulate and coerce us into leaving home, joining his cult and performing rituals and magic that would have frightened even the most adept psychic.

During this period of my life I 'lost' myself to the powers of the wizard. Over time, though, I slowly began to become suspicious of the integrity of his methods and through my God-given protection, my intuition, I was able to turn against his cultist regime. This resulted in a serious psychic attack and possession by malevolent forces, which caused a debilitating illness, insomnia and a digestive disorder which led me to lose two stone in weight. My family and friends suggested that I needed help, and for the first time since my meeting with the wizard, I listened to them.

I was not alone in this encounter with the wizard's wrath. I found two other victims and we set up ritual protection against his powers. We were then approached by a group of occultists who were members of the Order of the Golden Dawn, following the teachings of Dion Fortune and others. With their knowledge and protection, we managed to escape the wizard and return home. The members of the occult group offered healing, guidance and support, and through their knowledge and compassion I was able to recover from this ordeal. It took a year, but with their help I gained an understanding of the practice of magic, ritual and occult lore.

Since the 'wizard' had forced us to leave our family homes and stop all professional duties, I lost my place at university, took a job in marketing and my life took a very different turn...

I met Gillian Griffiths, a well known medium who used to run psychic development and healing groups. She also told me that I had a natural talent and encouraged my development. I would come to class with stories of haunted houses and other numerous psychic encounters which became the focus of the class each week. Gillian helped me to become adept at helping the spirits move on until I became involved in a haunting which was far too malevolent for purely psychic skills to deal with. It was then that she suggested that I call on a renowned ghosthunter and healer called Terry O'Sullivan.

THE ST MARGARETS POLTERGEIST

At that time, it was customary for my friends and me to socialize in the pub at weekends and later go on to a party at a friend's house. One night, my brother Paul, his girlfriend Sîan, Rick, a friend of ours, and I went to Matthew's house in St Margarets, a quiet part of town close to the river Thames. Matthew was a friend of my brother's and I had not met him before. I knew very little about him except that his mother had been a heroin addict and had died in the house, and his father had recently died of a heart attack.

It was a small Victorian terraced house. We all sat in the front room and put on some modern rock-type music that was popular at that time. Sîan, Paul, Rick and I sat on the sofa opposite the fireplace, which had a mirror hanging over it.

Within about half an hour the atmosphere began to feel a little tense, slightly chaotic. The boys started arguing over the music. Then suddenly I started to feel a pressure on my chest. I looked up into the mirror and instead of seeing the four of us on the sofa, I saw two old ladies, a white-haired man in his fifties, who I presumed was Matthew's father, and a woman I did not recognize. This startled me. Then Sîan started to complain of the same kind of symptoms.

The music on the sound system supernaturally transformed itself into the organ music that you would hear on the old black-and-white horror movies of the 1930s. The next moment Sîan and I had both been pinned up against the wall by an invisible force. The pressure on my chest was excruciating and I thought I was about to suffer a heart attack. I held on to Rick's hand and my fingerprints came out on his flesh as if I had burnt him with my hand! Then the plates in the kitchen started to smash on the floor, the windows and doors started to open and close and we all began to scream!

I had very little understanding of what to do under these unusual circumstances, as I had never been attacked by a poltergeist before, so I just thought I should summon the angelic beings to help! I prayed to God and to God's protecting angels, my guides and ancestors... From the moment I began to pray and concentrated my focus on calling upon God, the music stopped and the dark atmosphere that had entered the room disappeared. As the mood lightened, Sîan and I settled back down into the sofa. Everyone laughed hysterically and then pretended nothing had happened!

Later I asked Matthew if he had ever experienced anything like this before. He said he had, just after his father had died. During the night he had sometimes felt something get in the bed with him and on occasions throw him out.

The following week I went to my class and told Gillian about this encounter. She lit a candle for the spirits of the dead that had been trapped in the house and suggested that some kind of poltergeist, possibly non-human, was living off the life force of human souls. She believed that we had gathered enough energy for it to manifest its powers. Since I had been able to banish it from the front room and prevent it attacking us, she suggested I go back and check out what it wanted and examine the history of the house for any clues as to what it could be.

The following weekend I went back, this time during the afternoon, rather than at night. I felt I was being watched, but the poltergeist did not come close. I located the spirits of the two old ladies in the main bedroom upstairs. They were earthbound and afraid. I tried in my naïve inexperienced way to rescue them, but they felt trapped and I certainly did not have the power to help them move on.

After my invocation to release the old ladies, I heard plates being smashed in the kitchen. There was nobody in there and the moment I walked into the kitchen, it stopped.

The next moment, a loud bang came from the bathroom. Matthew went running upstairs to find out what had happened. Water was leaking all over the floor and the clothes from the airing cupboard had been thrown down the stairs.

I realized that this situation was bigger than I could cope with and left as fast as I could, yet I knew that from the time the force had attacked me, it had been aware of some kind of protection that I had so it never came too close.

Later that night, we were in the local pub and I asked Matthew for a little history of the house and his family. Matthew and two of his friends who had been living with him all said that they had been feeling unwell, tired and headachy, and one complained of being thrown out of bed. All that Matthew knew about the house was that his family had lived there for about 10 years, his mother had died at home and his father had died of a heart attack just a few months ago. They had bought the house from two old sisters. One had died in the house and the other had sold the property before going into a nursing home. The family had always felt the house seemed a little strange, but Matthew himself had not noticed anything different until his father had died.

I returned to my class the following week and Gillian suggested that I meet a friend who had been involved in soul rescue work for many years. This was Terry. I met him during a weekend workshop he was running for Gillian's students on psychic protection and asked if he would come and investigate the St Margarets poltergeist.

The investigation of the property suggested it was built over an underground stream. There are a lot of waterways in St Margarets, as it is so close to the river. In addition the area had been recorded as a plague pit site from the Great Plague of London.

The psychic activity in the house had been aggravated by Matthew's grief for his parents and by his own psychic energy. The poltergeist that had lived in the property had probably been active for many years, but had used Matthew as a doorway into this world.

This was my first lesson with a poltergeist and the power of my own faith and prayer. Terry visited the house and released the spirits of the dead, who were all willing to leave. We left the spirit force that lived under the house to return to the land.

After blessing the house and cleansing the main negative spots, which were in the kitchen and the front room, Terry sealed the energy with crystals to stop the poltergeist from entering the house and affecting the physical world. Shortly afterwards, Matthew decided it would be a good idea to sell up and move on...

This encounter was the beginning of my relationship with Terry. We made our connection through our spiritual interests and I began my initiation into soul rescue work with him. Since then we have travelled across the world and visited hundreds of homes, sites and ancient places, releasing the souls of the dead and healing the Earth.

MY WORK AS A PSYCHIC

My gift in communicating with spirits means that I can help people on two levels. Many of my clients come to me because I speak to them with the voice of an ancestor or a spirit guide who helps them to find within themselves a deeper knowledge of their purpose and destiny on this planet. In the process they come to believe in the existence of the otherworld and so they learn to trust the processes of life and learn to lead happy, fulfilled, successful lives through the connection they have with their soul and their ancestors.

On the other hand my gift has brought me many experiences with the dying and the dead. People come to me when they learn that they are dying or when someone close to them has died and I am able to help them approach death and bereavement as a spiritual rite of passage. People die in many different ways, but the soul undergoes a similar process as it journeys from this world to the next. I have had many experiences of souls coming to me in the days after death, in dreams and apparitions, either because they need my help to move on or because they want me to reassure their living relatives that they are fine.

I have come to understand that dying is very similar to giving birth. When I work with the dying, healing and talking with them, I am simply helping them to understand how to let go into death. In the same way as a birthing mother has to let go at a pivotal point in her labour to allow the child to be born, so we have to let go when we die. It is much less painful and traumatic if we do.

The newly dead often appear to me soon after they have died, even when they are thousands of miles away. Communicating with the living may help them to make their transition from the physical to the spiritual world or they may simply be saying goodbye. I am honoured to be a part of their transition, offering them some psychic support and guidance. I am also honoured to be able to use my gifts to help those who are dying. It is important that we all have some spiritual guidance to help us prepare for death. As society embraces a caring attitude to birth, it is also essential that the dying are made to feel safe so that the soul can journey on as freely as possible.

My talent as a soul rescuer is in communicating with those in the otherworld who wish to help their families and in assisting in the healing of those who have recently died. This work helps to prevent souls becoming earthbound in the first place. So even as Terry works to rescue the dead, I help to make sure that they do not need rescuing.

THE KALACHAKRA INITIATION

In 1989 we decided to take a pre-marital honeymoon to India, where we visited Delhi, Kashmir and Ladakh. In Delhi we visited a Hindu temple filled with icons and paintings of Krishna. We received a blessing from the priest, who anointed our brows, reminding Terry of the elation he felt at his first communion as a child. A great light touched us. It taught me that there is no difference in God, whatever faith you are led by.

We journeyed further into India and arrived in the north, in Kashmir. Here we realized we were surrounded by earthbound spirits, even at the mosque. Kashmir is a place of political and religious struggle. There are frequent outbreaks of war between various factions and this is reflected in the atmosphere and the number of earthbound spirits.

In Ladakh, at 12,000 feet, it was easier for the spirit to soar. The atmosphere was conducive to peace and the Buddhist lifestyle. It was Buddha's birthday the night we arrived and there was a procession of pilgrims going into the hills to the local monastery. Each held a lighted candle. This was a spectacular sight and an inspiration. It enhanced the beauty of the landscape.

During this trip we were invited by a high lama from Dharamasala to participate in a Kalachakra ceremony for world peace. We were the only Westerners in attendance apart from the Dalai Lama's official photographer, an American. This two-week ritual took us to the limits of our patience and egocentricity. We had to sit from 6 a.m. through the whole day chanting, singing, praying and meditating on top of the roof of the world. We had to walk down mountains, wade across deep streams, burn incense and seeds, rice and paper, purify ourselves in water and withstand hours of prayer and ritual to become initiated in the Tibetan method of liberation and peace. By the end of the first week, we were different people, the light shone from our faces and we had offloaded so much anger, rage and mental anxiety that we literally flew down the mountains back to Delhi and home.

Our next journey was through the Americas, meeting our Native American cousins who taught us the work we had to do with the land.

This book too is a journey, offering the opportunity of understanding the realms of spirit and the deep connection that we have with our ancestors. The physical and the spiritual co-exist, as beliefs throughout the world since the beginning of time confirm. Physical death is but a rite of passage into the liberation of the spirit, into the light, and the world of the in-between, the land of earthbound spirits, ghosts and ancestors...

Through the many years we have worked together, we have laughed and cried, shared stories and advice with many people. This is their story as well as our own journey.

Enjoy.

Terry and Natalia O'Sullivan

The

JOURNEY
OF THE SOUL

PART ONE

You would know the secret of death.

But how shall you find it unless you seek it at the heart of life?

The owl whose nightbound eyes are blind unto the day cannot
unveil the mystery of light.

If you would indeed behold the spirit of death, open your heart
wide unto the body of life.

For life and death are one, even as the river and the sea are one.

In the depth of your hopes and desires lies your silent knowledge
of the Beyond;

and like seeds dreaming beneath the snow your heart dreams
of spring.

Trust the dreams, for in them is hidden the gate to eternity.

Your fear of death is but the trembling of the shepherd when
he stands before the king whose hand is to be laid upon
him in honour.

Is the shepherd not joyful beneath his trembling, that he shall
wear the mark of the king?

Yet is he not more mindful of his trembling?

For what is it to die but to stand naked in the wind and to melt
into the sun?

And what is it to stop breathing but to free the breath from its
restless tides, that it may rise and expand and see God
unencumbered?

Only when you drink from the river of Silence shall you indeed
sing.

And when you have reached the mountain top,

then you shall begin to climb.

And when the earth shall claim your limbs,

then shall you truly dance.

Kahlil Gibran, *The Prophet* (William Heinemann Ltd, 1926)

THE SOUL

CHAPTER ONE

As a man leaves an old garment and puts on one
that is new, the Spirit leaves his mortal body and
then puts on one that is new.

The Bhagavad Gita

The Bushmen of southern Africa say that a star falls for the death of every human. When the hammerkop, a marsh bird of the Bushmen regions, sees the star fall into the water, he cries out. So whoever sees a falling star and hears that cry knows that one of his own people has fallen. A soul has started its journey to the kingdoms of eternity.

The soul represents the deep mystery, the universal connection that we all have with the divine, the Creator, the Great Spirit: God. The idea of the soul cannot be confined to any one religion, for it is simply the energy that animates all of life.

There is so much fear of death in the modern world because there is so little understanding of the soul as separate from the body and the mind. It is not that we have souls; we *are* souls born to fulfil a unique purpose or destiny in the physical world. Within the soul lie the qualities of peace, purity, love, wisdom and power which resonate with the never-ending spirit of the universe. Through meditation and prayer, breathing and listening quietly, we are able to touch this sacred space within. Spiritual energy work like yoga and tai chi further enhances our links with our inner soul. Soon entering this space becomes like entering a flowing river and, gradually, as the ability to go inside gets easier and easier, it brings with it a sense of extraordinary connection with the universal spirit.

The soul is our individual link with eternity. There is within all of us a silent knowledge that a part of us never dies. This understanding that the death of the body does not mean the end of the soul's journey has been common to all of humankind since the beginning of time. This deep knowing is expressed through religion, ritual and prayer as the living seek ways to communicate with the beyond and the origins of immortality.

The butterfly emerging from the chrysalis has served as a metaphor for death since Celtic times. More recently in a concentration camp in Poland where 300,000 people were put to death, hundreds of butterflies were found all over the walls, etched in the stone and the wood. In the same way that the butterfly struggles to leave the chrysalis to emerge into its brilliant exquisite self, so too the immortal soul leaves the mortal body and the dark mystery of eternity draws the spirit away from the cocoon of physical life.

MAPS FOR THE SOUL JOURNEY

Death itself has always been a focus for a spiritual vision of life. Belief systems in every culture and every time speak of the certain immortality of our soul essence. Whether it is the aboriginal belief that we simply expand into the everlasting Dreamtime, the Buddhist belief in the endless cycles of rebirth or the hope of Christianity to embrace Jesus Christ on death so that the soul may journey with Him to heaven, the key to immortality lies in the belief that death is a gateway into the realms of divine consciousness.

Ancient cultures were compelled by death and the journey of the soul. The tales of heroic journeys to the underworld, primordial battles between good and evil and the triumph over darkness and death explain humanity's place in the cosmos and describe the kingdoms of the dead.

This afternoon, when I sit down beside her, she cuddles up in my arms. I rock her gently.

'I'm afraid of dying. I don't know how to die. Help me please.'

I'm struck dumb. I do not know how to die, either. 'I think it's easier than we think. You could say that it happens of its own accord. Maybe there's something in us that "knows",' I say.

She looks at me with her large eyes sunk in their dark sockets. Suddenly she moves her hand toward my neck and takes hold of the Egyptian cross I wear, the one that's also called 'the staff of life' or 'the key of Isis'. She wants to know what it represents. I tell her about the bas reliefs in the royal tombs of Egypt, on which one can see the dead journeying through the underworld holding the staff of life until they start climbing again toward the light. 'Everyone has his or her staff of life, which will help to journey through death. You'll find yours too.'

Marie de Hennezel, *Intimate Death* (Little, Brown & Company, 1998)

Mythology rises from the imagination, reflecting the ideals, aspirations and fears of the culture and the age. It is the literature of the spirit which brings vision to the hidden journey of the soul. The stories which reach us from nomadic and pastoral people rest on the simple cosmology of nature, where to enter the otherworld was to be elevated into a paradise, a beautiful, abundant version of the mundane world, while sophisticated civilizations cultivate increasingly complex ideals of the afterlife – concepts of judgement, innumerable deities and various realms of heaven and hell which the soul had to traverse.

The journey to the realms of the dead is often a perilous one. The soul usually has to negotiate a difficult boundary: a river carried by an unkempt ferryman who demands gifts or payment for his service or a bridge of a single hair, which is crossed by Muslim souls on their way to paradise. The obstacles facing the souls of the dead include tests of judgement and temptation, demons and the hungry souls of the dead who try to prevent the soul reaching its heavenly destination.

In Christian and Buddhist teachings the dangers are usually that the soul might fall back into earthly desire, attachment or negativity instead of forward into faith. In *The Tibetan Book of the Dead* there are prayers, mantras and visualizations to guide the soul on the path to liberation as it reaches for the radiant light of awareness which shines brightly on us as we die but which, in our initial confusion, we may ignore, turning instead to lesser glowing lights which represent our habitual human fears and negativity.

The Egyptian Book of the Dead, a collection of highly illustrated papyrus scrolls found in the great tombs, also reveals magical incantations and formulae which the soul could use to open the gates of the underworld. The popular symbol of the ankh, key to eternal life, which symbolizes the divine union of masculine and feminine, comes from those ancient times.

Prayers, mantras, sacred texts and symbols are the maps and tools which help the soul to find its way to the divine. They are the ways humanity has created to strengthen the spiritual link between our mortal lives and the invisible and they help us to gather our courage at the edge of the void and fall into infinity.

CYCLES OF LIFE

The understanding of life as a cycle of transformation beginning at birth and proceeding through growth into death and back into rebirth reaches back to our most ancient ancestors. They understood that the seasonal cycles of the Earth, the moon and planets were a mirror of the human cycles of experience. Death was accepted as a part of the natural world, simply another transition on the wheel of life and a culmination of life's journey from birth through childhood, puberty, marriage, parenthood into the menopause and old age.

The mysteries of paganism and shamanic principles encourage a holistic attitude toward the soul journey through the cycles of life and death. Life changes or transitions are celebrated as gateways of the soul's transformation. While baptism, marriage and death are still celebrated as spiritual occasions in Western cultures, indigenous peoples still mark the transitions of puberty and menopause (elderhood) with initiation rituals. The word for certain Congo rites, *Kombosi*, also means 'resurrection', and these rites of passage are always concerned with death and rebirth, for they are about letting the old self die to make way for the new. The rituals themselves – which often push the initiates to the brink of death itself – are powerful ways of helping the psyche to accept, and celebrate, the transition from one state to another. For we cannot embrace the new unless we let go of the old.

Birth and death are the most traumatic transitions on the wheel of life for they are the gateways between the physical and non-physical realms, bridges between the known and the unknown. Both are profound experiences which require us to let go into trust at a moment when we

Out of life comes death, and out of death, life, Out of the young, the old, and out of the old, the young, Out of waking, sleep and out of sleep, waking The stream of creation and dissolution never stops.

Heraclitus

feel most vulnerable to forces beyond our control. We have to gather our courage and take a leap of faith. It is during these moments when we come into contact with our own mortality and learn most about the mysteries of the soul.

In all cultures birth is marked by a rite which places the child in context of family, culture and religion. Baptism welcomes a new soul to the Christian fold, while the Yoruba will call a priest to divine which ancestral soul has returned to the world. Birth is often considered more traumatic for the soul than dying for, after spending time in the beauty and light of the kingdom of the spirit, the soul has to get used to living in the harsh reality of the physical world, whilst the souls of the dead are leaving pain and limitation behind to be softened and comforted by spirit.

In the past many of the rites of death imitated those of birth and baptism. The body was often buried in a foetal position, as though it were waiting for rebirth, and water was trickled onto the head, as in baptism. Even today among peoples in West Africa the dead are buried upside-down in a womb-like chamber with an opening representing the birth canal.

Belief in the eternal regeneration of life means that death can more readily be accepted. In the West, where the reality of death is denied and repressed, it is almost always approached with fear and denial. And yet, when acceptance of death can be integrated as a part of our soul's journey, then we can liberate ourselves from the fears which prevent us from really living our life to the full. Life itself is a series of little deaths. Every time we change, a part of us dies. Every loss we encounter, every love affair which does not work out or project which fails, is a moment of death which causes us to grieve before picking up the pieces and moving on.

For Buddhists the contemplation of death lies at the heart of life. Preparation for death begins with living a meaningful life built on love, compassion and truth, for these virtues will ensure a positive death experience and an auspicious rebirth. Faith in the spiritual side of life makes it easier to let go into death. Meditation, yoga, prayer or a simple innocent faith in God brings awareness of the life force which exists beyond, around and within the body but is not dependent on it. Gathering our spiritual resources brings peace of mind and eases physical or mental distress as the soul becomes a place to which we can retreat. It is this connection to our inner divine nature which enables us to approach death with less fear.

The fear of death is a universal response to the unknown but as we learn to trust in the universal laws of creation which show us that birth, growth, decay and death are the everlasting cycles of life which govern our existence on this Earth we can begin to trust that our journey will be a safe one, that, as the scholar and teacher Joseph Campbell wrote, 'Out of the rocks of fallen wood and leaves, fresh sprouts arise, from which the lesson appears to have been that from death springs life and out of death, new birth.'

I want every human being not to be afraid of death, or of life; I want every human being to die at peace, and be surrounded by the wisest, clearest, and most tender care, and to find the ultimate happiness that can only come from an understanding of the nature of mind and of reality.

Soygal Rinpoche,
The Tibetan Book of Living and Dying

SOUL MIDWIFE

Claire Proust is a soul midwife who has also helped many souls cross the boundary between life and death. She compares the process to the labour pains of birth and as a soul midwife provides the practical, emotional and spiritual support for the dying and their families, helping them to face the forces of death with calmness, openness and strength.

As a former nurse, she found that almost all the deaths which she experienced in hospitals were deeply traumatic, thanks to the overwhelming fear of death which often results in unnecessary and invasive surgery and little compassionate preparation for the dying. For seven years she virtually single-handedly ran The Voyager Trust, which pioneered the provision of the holistic and non-invasive care for the dying and bereavement counselling for the families. She believes that the taboo around death in the West is so overwhelming that most

I have always found the actual moment of death to be blissful. Even people who have been terribly frightened of dying relax into death, which becomes something resembling euphoria. In my experience the moments of death and birth are the closest we come to deity.

Clare Proust

people are paralysed by it and yet she found that with simple honesty and compassion most people are able to quite quickly overcome their fears of both their own dying and the deaths of those around them, becoming instead empowered by the experience.

Clare advocates that each person must be given the space and the time to die as they want to die. Each death is unique and, as with labour and birth, each person needs to be allowed to die in their own way.

She describes an incident in one hospital where she was working a night shift which almost restored her faith in the medical profession's emotional ability to cope with death. An old man was gasping his last breaths. He had lung cancer and was confused and coughing phlegm. He kept calling out a woman's name and became distressed when she did not appear. One of the doctors on the ward decided to take action. He climbed into bed with the old man and held him in his arms. The old man said, 'Kiss me,' and without hesitation, the doctor kissed him and continued to hold him until he died very peacefully. Some of the staff criticized the doctor's behaviour, but for Clare it was a wonderful lesson in compassion and humility. 'The world did not end when meaningful physical contact was made with a patient. What did happen was that a tired, ill, confused and sad person was soothed and died in love.'

THE GATEWAY

The old and the sick mostly die in the quiet just before dawn as the metabolic rhythm of the body reaches its lowest energy point. It is the darkest moment before dawn, the time of the greatest peace. In Sweden they call it the hour of the wolf.

The Tibetan Book of the Dead gives a definitive description of the processes of death. As the organs fail, the senses shut down and the mind–body connection ends. At the moment of death the elements out of which the body is made are said to dissolve into each other: earth into water,

water into fire, fire into wind and wind into consciousness or pure ether.

Air is the element of the mind and as that begins to dissolve it feels as though the whole world is swept away by a great wind as it expands into consciousness and all inner energies gather in the heart in the moments before the end of physical life. There are three final breaths as the three drops of blood collect in the 'channel of life' at the centre of the heart. Then silence. At this moment an atmosphere of profound peace descends in the room.

For spiritual practitioners this is the moment of liberation of the spirit from the confines of the body. The Tibetans talk of the consciousness flying out of the crown of the head, sometimes with such force that a fragment of bone in the skull is displaced. The Native American describes death as though the body were an old coat which simply falls away to reveal the naked soul underneath. The Sadhus (Hindi holymen) will discard the body when it has lost its ability as a vehicle for enlightenment with no emotion at all. It has become a burden to their onward journey, so they are able to arrest the functions of the body and journey in one seamless movement from life into death. Certain Himalayan yogis will simply go and sit outside, enter a state of deep meditation and allow their body to freeze around them.

Emma Restall Orr, a Druid priestess and poet, explains that in the mystical tradition of Druidry the adept hopes to reach a state of ecstasy – a profound communion with the divine – at the moment of death. This moment of ecstatic union is said to cleanse the psyche of all the events, hopes and fears of the last life so that the lessons and emotions are not continued into the next. At the point of death you call out the name of your God. In Hindu tradition the aim at death is the same: to consciously give yourself over to the divine. When Gandhi was assassinated his last words were, 'Ram, Ram' (God, God), which according to Hindu belief ensures his soul's place above the trials of rebirth.

There's no real training for a soul midwife other than just doing it. I know that there are hundreds of people, men and women, who have dealt with just one death as a soul midwife. They were just there at the right time and were capable and moved to say and do the right thing.

Clare Proust

BRIDGE OF FAITH

Helena was not a spiritual person at all, although her husband Patrick has 'enormous, unshakeable faith' in Catholicism. She was diagnosed with cancer in January, just before she gave birth to twin boys. She was 28 and she had two other sons, a five year old and a three year old. Julia, her sister-in-law and an expert in palliative care, had helped many people cope with the fear of dying but the acute suffering of someone she loved was unbearable. 'In the middle of the night she would come down to the kitchen and scream at me: "Please don't let me die, please don't let me die. I've got four tiny babies. Please don't let me die." And there was nothing I could do to save her.'

Despite his desperate sadness Patrick accepted Helena's pending death from the moment of her diagnosis; he felt that they had been given this 'cross to carry' for a reason to which they were currently blind. He cared for her at home and sustained her during her darkest moments. He did not try to hide the truth of her sickness from himself or her and encouraged openness with the children. And he prayed and prayed that she might get better.

In the course of her illness Helena underwent an extraordinary transformation which began when Julia took her to Lourdes, which is renowned as a place of profound spiritual healing. Helena's transformation was dramatic. Suddenly she became more peaceful. She had resolved something in her mind. The fear had gone.

Father Edward, the priest who had married the couple and who would eventually convert and finally bury Helena, describes her as being bestowed by the 'grace of faith'. None of her friends could believe the sense of peace which she carried with her until her death.

In September Cardinal Hume said he would say a Novena for her. A Novena is nine days of prayer for a specific intention. On the first night Cardinal Hume held a mass in the crypt at Westminster cathedral with all the family's closest friends and relatives, many of whom had never prayed before, and they prayed that Helena might get well. Then, each day for nine days, all of them repeated the prayer for a miracle.

Helena was amazed that so many people were praying for her and her faith, grace and peace grew day by day, even though she was getting sicker and sicker. When she came to the cathedral for the final prayer of the Novena she could just about walk from the car to the crypt, where she stood surrounded by all her friends and family praying for one last time. Hume anointed Helena with oil on her forehead and on her hands, a rite which is healing as well as bringing to the recipient the special graces that Jesus brought to the sick as he moved among them, healing and touching them.

Helena died in November, three weeks after converting to Catholicism. She died while Patrick was holding her hand and they were saying a rosary together, at the very moment of saying, 'Help us now on the day of our death...' Patrick still remembers her death as the most powerful moment of his life. At her funeral he asked everyone not to mourn her memory but to close their eyes and feel her presence as he had done at the moment of her death.

Despite the catastrophe of his wife's death and having four young boys to look after, Patrick's faith never wavered. He had grieved so much with Helena when she was alive that he was able to return to his life quite smoothly. Some months later a friend suggested that her cousin come to help him with the children. 'She is very together and very loving,' she said, 'and she adores children.' She moved in in January and Patrick married her in May. The kids adore her and every Sunday when they light a candle and say their prayers they say one for their mother in heaven and one for their mother on Earth.

St Augustine said that prayer was when heart speaks to heart and during all those weeks of prayer Helena's heart opened wide to the body of faith which helped her to leave this life in a state of grace and peace. No doubt she is watching over her family.

> Death is the ending of one phase of consciousness. It is only a process whereby we have to hand ourselves over to something bigger than ourselves. We have to be willing to die to our own selves so that we can grow into the next phase of consciousness. This is a process which goes on all our lives. Every step of trust and surrender where we give ourselves over to something bigger than us – love, children or compassion for humanity – is really just a practice and preparation for dying.
>
> Bishop Barrington Ward

Simon Barrington Ward, former Bishop of Coventry, describes the ideal death as perfect surrender. It is, he says, the ultimate healing when we can leave all our pain and limitation behind. As he traces the cross with oil on the foreheads of the dying he is performing a final rite of blessing, healing and grace as they hand themselves over to God. When he visits the dying he describes to them the idea of giving themselves up to a wave or stream of love which will envelop the soul on death. He invokes a God who is walking through the valley of pain and despair with them, ready to gather them to Him despite all their sins or failings.

Mother Theresa saw the face of Jesus on the poorest of the poor whom she rescued every day for more than 20 years from dying in the streets of Calcutta. She believed that to minister to the dying was to minister to Christ on the cross. This belief is uniformly shared by the nuns who move around her home for the dying silently and efficiently, washing those unable to wash themselves, massaging the legs of those unable to walk, comforting those who by tomorrow will be dead. She taught them to see in their suffering the suffering of Christ.

Although the Missionaries of Charity do not claim an explicit mission to deliver the souls of the dying to Christ, Mother Theresa has probably helped thousands of them move on to eternity thanks to the tender care and gentle faith of her nuns. They bring a dignity and calm to a death which otherwise would be agitated and painful.

The dying often choose to go through the gateway alone. Children and the old especially seem to find it easier to let go when they are not in the presence of the people who love them. The family may feel terrible that they were not at their side, but usually the dying do choose their moment of death.

In *The Tibetan Book of Living and Dying* Soygal Rinpoche recommends a simple but extremely powerful visualization practice known as *phowa* for both those who are dying and those who are caring for them. *Phowa* means the 'transference of consciousness' and is a simple meditative process of relaxing the body while the mind invokes an embodiment of whatever the practitioner believes in. This can be Jesus Christ, Buddha, Mary, St Francis, a guardian angel or simply a vision of pure golden light. Everyone is encouraged to visualize their own embodiment of the divine filling the heart and mind with a peace which allows the soul to merge with a pure body of light.

For the rest of us the monks advise that we reach our death thinking loving and compassionate thoughts, praying to be reborn in the realms of golden light or as another human being on the journey toward enlightenment and holding our own vision of Divine Truth in our mind's eye as darkness comes.

The breath of life which enters our bodies at birth in a great inhalation then leaves us with a sigh.

DEATH

What does death feel like? More than eight million people have died and come back to life again and they come back with extraordinary tales of the world beyond. What is remarkable is that most people tell similar stories and remember the whole experience with astonishing clarity. Dr Raymond Moody's collection of case studies, *Life after Life* (Mockingbird Books, 1975), one of the first books on the subject, identified a number of what he called 'core experiences'.

In every instance people describe the sensations of dying as feelings of peace, stillness and serenity. Once out of their bodies, when they hear the doctors or onlookers pronounce them dead, they move toward a long dark tunnel at the end of which is a brilliant white light which draws them onward and envelops them in an all-consuming love. Even those with no religious convictions or belief in an afterlife have similar experiences and describe the light as emanating from an ancestor, angel, religious figure or other spiritual being.

Some people have come back describing encounters with pure light beings or angels who look like the angels of classical art – people of extraordinary grace and beauty with wings growing out of their shoulders. Others claim to have met spiritual masters like Jesus or Buddha. Usually they are asked telepathically what they have done with their lives. Few feel judged or afraid and most feel such peace that they do not want to return. Most of the 'near dead' feel unconditional love and safety in this light. Few of them want to return and yet all of them are turned back. There is usually a boundary, a wall, a river or a great sea beyond which they cannot pass. It is usually here that they are given instructions or the choice to return.

Soizic Aureli remembers the terrible shock of plummeting back into a body wracked with pain after dying during an operation for cancer when she was 33. When she left her body she had been given a clear choice:

This angel-type person said to me: 'You can stay if you want in this dimension, but you have not done anything that you came to do in your life yet. If you choose to go back you have to change your life completely and make sure that you carry out your mission in this life.'

Going back wasn't easy for Soizic. She was unhappy in her marriage and dissatisfied with her job. She felt trapped by her life and hated working in the corporate world. The cancer and the radiotherapy had made her weak and tired. She really wanted to stay. But she suddenly remembered her youngest daughter, who was only three-and-a-half years old. 'I had to go back to be with her because I knew that no one else would look after her. I also knew that whatever happened I would change my life completely.'

When she came back she did just that. She decided not to listen to the doctors anymore, stopped taking the pills and discharged herself from hospital when they told her she would have no more than two months to live. She called her homoeopath, changed her diet, took alternative remedies, got back on her feet quite quickly, then left her marriage and changed her job.

Today she is a counsellor who works with psychosynthesis, which she describes as 'soul psychology'. Many of her clients have cancer.

===

The vast majority of people who leave their body give compelling descriptions of the unearthly light and blissful atmosphere they encounter. P. M. H. Atwater, who wrote *Beyond the Light* after she herself had died and come back three times, found that nearly everyone who had seen this extraordinary light felt that they had been in the presence of God, no matter what their previous beliefs.

For most people the experience of 'near death' is overwhelmingly positive, but people have also gone to places which are dark and frightening. Survivors have described falling through a vortex or being on the edge of a dark whirlpool surrounded by swirling clouds, being surrounded by the noises of groaning and screaming, and seeing grotesque human or animal forms. Panic, loneliness and fear overwhelm them and the people they meet are often shadowy figures who do not recognize them and who seem trapped and unhappy. In these cases the survivors fight to get back, struggling against forces which seem to hold them in order to prevent their return.

===

When Joey Rae died for some 30 minutes after a heart bypass operation she saw everything in the operating theatre – bells ringing, machines flashing, a flat line on the monitor and the panic. Her first feelings were relatively calm; she felt very light and knew that she was either going to die or was already dead.

A man she did not recognize came and took her hand. It was her biological father whom she had only met once when she was four years old. As she saw this

This inner knowing just took over. I was not scared anymore and I wanted to take charge of my life for the first time. I wanted to stop being the victim I had always been.

Soizic Aureli

dark man leading herself as a young girl toward a bright illuminated tunnel she began to feel scared and a huge sadness came over her. She rapidly recollected her family and a sense of loss engulfed her. She became acutely aware that they really needed her, especially her five-year-old grandson. 'Then I became very upset and angry. It started to feel as though I was in a nightmare. I really had to struggle to get back into my body.'

She hovered between life and death for days. Her family focused their love and attention on her. The illness had been sudden and Joey Rae was still young. They were all deeply afraid that she might die and absolutely unwilling to accept that she was going to leave them.

Joey Rae's brain had suffered some damage and she had lost sensation in the left side of her body, but after 17 days in intensive care she was taken off the critical list and returned to the ward. After only a few weeks she was completely back to normal. Her personality, sense of humour and determination came back in full force but she had changed in the way she approached life and her family.

The experience has also completely changed her daughter Nikkita's vision of life:

I realized the power that will, the mind and love have over our destiny. We have a choice. Nothing is predestined. It has taught me about the power of love and how love can act as a really strong magnet to the confused and injured spirit.

═══════════════

People always return changed. In shamanic cultures the near death experience is created on purpose by putting initiates through life-threatening situations and debilitating physical hardship in order to make them aware of other states of being. They are the teachers and healers of the rest of the community because of the knowledge that they bring back with them from the realms of infinity. In the West survivors of 'near death' also often change their life course and become healers and spiritual teachers, helping others to overcome their fear of death.

Denise Linn, the internationally renowned healer, lecturer and writer was shot and almost killed when she was just 17. When she got to the hospital she was in an incredible amount of pain and she was aware of people shouting around her. Then she left her body.

Suddenly everything seemed to get very quiet and dark and the pain subsided. I felt like I was inside this very soft velvety black bubble. Then instantly, as if the bubble had burst, everywhere there was golden light. It was the most brilliant light. It made the sun in the Sahara pale in comparison except that it did not hurt your eyes. Infused in the light was the most beautiful melodic music I had ever heard. It was as if each note was a precious drop of dew or nectar. Just as the light was so bright, the music was so sweet and crystalline and pure. What was remarkable was that I didn't seem to be separate from the light and the music. I had no boundaries – I experienced myself to be everywhere. Although it doesn't make any sense to my conscious mind now at that moment it seemed so real and natural.

I was unable to think of the past or the future because everything existed right now. There was a sense that every person who had ever lived and every person who was going to live was there and yet we were not separate from each other. We were all individuals and yet a part of a great loving Oneness and infused in this experience was the most blissful feeling of love. I was enveloped in a kind of love which was different from the love that we experience on Earth because the love we have here is a love of separation, as there is always distance between us and the people we love. In that place there was only love.

The remarkable thing was that it was all so familiar to me and it made my physical life up to that point an illusion. In a blink of God's eyes my life had become like a dream and this had become my reality.

Then I came to a beautiful golden river of light that shimmered and sparkled. I could see through this golden haze to the far shore and I knew that

I would never return to my body if I reached it. I stepped into the river and I could feel this golden light parting on each side of my body. I was desperate to reach the other side but when I got halfway across I felt a huge tug around my waist and I was being dragged out of the river. I heard a voice which said, 'It's not your time now. There are some things you need to do.' And I found myself instantly yanked back into my body.

Her body was badly damaged and she suffered a great deal of pain.

One night I was in so much pain that I was desperate and suddenly I felt some-one's hand slip into mine. As soon as this happened the pain disappeared. I thought it was a kindly night nurse, but when I opened my eyes there was nobody there. Even when I wiggled my fingers I definitely felt as though some-one was holding my hand. Then I fell into a deep sleep.

Throughout her long convalescence she would find herself drifting into altered states of consciousness:

I could hear music that other people couldn't hear and see things that they couldn't see. Once when they took me outside for some fresh air I began to hear this remarkable hum. I looked around to see where it was coming from and around every blade of grass there was this radiant light and I realized that I was hearing the sound of the grasses. Then I looked at this tiny sapling and I saw the same light glowing around the tree and the leaves and I could distin-guish a beautiful sound as the sap was rising up and as the sun was entering the leaves and going down the tree. Then a small breeze came up and as the leaves twisted and turned I could hear a pure crystalline sound like a chime.

Denise Linn has extended her vision of the eternal nature of spirit to the world in the form of healing workshops, books and lectures. It brought her in touch with her Cherokee heritage and helped her to understand the vision of life held by most tribal peoples throughout the world. She considers her near death experience a special gift:

When I had my NDE I wasn't given something which I did not already have: it just allowed me to remember who I am. It is as if inside each person there is an ember of remembrance and there are ways to allow that ember to become a flame, a flame that says we are infinite and immortal. That we are spirits.

RITUALS AND RELEASE

Do not stand at my grave and weep
I am not there. I do not sleep.
I am a thousand winds that blow;
I am a diamond's glint on snow.
I am the sunlight on ripened grain;
I am the gentle autumn's rain.
When you awaken in the morning's hush,
I am the swift uplifting rush
of quiet birds in circled flight.
I am the soft star that shines at night.
Do not stand at my grave and cry,
I am not there.
I did not die.

Anonymous

The ancients grieved over death and yet their belief in death as a positive transformation when the soul begins its journey to the afterlife led them to create rituals as a bridge which the soul could use to move between worlds.

As a child, Aggie Richards, a nurse and member of the Spiritualist Church, would find herself drawn to funerals, where she would see the spirit of whoever had died shimmering above the mourning guests. Sometimes she saw something which resembled an umbilical cord trailing from the spirit into the coffin; as the coffin was lowered it would slowly dissolve. She knew that no one else could see this and would always say a prayer for the spirit as it disappeared. Her vision corresponds with the spiritual belief that the souls of the dead attend their own funerals and even as the living are saying good-bye they too are preparing to take their leave.

The religious custom of reading sacred texts and prayers at funerals reminds the soul that it wishes to seek reunion with God and the European custom of keeping candles burning around the coffin light the way for the dead to the invisible realms. The clothes, food, gifts and messages which are often buried with the dead reassure the spirit through lingering memories of their earthly existence and stop them feeling lonely on their journey.

From ancient Egyptians to Buddhists and the many tribal peoples of the world, many cultures have considered the newly disembodied soul to be at great risk, not simply from external forces but also from its own fear and confusion. The living are also held to be at risk at this time.

Many rites have grown out of the fear of the ghost of the dead returning to haunt the living as the gateway of death opened from the visible to the supernatural world. The original reason why mourners, pall bearers and undertakers dressed in black was to make themselves as inconspicuous as possible in order to protect themselves from the ghost and any other spirits hovering near. Even today undertakers will take the coffin to the house of the deceased on the way to the cemetery to make sure that the soul accompanies the body, and the corpse must always be taken from the house feet first, otherwise, looking back, it will beckon one of the family to follow it into death. In Haiti the cortège will break into a run as if being chased to the cemetery. Twisting and turning through the streets, it takes the most circuitous route, trying to make the soul lose its sense of direction so that it can never find its way home again. Gypsies pile thorn bushes over the grave to prevent the soul rising out of it and in the past would always burn the possessions of the dead so that they would have nothing to return to.

THE FUNERAL

The funeral ceremony is the final and most sacred rite of passage on the wheel of life as the body is returned to the elements and the soul is released. Funerals serve the same functions throughout the world: to dispose of the body, to ensure the safe passage of the soul and to comfort the living. The prayers, rituals, magical incantations and celebrations help to divest the soul of emotional attachment and empower it to continue its journey toward the light.

THE SOUL THAT WAS MINE IS NOW YOURS

The Indian custom is to let the soul go and not to hold on to it, so we set aside 13 days for mourning, for it is thought that it will take that number of days to heal. In Hindi the word for 13 – *thera* – also means 'yours' and on the thirteenth day we release the soul that we love back to the keeping of Baba, God, our spiritual parent.

Mainly I help the mourners to let go of the person who has died and allow them the freedom to go on. I teach people that by our distress we may be blocking the soul's path and not helping ourselves to heal. There are many people who never heal from death but there are others who come to the understanding that their soul connection to the one who has died is eternal. That we never perish.

By sharing our spiritual knowledge, helping the mourners to meditate and make connection with their own God, we teach them how to help the spirit to go, which heals their own spirit at the same time.

On the thirteenth day the mourners will put oil in their hair, change their saris. They will prepare all the favourite foods of the soul that left the body and invite their friends and family to enjoy the feast. One of our sisters will sit in meditation and powerfully remember Baba as the food is being blessed and then we will feast. When we have given to the soul one more time, all that they desired in life then we let the soul go to Baba.

It is a time of freedom and release and energy. Everything changes after this ceremony: attitudes, thoughts, sadness. You often realise that until the thirteenth day you have been holding on but on that day you can feel that the soul has moved on: We can finally say: 'God, the soul which was yours, I offer back to you.'

Sister Jemini of the Brahma Kumari Organization

Messengers from the spirit realms invoked during funerals to guide and protect the soul include angels, deities and the souls of the ancestors. In Christian rites it is the figure of Christ in particular who brings hope of life after death. He is the aspect of Love into which the soul is safely commended. In Catholic tradition the requiem mass is believed to have the power to ritualistically bring the soul to repose and peace in immortality. Requiem literally means rest and the rite divests the soul from the sins of life so that it can release itself into the arms of God.

For pagans it is the magic in the forces of nature which gives the soul the powers of transformation. In Druid rites the spirits of nature and the ancestors are invoked during rites held on open land and in groves. The many deities who might come forward to protect the souls of the dead are linked to the power of elemental forces and connected to the land. In the British Isles it might be the Celtic gods and goddesses, Brigid, Cerridwen and Cernunnos who are invoked, while in the Nordic traditions Odin or his consort the earth goddess Freya may lead the dead to the otherworld. They bring the gifts of the wind, sun, growth and change to help the soul on its way.

Throughout the pagan world, the ancestors receive the dead, completing another cycle of life with their reassurance and wisdom. In Africa funerals celebrate the rebirth of the soul as an ancestral spirit but it is up to the living, through their ways of mourning, to ensure safe passage. The mourning dances which kick up the dust of villages throughout the continent generate the necessary energy to push the dead into the arms of the ancestors, who are the true elders of the community. The living benefit from their advice and protection, so a good send off is crucial in order to get the relationship off to a good start. The body is usually buried close to the living so it is easy for the dead to watch over them. In some cases a beloved grandmother or grandfather may even be buried under the family home.

Burial is traditionally linked with cultures who identify with a belief in the ancestral realms so, as the body dissolves into the earth, the soul does not begin a restless search for its origins. The earth is the Motherland where the regeneration of the soul begins and for the living the grave becomes a focus for grief and a place of pilgrimage.

In the British Isles the burial grounds of our ancestors and the tombs, cairns, long barrows and tumuli are invariably found near the enigmatic standing stones and circles have become sites of pilgrimage for modern pagans, wiccans, tourists and travellers. As paganism becomes increasingly acceptable, people are choosing to bury their dead away from the consecrated graveyards in gardens or woodland. Thanks to the early Quakers of the seventeenth century, who were usually buried in their gardens, it is perfectly legal to be buried on your own land – although it will diminish the value of the property. Princess Diana's burial on a small island in the middle of a lake in her ancestral home of Althorp in Northamptonshire rather than in the family mausoleum was a significant break with tradition. The vision of her burial place carpeted with flowers and reached only by boat echoed the ancient mythology of the journey of the soul across a river to the Elysian fields of myth.

For Buddhists and Hindus the slow disintegration of earth burial is thought to make it difficult for the soul to detach itself from the physical world, but if the body is consumed by fire the soul is released like the mythic phoenix into the spirit realms. The banks of the Ganges in the holy city of Varanasi in India are filled with pyres on which the bodies of rich and poor are burned, filling the streets with the sweet smell of burning flesh mixed with exotic incenses and woodsmoke. Three days after cremation the ashes are

Instead of treating the last act in our life in terms of fear, weakness and helplessness, think of it as a triumphant graduation. Friends and family members should treat the situation with openness rather than avoidance. Celebrate. Discuss. Plan for that final moment.

Timothy Leary

scattered in the flowing river. Cremation invokes the power and beneficent grace of Shiva, one of the most powerful gods of the Hindu pantheon, who dances the dance of destruction and creation which fuels the wheel of life. Fire is considered to be the most liberating and purifying of the elements, the closest to the energy of the spirit, and so through fire the soul is more easily able to expand into its divine self, purged of the events of this life.

In a tradition which may have originated in Asia most of the Native American tribes chose sky burials, placing the bodies of the dead on wooden platforms with their feet towards the rising sun. Their profound love of the natural world and understanding of the notions of the 'give away' or sacrifice meant that they welcomed the surrender of the body to the elements. A body above ground had no coverings to separate it from the Creator and so the soul, the breath of life, could easily merge with the wind from whence it came. When the scaffolds decayed, the skulls would be taken to the prairies and placed with others in circles of hundreds or more. With the faces turned inward, the skulls created a sacred space which became a place for affectionate veneration. When the Native Americans had to move away from their lands they believed that they were being torn away from their loved ones and forced to leave them alone forever on the plains.

From the earliest graves of the Palaeolithic era to the most modern rites, humanity has ritualized death as a sacred transitional journey. As we release the bodies of our dead there is a powerful awareness of the soul essence which continues beyond the physical, visible world. The rituals and prayers which we offer up to the dead are the beginnings of a soulful connection with the souls of the dead as we help them make their journey into the unknown.

GRIEF AND LETTING GO

As the souls of the dead make their way towards their destiny in the world of spirit they are uniquely sensitive. It takes some time for them to become used to their disembodied state and realize that they are free to embrace liberation. During the few weeks after death they look back and process the events of their lives and say a final goodbye to those they love. Without their bodies to anchor themselves to the world they are deeply affected by our emotions and thoughts. They can feel our grief, as it reflects their own sadness at leaving those they love. So the spirit will often visit familiar people and places one last time.

For Malidoma Somé, shaman and author, grief is an important rite of passage required by both the living and the dead to recover from the trauma of death. Without it the separation between them never actually reaches that stage when the living accept the fact that a loved one has become a spirit and therefore the dead cannot become free from their earthly consciousness. Tears carry the dead home, for they release a powerful emotional energy which provides them with a sense of completion and closure.

When someone dies among Malidoma's people in West Africa the village erupts with emotion as the women begin a guttural wailing to announce to the village and the spirit world that a death has taken place. The rituals of communal mourning which follow allow everyone the opportunity to reach a cathartic peak of grief and release all their emotional pain and loss. A prolonged expression of grief exhausts the body to the point where rest is needed. It mellows the mind, heart and body and leads us toward an acceptance of death, separation and loss.

Why did you leave us?
What did you lack to
   make you happy?
Look with pity on the
   children you have left.
Long is the day without
   you.
Dark is the sun since you
   are gone.
Never will your like be
   seen in this world
   again.
   Traditional mourning song

CHILD OF PEACE

Isobel's daughter died at only three weeks old. She found herself at odds with both the medical professionals who surrounded her and her partner as she tried to follow her instincts to commemorate and honour the soul of her child. Although her approach was seen as unorthodox and uncompromising, she emerged from the death of her daughter healed and able to resume her life.

I was in this place of shock as I had to synthesize the experience of birth and death very quickly. Both are powerful experiences. My milk was still coming and my body was still suffering from the birth. She died in hospital on midsummer's night as I watched over her in an emergency unit, but it was two hours before they finally switched off the ventilator, before my husband could finally bring himself to ask them to turn it off.

I couldn't bear the thought of leaving her there alone, so I told them that I was taking her home. The hospital was reluctant to agree, so I found myself saying that it was for religious reasons although I did not truthfully know what I was going to do when we got home. My other daughters received the dead body of their sibling with the openness and acceptance of the very young, but friends were still calling for news of the birth and when a neighbour dropped by with something she had knitted for the baby I realized that I could not stay there. I was inspired to call the Buddhist Society for advice and they suggested that I go to a Buddhist temple on the outskirts of London. I phoned the abbot and he invited us to go and stay with them.

When we arrived I was invited to place my baby at the feet of a statue of the Buddha in the meditation room. I laid her down among all these summer flowers freshly picked from the garden and I knew I had come to the right place. We arrived from this awful hospital situation to this peaceful place which is called *Amaravati*, meaning 'Deathless Realm'.

That night meditation practice continued as normal with all the monks and nuns and ordinary people chanting with my baby lying at the feet of the Buddha in front of them. I spent most of the first night there in vigil there with my baby. I felt totally destroyed. My child was born and now it was dead. I knew that I needed to go beyond this tremendous pain of letting go of her but I had no idea how I was going to do it. Early the next morning I came down to discover that someone had placed a tiny Buddha and a poem on her heart.

The daily round of meditation continued around us until the day of her funeral, when I organized a dinner for everyone at the temple and invited a few of her friends. There was a special meditation and a huge meal and then we carried her to the crematorium. I did not want black cars and coffins, just a simple drape over the tiny cot which had been made before she was born. Many of the monks and nuns from the community came with us and we all stood around in a circle. Many people asked to hold her and said some words, some poems and words from the Buddha. There was nothing so difficult as putting her into fire, but the support of the temple community made it bearable.

Many of the nuns thanked me for the great teaching they had received and some of the younger nuns left the order to marry and have children themselves, inspired by the closeness of death to realize what they wanted. Many had never seen a dead body and they asked me if they could touch her. It all gave meaning and purpose to my daughter's short life. She had already become a teacher. Everybody was learning from the experience of her death. One woman was inspired to plant some bulbs for her son who had died in similar circumstances 25 years before and others mourned their own dead children for the first time.

She was very powerful. From the first moments I felt myself being led by her. I am sure that she led me to the temple because I cannot rationally remember how I made any of those decisions. I just knew we needed to be in a quiet place together. She took me there and brought me to learn a lot about truth and life and death. All along some deep part of me recognized that she did not belong to me, but that as her mother I should be with her on her journey to the very last minute. From the first moment when I knew that she was not going to make it I knew that nothing else mattered but this. I was changed on many levels. I am more reassured that there is more to life and death than what the eye can see and what science can prove.

In a similar way the mourning which erupted on the death of Princess Diana became a powerful catharsis as thousands of people went on spontaneous pilgrimage to Kensington Palace and other places linked with Diana's memory. Many people were surprised by the intensity of their grief, which they expressed in the most religious and archetypal ways. Flowers, candles, incense, banners, icons, paintings, gifts and offerings transformed the park around Kensington Palace into a massive universal shrine far removed from late twentieth-century London. It became simultaneously a Hindu pilgrimage, a Mexican shrine, a Catholic vigil, an Irish wake and a pagan ritual.

In this atmosphere of communal mourning many were able, sometimes for the first time, to grieve for private losses of their own. Our natural processes of mourning can be interrupted for many reasons but if we do not fully grieve for the dead a part of us holds on to them. With her death Princess Diana performed her final act of service for the community. She triggered a healing release of grief which soothed the troubled hearts of thousands of people as well as helping them to finally let go of the souls of the long dead.

Among Buddhists the onus is on the mourners to forget about their own anguish and to help the dead rise up and move on into the great light through meditations and showering love onto the deceased. This was especially important in cases of sudden death, which causes such a great shock to the soul that it can become trapped in the moment of death and unable to move on towards the natural processes of rebirth. Soygal Rinpoche urges us to 'imagine rays of light emanating from the Buddhas or divine beings pouring down all their compassion and blessings. Imagine this light streaming down onto the dead person, purifying them totally from the confusion and pain of their death, granting them profound and lasting peace.' After death the mind of the soul is intensely clairvoyant and can pick up the tiniest thought and emotion. Loving thoughts are like a silken cord to which they can cling as they move through the first phase after death.

Grief is an active, not a passive, process. If we are given the space for our grieving then our hearts can begin to heal. Our natural ability to integrate our loss can begin to work its magic. There comes a time when we need to stop grieving and release our attachment to those we love. The dead need us to let go.

Just recently, as work on this book drew to a close, we were told about a man who had been suffering from a recurring dream ever since his eight-year-old daughter had died when she had been knocked over by a car. She had been a vibrant, popular child and the whole school had come to the funeral. In the dream the man would see his daughter on a hill surrounded by thousands of other children holding candles. All of them were alight except for his daughter's. He could not understand why it was that his daughter's candle was never alight. Then one night she came to the front of the crowd and he asked her why. She said to him, 'I keep lighting it, Daddy, but your tears keep making it go out.'

CELEBRATION OF THE DEAD

The instinct to praise the dead is natural and ancient and one of the most important elements of any funeral service is the opportunity to celebrate the achievements and the character of the one who had died. Among the Egyptians the act of praising and lifting the atmosphere after death was part of releasing the soul of the dead to a higher place. In Ireland and elsewhere the lamentations to the dead told of their great deeds in life; their sense of humour and successes, good looks and kind hearts were praised in long rolling rhythmic phrases. Throughout the world dancing and singing is common at funerals as an expression of the belief that the soul really is moving on to another dimension. Despite the sadness and grief of death, wakes and fiestas release the weight of mourning and change the atmosphere from one of loss into one of celebration.

The Buddha himself exhorted his followers to celebrate rather than mourn his passing: 'It is not appropriate to grieve in an hour of joy. You all weep, but is there any real cause for grief? We should look upon a sage as a person escaped from a burning mansion. My time has come, my work is done. My teachings shall last for generations so do not be disturbed.' Releasing his disciples from grief, he encouraged them to celebrate death as the moment when knowledge dispels ignorance and the spirit is released to peace.

The natural instinct to praise and honour the dead at funerals, wakes and memorials pours a positive energy onto their memory and sheds light onto their souls. By praising the spirit we help the souls of the dead to seek their own liberation, safe in the knowledge that they were well loved and had fulfilled their promise in life.

After the funeral the soul takes its leave, divesting itself of the last emotional attachments to the physical plane. But there is always a choice: to move toward liberation or to stay. Sometimes it is not always easy for the souls of the dead to move on. Some do not wish to leave and others find themselves unable to and are pulled back by grief or regret. Reluctant to leave family and friends, they linger around the familiar places and people, wondering why no one is talking to them.

Such a soul, confused and disorientated, finds itself unable to expand into the eternal spirit of the universe. Instead of entering the river of endless life it becomes frozen in its own individuality and, still stuck in the daily habits of the human world, becomes literally 'bound to the earth'.

There is only one true form of greatness for a man. If he can bridge the gap between life and death ... if he can live on after he's died, then maybe he was a great man. Whatever's the truth, you've got to live fast.

James Dean

THE GOOD DIE YOUNG

TERMINAL VELOCITY – CELEBRATION FOR A FALLEN WARRIOR

Adam was one of the torchbearers of rave culture. George, his friend, producer and DJ, remembers him: 'He was one of those magnetic characters who drew people to him. There was this huge energy about him. He came into your life like a bolt of lightning. He wanted to break down barriers; he wanted to communicate.'

It was the summer of 1992, dance music had come of age and the scene was bursting with creative energy. Adam, George and a few close friends were putting on parties for 2–3,000 people or more and were talking about setting up a record label.

When a couple in the group who had been in love for years announced that they were going to get married in August it seemed as if it would be the perfect ending to a perfect summer. Adam and George began planning the stag night at a massive converted barn near Polzeath, a stunning rugged beauty spot perched on 300 ft cliffs in Cornwall. The day of the party they went down with James, the groom-to-be and a couple of other friends to set up the decks and the sound system and prepare the room for a massive sit-down banquet. Then they headed for the cliffs to chill out and wait for the big night. George remembers:

It was the most beautiful day. We were playing frisby up there and flying kites. Adam was sitting right on the cliff edge. We wandered off to the special place around 500 yards away to have a smoke and came back over the headland. Adam wasn't there. We assumed that he had gone for a walk so we started playing frisby again. Then the wind caught it and it went over the cliff. Grant walked to the edge and looked over. I remember him saying, 'Adam is down there!' I saw the look on his face and I realized that the worst thing possible had happened. I crawled over to the edge, looked down and saw Adam's body all broken on the rocks.

James ran to phone the coastguard while George and Adam's best friend Dominic climbed down the lethal cliffs to rescue Adam from the encroaching tide if he was still alive. The coastguard helicoptered him to the local hospital and radioed that he still had a pulse but by the time they got to the hospital he had died of massive head injuries.

George was mainly in shock, while Dominic fell to pieces after identifying Adam's body. They slowly returned to the farmhouse to greet the guests.

'We just had to walk in and tell everyone that that Adam was dead. Most of them were friends of Adam's. First they didn't believe it and then they were devastated.'

The huge banqueting table which had been laid out for a celebration of life now became the setting for a wake.

Suddenly we are not there to celebrate a marriage, we were there to mourn a friend. I have never felt so tangible a presence of grief. You could feel it – it was thick, heavy energy. Everyone was trying to ground it. You could see it in some-one's eyes and yet in a very male way we would try to bury it, try not to show it, to deal with it and not get thrown off, to take it all in a really strong way. But we couldn't, it was too much. Every few minutes it would boil over and we would lose it. I felt emotions which I had never felt.

The evening which had begun in numb devastation began to transform as everyone was able to grieve and comfort each other.

As one person started crying so did others. You could see the grief rising in their faces and their stomachs. There was this feeling of incredible generosity between us – as one broke down, others would support them. And then as the evening wore on this generosity became more evident than the grief. The night was transformed by this amazing feeling of love and sharing into this incredible beautiful experience.

Looking around the table it was as if it were an ancient celebration for a fallen warrior. The fact that we were all male seated around this massive ban-queting table made it feel as though we had all been to battle. It was a ridicu-lously fitting way for Adam to die. He was a full-on warrior. He had already done so much in his life and he was just reaching a turning-point where the record label and the music were about to come to fruition. And now he had died at a moment when we had all come together. It was almost perfect.

Afterwards they went upstairs to where the decks had been set up. Dominic and James began to play all the music which had inspired them through the years.

That was the best moment of all. It was the soundtrack of our lives, the whole backdrop to our coming of age and it was everything that we had worked towards in the UK and around the world, making music and celebrating life. It was where we had all met. We sat there for hours with the music and the memory of Adam as a tangible presence in the room. It was healing everyone.

In the car on the way home George, Dominic and Mark formed Flying Rhino Records, named after a clothing company Adam had started in Australia. The company has gone on to become a legend on dance floors around the world.

Flying Rhino has been a healing experience for all of us. It is as if Adam's energy dissipated into all of us. We carry it now. When we hit problems we remember what he would say: 'We are here, we are alive, we are here for a reason, so get on with it. Let everything go and live in the moment.' That is how he was.

His death was the furnace where we were born – the fires of experience have bonded us completely. We went to the bottom of the well to drink and we have come back transformed. Adam's death reminded us that the darkness is always there – that you can't always live in the light – and we found that moving between those two places – between the darkness and the light – is where creativity lies. As you move from darkness and step into the light, that is when energy crackles, that is when things get born. Adam always knew that.

On all of the CDs and the vinyl the team produce, they scratch a message to Adam, their 'spiritual manager': *'Big love to Adam. Boom Shankar to Adam. All life to Adam.'*

═══════════════

EARTHBOUND SPIRITS

CHAPTER TWO

Those who are dead are never gone;
They are there in the thickening shadow.
The dead are not under the earth;
They are there in the tree that rustles,
They are in the wood that groans,
They are in the water that sleeps,
They are in the hut,
They are in the crowd.
The dead are not dead.

Those who are dead are never gone:
They are in the breast of the woman,
They are in the child who is willing
and in the firebrand that flames.
The dead are not under the earth:
They are in the grasses that weep,
They are in the whimpering rocks,
They are in the forest,
They are in the house.
The dead are not dead.

Birago Diop, Mali poem,
from *Indigenous Religions*

The Australian Aborigines believe that at the moment of death the soul splits into three: one is the animal or bush soul which returns to the earth and another is the immortal part of the soul which leaves the visible world and expands into the shimmering realms of the Dreamtime where mind and matter merge in an energetic resonance. The Dreamtime is the equivalent of eternity, a boundless state of being from where the first people came and to which the last people will return.

The third aspect of soul the Aborigines call the 'trickster' and it is known to interfere and cause problems for the living. This is the human ego soul which needs all sorts of persuasion to move on and relinquish its attachment to its familiars and its home. Every year communal rituals clear the territories of souls that remain earthbound. Today many elders in their communities believe that the Earth is saturated with earthbound spirits as the understanding of the transitions of the soul has dwindled. The Dreamtime has become cluttered with the fragmented and disembodied energies of the departed.

The Buddhists believe that after death the soul has a kind of intuition like a streak of lightning. If it can seize the light it is set free, but usually it is dazzled. It shrinks from it and is pulled backwards by false conceptions, attachments to individual existence, habits and pleasures. For some souls, the significance of death completely escapes them and just like a man absorbed by his own preoccupations, they will simply fail to notice what is going on. For several days the newly earthbound soul will continue as it has always done, talking to friends and family, living in the house, and it will be astonished that no one answers it or seems to be aware of its presence.

In Tibetan Buddhist belief, a soul which has just left the body is uniquely sensitive and vulnerable. Still connected to the Earth plane, it can pick up the smallest emotion, hear thoughts and feed off the atmosphere. The clairvoyant consciousness of the person in this 'bardo of becoming' state is thought to be seven times clearer than in life. Consequently loud and frightening displays of emotion by those left behind can confuse it, while loving thoughts and compassion are believed to be of great benefit in helping it reach towards the light.

Once it was common practice to open a window in the room where a person lay dying to enable the soul to take flight. The Hottentots of South Africa, the Fijans and the Native Americans all made a hole in the hut to allow the passage of the spirit, but cautiously closed it again after it had gone to prevent its return. Throughout history the widespread belief in earthbound spirits, unable to leave the human world, is expressed in the taboos and customs which protect the living from the unwelcome influence of the dead.

Healers and psychics encounter earthbound spirits everywhere living alongside us in a different dimension, completely caught by their own world. Some of them remain attached for generations, causing harm to no one but themselves, while others can cause physical, psychological or spiritual interference. Our clients have suffered innumerable annoyances, illnesses, failing relationships and bad luck when they have moved house only to find an angry earthbound spirit already living there...

Some earthbound spirits who were accustomed to certain places in life may wish to remain there; others may be confused or lost and simply not know what to do other than go back home, so the departed and the living co-exist under the same roof. Earthbound spirits can haunt the places where they died as well as where they are buried. They are found wandering hospital wards and corridors as well as inhabiting graveyards and cemeteries.

For seven years, when I was working in a London hospital, responsible for the purchase and distribution for supplies, I would rescue souls from the wards and the morgue. I was continually surprised by the awareness of the people who cared for the dead.

I remember on one occasion when I had to make a visit to the hospital morgue, the attendant, Martin, began talking about his job in a very serious manner, keen to display his knowledge and authority. He explained how he had to determine the religious persuasion of the deceased in order to attend to the altar and ensure that visiting family and friends would not be offended. 'It would not do to set the altar for a Jew and find the deceased was a Muslim or a Roman Catholic,' he told me. 'People do take death very personally, you know. It only happens once and you've got to get it right first time.'

It struck me how much he enjoyed his work, dealing with death as though it were a personal hobby. I watched him for some time, invigorated and inspired by his interest and enthusiasm. Then the door opened. You could hear the hinges squeaking but the doorway was out of view so nothing could be seen. I felt it was an appropriate moment to ask Martin whether he had ever seen a ghost or spirit. He stopped in his tracks as if poleaxed, turned white, looked towards the ceiling and fearfully replied, 'No.'

It was Harry the stores assistant who had opened the door. Coming through it, he joked, 'Better get that squeak seen to. It feels cold in here, as if someone has just died!'

I thought how afraid Martin had been of the idea of the dead haunting the living, whilst Harry took every aspect of death in his stride. Harry was approaching retirement, so he had seen many of his friends taken out of this world whilst serving in the Second World War. He told me that he was looking forward to rejoining the friends he had lost in his youth. He recounted the death of a good friend whom he had seen lying mutilated on the ground and then getting up again: 'He looked to me like a shadow of himself. I blinked, then he was gone.' Since then death had held no fear for Harry.

During my time at the hospital it felt as if I were employed just to rescue the souls who had passed over. I am quite sure this task is carried out by many who walk among us. Some will not realize they do it, like Martin the morgue attendant, yet with loving care and attention they too become a doorway between worlds.

We have encountered earthbound spirits all over the world and helped them to be released from their attachments and move on. There are numerous reasons why some souls are unable to move safely into the otherworld, regardless of the method of death, but we have found that expectation of an afterlife is a key factor. During our travels to India we found that regions which looked to Christianity, Judaism or Islam, the monotheistic faiths, were filled with discarnate spirits, whereas the cities of Buddhist, Hindu and tribal cultures were less troubled by earthbound spirits. We concluded that belief in a cyclical soul journey, rebirth and reincarnation made people feel safer than the idea of judgement inherent in monotheistic faiths. A belief in a certain afterlife means it is safe to die and the soul can move on more easily and not hold on to this life of limitations.

BOUND TO THE EARTH

There are many reasons why souls are unable to find their way once in the spirit worlds. Their memories can keep them attached to a person or place. The manner in which they died can also hold them back. To experience a sudden or violent death can be a tremendous shock, stunning the soul so that it is unable to recognize that death has happened and continues to live as though it were still alive. Ghostly sightings in locations of war, from the Somme to Vietnam, in villages and towns destroyed by natural disasters and in other places of national tragedy are common, as the souls of the dead remain trapped by the shock of their deaths.

A MESSAGE FROM AN EARTHBOUND SPIRIT

When I died I experienced immense grief. That is what pulled me back to the world of the living. I had unresolved business and a great deal of guilt because of leaving those whom I thought needed me. With the passing of time I believed I had made a mistake in coming back. I noticed time changes everything and I wasn't needed. I then felt deep regret followed by pain. I waited for my wife to pass over, but as time went by, she never did. In fact she sparked up a friendship with another man, which was more than I could bear to think about. So, as a Christian in life, I prayed hard in death.

Suddenly it was as if a great wind touched me from behind. I felt myself being levitated away from personal issues. My heart felt lighter, I felt restored. Then I saw the light and knew I was safe. I discovered the Saviour works in a mysterious way and realized there is a loving God.

Stanley, died 1957

Emotional attachments also weigh heavily on the soul. If the soul is haunted by failure, fear or regret it can be drawn into the shadow of memories which causes it to feel unsafe and unable to heal the past.

A spirit may also refuse to leave a place because of its ancestral connections or the failure of descendants to carry out its will. The belief in ownership does not necessarily die with mortal death and nor does an attraction to objects or places, love ties with family and friends or the desire to celebrate life in a human way. Most often, though, it is simply a case of becoming so accustomed to the habits of life that we simply cannot see another way of being.

RESCUING THE DARK AND THE LIGHT

Early on in my career I rescued two spirits who could not have been more different. The first was wandering in the Whispering Gallery at St Paul's cathedral. He introduced himself as Joseph Mallord William Turner, the celebrated artist of the nineteenth century, and over the next three days, as I helped to relocate him to his ancestors, he talked about his life, in particular his friendship with Byron. I assumed quite naturally that he mean the poet, but when I suggested this he was affronted and condemned him as a cad and a bounder. It was the poet's father who had been his friend. By the time of his death he had become spiritually confused. He told me that he had become disenchanted by his traditional religious beliefs and instead had announced, 'The sun is God.' When he died the confusion in his consciousness meant that any chance he had had of moving on had been lost. Finally I was able to help him to move on and meet his ancestors.

Within a week of rescuing the great artist I was confronted by a very different sphere, one of great darkness. I was in an art gallery when quite suddenly I felt overshadowed by a spirit. The hairs on the back of my neck started to twitch, I felt physically nauseous and the taste of metal stained my mouth. A moment later a voice whispered in my ear, 'Help me, please. I am a killer.'

I soon started to feel the spirit's criminally evil instincts take a grip on me. What was remarkable was this killer did genuinely want help. Somehow he had become aware of his past evil and he was able to describe to me that before he killed anyone he would have a dark feeling or presence crawl over him and manipulate his actions. He believed that he was possessed by the Devil. After he had killed, the darkness which overcame him fell away as if it were a cloak and then he was full of remorse for his actions.

Although he never stated this, my belief was that he committed suicide and remained as an earthbound spirit hiding in the shadows for fear of being taken over by the Devil. Even after his death he still experienced this fear of being possessed. Even though he could not kill anymore, nothing in death gave him peace of mind.

I carried his spirit with me to the home of a co-worker and we began to pray for his release and for someone to come forward to help. Surprisingly, a band of monks came forward dressed in dark brown robes. They were chanting, which seemed to resonate with some buried memory in the killer's mind. He walked into their midst and a moment later they all disappeared in a flash of light.

REASONS FOR ATTACHMENT

CRYING BACK THE DYING

An excessive display of sorrow was once thought to hinder the soul's departure by strengthening earthly ties. Rituals of grieving for the mourners are vital moments of separation but there comes a point when to grieve is to hold on too tightly to the soul. We need to understand that there is a soul connection between us which reaches into eternity. But for now the departed need us to let go.

RESISTANCE TO CHANGE

Many earthbound spirits have no idea that they are actually dead. They become caught in a time warp, a shadowy world that is a grey projection of their own imagination, which has become stuck at the moment of their death. If they have died suddenly with no preparation they may simply carry on with their usual routine. They go to the office and down the pub; they watch television and play pool and cards. They act exactly the same as they did in life, with all the same attitudes, beliefs and even jokes. They might continue this way for hundreds of years!

Such earthbound spirits are aware of little or no change around them and continue to enjoy a surprisingly physical existence. They love the things dear to them, enjoy the same smells and feel as though nothing has happened. Gradually, though, their habits of convenience will become stilted and they will begin to feel wary and unable to move about easily. They will start to lose their memory. Friends won't seem to call anymore. They will feel some activity going on around them but they will not understand what it means.

It is when earthbound spirits' routine is broken, their habits interfered with, that they start to raise questions as to their state and perhaps express a wish to move on.

Poltergeists are sometimes souls of the dead who have become frustrated by their situation and want to draw attention to themselves. They cause havoc in an attempt to exert some control over their environment for, as a ghost, they have realized that they are ineffectual and invisible. They are usually happy to move on and breathe a sigh of relief when we begin to actually talk to them, see their presence and ask them what the matter is.

FRED AND GEORGE

I had a phone call: 'Terry, could you remove a ghost from my house in London?' During this working period I was constantly being called to London, a place so haunted that the majority of properties have earthbound spirits.

The following day I arrived at a large Georgian house in Eaton Square. The rooms were large and delicately decorated in a style that would suit a wealthy person from either the Far East or western Europe. The atmosphere was cool but not uncomfortable.

My client introduced herself. She was Chinese and had spent most of her life in Hong Kong. Her family were practising Buddhists and she had kept her religion and traditions even though she had married an English aristocrat. The heritage of the house was that it had supported the English gentry for many generations.

Unlike many Westerners, who find it hard to believe in the reality of psychic interference, let alone cope with it, my client knew that what was occurring in her house was certainly interference from the otherworld. Although she had moved in only a few months previously, the problems had not started immediately. This is quite often the case. But recently the lights had been switched on and off and the most irritating sounds had come from the central heating system, even when it was switched off. The maids and housekeeper had complained about the noises and a man who appeared and then disappeared from their rooms at night. My client was worried about losing her staff as well as coping with the noises, which were driving the family mad. She had already sought the advice of electricians and heating engineers and they could find no reason for the disturbances. It was evident that the last resort was to call in an expert on the paranormal.

As we made our way around the ground floor, I sensed a source of great psychic energy in the house. I was invited to take a look at a room filled with some remarkable antiques from the Far East, the centrepiece being a carved door. I was standing in front of the door, admiring the skill of the craftsmen, when I became aware of a spirit guardian watching me. He was dressed in period finery and was very tall, perhaps seven foot, with broad shoulders. I also noticed he was wearing a sword. Whether it was costume dress or for military use, I never asked. He walked straight up to me, smiled and introduced himself as the guardian spirit of the door, representing the sacred protection for the house, and also the guardian of my client. He told me the troublemakers were upstairs on the top floor and that he would be most grateful if I would take them away. As they had been here before the present family moved in, he himself did not have the right to ask them to move and they would not have gone even if he had.

I asked my client whether there was anything significant about the top floor of the house. She told me it was a self-contained flat which was used by her family when visiting London and agreed to let me take a look around it. As soon as I walked in, I felt agitated, jittery and angry. I walked around, searching for the source of the interference. I was about to sit down in the main sitting-room and link into the atmosphere to find out where the ghosts were located when I heard a spirit shouting at me, 'It's the bloody foreigners!'

With a little coaxing he explained that his name was Fred and he and his brother George had shared the house and been very happy. Then the new people had moved in. 'This upstart of a foreigner [the spirit guardian] insisted that we leave, so we thought we would teach him a lesson or two. We began by messing up the electricity, then turned to the boiler and the radiators, which really aggravated them!'

What had happened in this case was that two different cultures had clashed. The two English bachelors had not created any paranormal problems for the previous owners, even though they had been living in the house since their death in the early 1960s. But the arrival of a family who brought with them a spirit from a different culture was intolerable to them. After a long debate they agreed it was no use staying in an antagonistic environment and agreed to come with me.

───────────

Liz Whiston is a natural psychic, but when she moved into a new flat at first she wasn't sure what was going on:

Almost immediately I began to hear crashing noises, as if a huge pile of furniture had been pushed over, but nothing ever seemed to have moved. It happened in the middle of the night, with my cats jumping with apprehension as much as I did, and then it occurred again during the day. At first I wondered if it was builders, then someone in the car park, but no. I had bought the flat from someone who had stayed there for only six months and moved out due to illness. I wondered if they had had similar experiences...

One evening I walked in the front door and there was an immediate crash in the room beside me, worse than any of the others. I sat down and as Terry and Natalia had taught me I called down my spirit guides for protection and asked who was there.

It turned out that there were three girls who had worked in the building around 1910, when it had been a match factory. They had returned there after they had died to be around their friends. They were annoyed with me because I was moving things around and disturbing them. More than that, they wanted some sort of attention. Interestingly, they told me that they had been far worse to the person who had lived there before because he had been homosexual and they found this disgusting. Perhaps this was the reason why he had left so quickly?

My spirit guides talked to them, helped them realize they were dead and guided them out of the building through what apparently had been the door of the factory. I have never heard another crash since.

THE HOUSE GUEST

Cornelia, a therapist and healer, discovered that she was living with an earthbound spirit only weeks after she had moved into her new flat:

I was first attracted to my flat because of the large bay window facing the trees in the garden and it was there that I first saw her: a small, very delicate and elegantly dressed old lady with a lilac rinse in her hair and little pearl earrings. I looked again and I noticed that the furniture arrangement was different: there were two dark wooden armchairs and little round tables. She sat in one of the chairs, with the table laid for tea, and as she sipped tea from a dainty porcelain cup, she smiled at me and nodded.

A few weeks went by and since her presence had hardly been threatening, I chose to forget about the whole thing. Then I decided to call in a feng shui expert to advise me on my home. As soon as he entered the bedroom he picked up that there was a ghost there. He was adamant that it would be bad for me to share my living space with her and began rubbing sulphur stones in the corners of the room. I had a brief flash of the old lady again, this time very distressed and asking me why I was doing this to her. Then the vision disappeared. For the next three nights the energy was very turbulent until it began to be disruptive and disturbing.

I called Terry and asked him what to do, telling him about the feng shui incident and my vision. He suggested that I brought the lady along to see him and said that he would help to free her.

Later I sat on my sofa and talked into seemingly nothing, asking the little old lady if she would like to meet a kind man who might be able to help her on her way to join the rest of her family. She appeared and smiled at me, saying that she would like that very much. Then I saw her packing a small brown well-used overnight case. She told me that she used to live in the flat below mine but as it was now occupied by an alcoholic she had moved upstairs to my flat. She said that I was her favourite of all the people she had ever lived with.

We left the house together and she was very real to me. Even on the bus ride I could see her clearly sitting next to me. In fact, she was so real I almost made her a cup of coffee when we got to the house where Terry was waiting. Having made sure that she was safe and ready to move on with one of Terry's soul rescue guides, I said goodbye and left.

Two months later the block's cleaner, who has worked there for 29 years, pointed to a flowering bush in the garden, told me that a Mrs Chapman had planted it and asked me if I had known her. I asked her to describe her to me and she said she was a frail old lady who was always smartly dressed with a lilac rinse and pearl earrings. She had lived in the flat below mine since the block had been first built early in the twentieth century and she had been best friends with the tenant in my flat who had moved away. They used to sit in the bay window drinking together. She had died sometime before I moved in.

STATUS AND POWER

Earthbound spirits may be attached to many aspects of their earthly life, not only to people and places but also attitudes. They have often become stuck because they are concerned only with personal gain and desire, seeing no further than their own self-importance and experiences in life. They become attached to their achievements, their status and egocentricity, and often cause problems for their families. These are the control freaks of the spirit world.

In one of our cases an old grandfather decided to still live on a family estate after his death. In this case it was his sense of his own self-importance which held him back. He had no real love for his family, but he was a strong personality who wanted to hold on to his power and his land. He wasn't going to go quietly. It was his house, his domain and he was never going to let anyone else into it.

Everything appeared normal until the family decided to try and rent the houses on the estate. Then the trouble started. The family started fighting with each other over the property and the grandfather began making demands on them through dreams and appearances. In particular he managed to make the family house unpleasant to anyone who wished to rent it. People felt uncomfortable just by going into the property as he had created an atmosphere which made them feel unwelcome. Even his daughter felt uncomfortable going there. He was furious at losing control.

His granddaughter called us in desperation as people kept coming to see the property, but refusing to make an offer. We came to investigate and found the old man in his study, which still smelt of the cigars he used to smoke. A trapped bird was flapping around the hallway, which seemed symbolic of his earthbound state. We explained to him that the house had to be rented out to pay for its upkeep so that the family did not have to sell the estate. But he was still determined to hold on, even as we called on those ancestors who wished to help the family and assist him. It was his wife who came. She had died many years earlier and I sensed that she had been waiting for him for a long time but he was too blinded by his status to even notice that she was there.

In the end he went reluctantly, understanding that he didn't have a choice because of pressure from his wife and other ancestors who did not want the estate to move out of the family's hands. As he passed over a dark cloud lifted from the property. Within a week of our visit two offers were made and the property was rented to a family with young children who loved the property so much that 12 months later they renewed the contract.

WAYS OF DEATH

SUDDEN DEATH

When someone dies suddenly they go into shock and cannot find their bearings. The soul hangs around its most familiar surroundings, which are most often its own body. There is a palpable feeling of the soul around the body for hours, sometimes days, after death.

Harry Oldfield, inventor, scientist, thinker and healer, has for the last 20 years been conducting research into the human aura and energy fields, seeking to prove that they have a strong scientific basis. To this end he has developed scanning devices which are able to 'read' and photograph the human energy field and diagnose illnesses from cancerous tumours to broken bones. A senior physicist cum pathologist at one of his lectures in the South of France invited him to bring his polycontrast interference photography equipment to a mortuary to observe changes of body energy after death.

An enlightened mortuary official there told me that they witnessed a lot of dis-carnate spirits walking around there during the night. We set up our videos around the six dead bodies we were allowed to observe. They were of various ages with different causes of death ranging from a young man who had died from a drug overdose to a car accident victim and an old man who had died natu-rally.

It was with the violent death of younger people that we picked up force fields and energy patterns of unusual quality. Some were shaped in human form while above the man who had died peacefully in his 80s we picked up nothing but a warm pulsating light. In the case of the overdose victim there was nothing at all hovering above the corpse. It was dead energy.

Harry picked up a bright and brilliant energy not usually associated with a mortuary. Where was this light coming from? Could this be the light that the dying talk about at the end of a long tunnel? He was delighted by his recordings which seemed to provide evidence that the soul hangs around the body, especially in the case of violent or sudden death. But it was the final image which stunned him:

In the past I had been told that after some time soul collectors come from the spirit world to bring souls into the light. When I was first told this I was scepti-cal, but then early one morning I went into the consulting room to check the equipment and suddenly against a white background, I saw this priestly figure holding a staff rather like a pope. He was wearing a special head-dress and had beautiful colours around him. I called him Angelos. He looked to me like a fig-ure described to me by a clairvoyant, who said that this figure was often mis-taken for the Angel of Death but was really a being of serenity and of light who comes to guide lost souls to their final destination.

VIOLENT DEATH

Violent death, whether through accident, murder or war, can trap the soul in real torment and shock. Not only are such souls usually stunned by their death and often unable to come to terms with it, but they also leave behind unresolved issues and terrible grief which makes it difficult for them to move on. The shock can cause them to stay where they died on the battlefield or in the accident or else they will try to find their way back to their living relatives, drawn by their grief.

Sudden death causes great trauma for the soul, but prayers and rituals from any tradition can help it to realize that it has died and to move on. Simply by bringing flowers and incense to the place of death and pouring our love onto the memory can help lift the soul's consciousness, thus assisting it towards the light.

Being unprepared for death leaves many souls unable to move on, yet those who are aware of their immortality have a natural spiritual knowledge of how to pass through the spirit world moving toward their ancestors and into the light, however sudden their death.

MURDER

Murder always leaves a violent imprint on the psychic atmosphere of the place where it has happened. It is almost always immediately apparent to a psychic that this kind of violation has taken place. In the flat where our friend Kadamba was killed an unsettling atmosphere pervaded the place for months after her spirit moved on and this will need to be psychically cleared before anyone can live there in peace. We were able to help Kadamba through the stages of the death process because of our strong emotional bonds, but usually a murder victim is trapped at the place where they died.

In 1990 Marlon Brando's son was charged with the murder of Dag Drollet, the lover of Brando's daughter Cheyenne. Soon afterwards the American press began speculating that the family was being haunted by the angry spirit of the dead lover. Brando spoke of sheets mysteriously flying off his bed and 'cold ghastly lips' whispering, 'I should not have died.' The actor's former wife, Anna Kashfi, said he was convinced it was the ghost of Dag Drollet.

'It's terrifying,' Brando is said to have admitted. 'I know it is Dag's angry spirit.'

This problem for Brando's family did not cease until Cheyenne committed suicide the following year.

Sometimes earthbound spirits can be so resentful of the manner in which they died that they will haunt the living until they feel that their revenge is complete. One of our clients, Tom, was having difficulty in renting his house in West Hollywood, LA. Within weeks tenants would insist on leaving. We discovered that the previous owners were two lesbians who had murdered an old lover in the house. The kitchen was particularly haunted by the memory of the murder. Although neither Natalia nor I could detect an earthbound spirit, the atmosphere was thick with hatred and anger.

After purifying the house and cleansing the space, suddenly we felt the room become really dark and cold. I recognized the spirit of a young woman who was indeed the murdered lover. She was very angry at her early death and admitted to causing the problems in the house. I managed to communicate with her and after some time enabled her to release some of her hatred and anger. I convinced her that she was doing herself no good by haunting the house, especially as her murderers had been detained in custody. I suggested that she sought guidance from her ancestors to see if they could assist on the case, which was coming up in court shortly. She agreed that this was a positive way forward and left the house with an ancestral grandfather whom she was delighted to see again. The atmosphere of the house changed within days and Tom was able to persuade an old tenant to move back in.

ACCIDENT

Accidents also confuse and disorientate the soul, often leaving it wandering near the place of death waiting for some recognizable figure to help it find its way.

The Druid priestess Emma Restall Orr recounts passing a motorway pile-up and seeing the soul of a woman picking her way through the wreckage. Unable to stop but traumatized by what she saw, Emma began intoning a prayer: 'Be with that soul, whoever she may be, show her the way, by the power of three, oh my Lady of sweet serenity, be with that soul.' Later that night the woman's soul visited her. She had died with her child as their car had been crushed under a truck and she had come to thank Emma for her helping her to see the way.

The Lockerbie Child

I was called in to help one family soon after the Lockerbie disaster. A child, presumably killed in the crash, had attached herself to the father of the household, Ashley, who had been on a business trip in the area. She had become attracted to the colours in his aura and, as with all spirit children, was willing to trust him because of her innocence. She followed him home because he 'seemed like a nice man'. Ashley remembers the events vividly:

One evening my wife Bobbie heard the sounds of children's toys being played with, long after our own sons, then aged one and four, were asleep. She checked on them but found nothing. When she went back to bed she heard a child's giggle outside the door.

A couple of nights later I was also awakened by a child giggling just outside the door. It was definitely a girl's voice. I wasn't frightened, although I remember thinking clearly, 'I am not dreaming.'

The next evening we were out to dinner and suddenly I seemed to receive a rush of information. In a vision I saw a little blonde girl and heard the name Rachel. I turned to my wife and described the laughter I had heard. She went as white as a sheet.

By coincidence, Bobbie met Natalia and mentioned our little 'problem'. She told us Terry could solve it. He turned up one evening. Very quietly and without us telling him anything, he went straight to our younger son's bedroom. He asked not to be watched and in about five minutes emerged, saying he had sent the child on her way to the otherworld. There were no flashing lights, nothing dramatic, our children were running around as normal. We never heard another sound from the little girl and what convinced us that she was gone was that our younger son slept through the night, which he had not been doing ever since she had appeared.

From the moment I arrived in the house I sensed a child in the boy's bedroom. She was untroubled and felt safe with the family, which was extraordinary considering the way that she had died. It struck me that she was treating this situation like a holiday rather than a dreadful experience. She was content in herself and very lively and liked playing with the toys. It was very simple to call her family and explain to her that it was time for her to go with them. It was her grandparents, who had passed over several years before, who came to collect her.

SUICIDE

Suicide has always been a matter of grave concern among most religious and spiritual traditions, for it is believed that only God can give and take life. Buddhists believe that taking a life, whether it is your own or that of another living creature, is breaking natural law. Special rites and fire ceremonies are conducted in Tibet to free the consciousness of a suicide as it is said that they will almost always meet negative karma. But it is important to recognize that the souls of suicide victims need healing, love and prayers so that they do not remain caught in their own pain.

The international trance medium Colin Fry has found through his work communicating with the dead that many suicides do see the light when they die but they do not accept it because of their own pain, guilt or despair. 'They need help from this side of life to move onto the other side,' he says. 'I believe that life has punished them already and they do find through the support of ancestors and guides time to heal what could not be healed in their lives.'

Many who die in this way are not able to liberate themselves from the pain which caused them to commit suicide in the first place. In one of our cases the spirit of a suicide victim nearly persuaded a young girl to take her own life because he was making her so depressed. Her family had just moved to a large house and Alexandra had just turned 13. She was a sensitive and artistic child, always happy and enjoying life; she made friends easily and she had no problems at school. But over the few months that the family had lived in the home, her personality had changed and she had become moody, depressed and anti-social. She feared going to bed, suffered nightmares, would wake up every day exhausted and was unable to concentrate at school. For some months her mother had pursued medical and other professional avenues, including a child psychologist, but each new method brought her daughter only temporary relief. She began to suspect that the problems might be due to a supernatural influence. When she found Alexandra's diary with a recent entry implying a suicide attempt, she knew that something had to be done. At that point she approached us for help.

While Alexandra was at school I investigated the property and the surrounding land. I eventually found the soul of a young man who had died some years before occupying Alexandra's bedroom and I immediately recognized the symptoms of suicide. The soul was depressed, alone and frightened. He explained to me that he had committed suicide on a business trip in the Far East. On his death he had made his way home but as a disembodied spirit it had taken him 11 years to find his way back. When he eventually arrived home he discovered to his horror his family didn't live there anymore. At that point he realized that he had succeeded in taking his own life and now had nowhere to go. He recognized Alexandra as a sensitive child and tried to communicate his problem to her. This was the cause of her physical, emotional and psychological symptoms.

The work was not complete until I was able to heal any connection that this soul may have had with Alexandra, so when she returned home from school, her mother and I lifted her energies with massage and spiritual healing. Within three days she was back to her normal self. Her bedroom also had to be purified as the deceased man's depression and grief permeated it. I cleared it using herbal mixtures and crystals and, as the family are Greek Orthodox, they added icons and other religious artefacts to seal off and protect the bedroom, making Alexandra feel safe within her own religious beliefs. The mother later discovered from neighbours that a doctor who formerly owned the house had had a son who had committed suicide some years earlier.

As a general rule children are more sensitive to the world of spirits than adults and can often be disturbed by them. Parents may put change of behaviour down to school problems, illness or unfamiliar surroundings if they have just moved house but, if children are suffering from nightmares and do not appear to be themselves, it is just as likely that they may be troubled by an earthbound spirit in the home. Parents should listen to them and watch their symptoms. If they do not go away then it is worth calling a soul rescuer to check if there is a paranormal problem.

Another case with the soul of a suicide victim involved the possession of an adult. Christina and Genie have worked and studied with us for a long time and they were visiting us in Scotland for a private retreat. One afternoon they went down a secluded track, got lost and decided to find the nearest pub for a drink.

As they entered the pub they realized that they were interrupting a funeral party and were about to leave when an elderly man asked them to stay and enjoy his hospitality, even though it was a sad occasion. He turned out to be the father of a young man who had committed suicide by gassing himself in his car, leaving a wife and two young children. During the short time they spent at the pub Christina started to find the atmosphere stifling and soon told Genie that she wanted to leave as she did not feel very well. They asked directions to their hotel and left.

As they drove back Christina began to feel worse and worse. Her breathing became erratic and she wanted to vomit. She had a bad taste in her mouth and a knot in her stomach. During the night she became worse and was unable to sleep or eat anything. They left the hotel in the morning and decided to stop off at our cottage before continuing their journey.

We took one look at Christina. It was obvious she was haunted just by looking at her dark and hollow eyes and grey-green pallor. We helped her into the house and checked her aura with a dowsing crystal. It picked up that she had drawn a spirit into herself and we realized that it was the young man who had committed suicide. Christina's compassion had drawn him into her aura and he had pushed himself so close to her physical body that she was now mirroring how he was feeling. The way he died was haunting him, as well as the realization of what he had done. The heavy feeling on Christina's chest and foul taste in her mouth confirmed the diagnosis. The soul was very sad and depressed and unable to communicate coherently with us, but we were able to lift him gently out of Christina's energy field and pass him over to the otherworld. Within a few moments Christina felt fine and greatly relieved to be freed from her first possession by a spirit.

In situations where many people die at once in national tragedies, massacres and war the spirits will often all become earthbound together. Keeping each other company they can be even less likely to find their way into liberation because as they are all in the same situation they are less likely to notice any changes going on around them.

Recently I was invited by a ghosthunter Paul Southcott to attend an investigation at the London Dungeon Museum, a museum of the macabre which demonstrates some of the tragedy, sadness and darkness of London's past. Undoubtedly the building is haunted by many generations of disturbed ghosts, but it was not the darkness which interested me but how I could bring a little light and compassion into these spine-chilling surroundings.

Paul had located a considerable number of spirits trapped in a time warp. He led me to the place where he had picked up the psychic activity. It was in a long tunnel around the back of the museum which had been used as an air raid shelter during the Blitz bombing of the Second World War. The building had taken a direct hit, instantly killing 61 people who had been taking shelter there.

As soon as we entered the tunnel I could see them and feel their huge pain and panic. They were all caught in the moment after the bomb had exploded. None of them realized that they were dead, all thinking instead that they were wounded and waiting for the rescue services. Their pain filled the tunnel.

To rescue these souls the only way forward was to create a reconciliation, which has to be organized and carried out by field workers in the otherworld. These spirit workers are akin to guardian angels. They aid most healers and soul rescuers, ensuring that the souls that are rescued are moved forward to a safe place within the otherworld. In this case, with so many souls to rescue at one time, the only way was for them to be directly connected to these spirit workers. My job was to make contact with these people and call them out of their pain. Assuming them to be Christian, I prayed in the name of Jesus Christ for their freedom and safety. I directed my voice into the midst of their lonely world to resonate consciously with them so that they could hear my voice and be drawn to my physical magnetism. In hearing me they came forward. I explained that they were to be rescued and should follow the field workers who had come with me. These workers were wearing uniforms of the Second World War so that no shock would affect those being rescued. At this point I liaised with my inner world guardian, who told me that the rescue was underway and that I could leave them to tie up the loose ends.

One by one the trapped souls were lifted out of their limited memory of the time of their death and reunited with their ancestors and loved ones. As they left there was a huge wave of emotional release which was deeply moving for the people with us.

Hottentots

In South Africa we came across a similar situation when we helped to clear a friend's house in Cape Town. She had been suffering from excruciating back pain and recurring nightmares. The family were trying to rent the house for the summer but could find no takers.

Our investigation began by dowsing the basement. After an hour we suddenly saw hundreds of haunted faces peering up at us from a great pit in the earth. They looked like Bushmen or Hottentot tribespeople. They had died in great fear and appeared to have been killed in a massacre. It was now time for them to reconnect with their ancestors, who had been calling out of their compassion for them as time had passed. It would take the entire night for them to move on as there were so many of them.

In the morning the family phoned us to say that during the night they had heard a terrible commotion in the basement. When they went down in the morning they found that all their furniture, boxes and shelves had been thrown across the floor as if a burglary had taken place. We explained that often when there is such a powerful rescue, the energy which has been trapped for so long has to be released and shake itself free. This is what had happened.

The family were delighted with the change in atmosphere and our friend's back pain cleared in days. After a week the house was taken on for the summer.

TRAPPED BY WAR

So many souls who have died in war feel that their lives have been wasted. They haunt the battlefield where they died or try to find their way home, believing themselves to be only wounded or stunned by shrapnel.

When we lived in Scotland we rescued a spirit who had managed to return to his family home after his death during the First World War. He had been a soldier in one of the Scottish regiments and he had never ceased to be angry at the way he died. He told us:

I was sent behind enemy lines and returned to base. The commander insisted that I go back out again straight away to gather further information. I knew that if I went out there again I would die and I argued my case with the officer in charge and reiterated my fear. He insisted that I return or be accused of being a traitor to my king and country. Against all my instincts I returned to reconnoitre enemy lines when I met my death crossing no man's land. As I felt my spirit rise out of my body, I tried to call out, 'You'd better not send me back!', only to notice my voice gave out no sound as if I was struck dumb. The realization of my death struck me instantly and I was filled with abject anger and rage towards the officer who had ignored my plea.

This soldier had spent many years reliving that situation and been unable to liberate himself due to his hatred for the commanding officer. Finally he realized that this could not go on any longer. He decided that he must change his attitude and release himself from his rage so when we discovered him he had reached the point where he was willing to let go.

Out of gratitude for his rescue he decided that he would dedicate himself to working with us to free souls who had died in similar situations to his own. Since then he has been a very valuable member of our inner world rescue team.

In war when large numbers of the same regiment are killed at one time on the field of honour it is often the case – particularly during the First World War when men from the same town or village were killed together – that they find each other and, believing themselves to be still alive, wander the battlefields fighting what to them is a lost cause. Others try to return to their homes, believing that they have been given leave due to being wounded in action.

During a recent visit to an old estate in Cornwall we discovered a group of First World War veterans. The house had been a convalescent home for returning soldiers and the main bedroom, which was connected to the living room, felt oppressive and seemed to have shadows lurking in the four corners. It was dark even during the day and a heavy mist hung over both the rooms. As I walked in I could see beyond the shadows and grey damp atmosphere to the spirits of six elderly gentlemen. As soon as they could sense that we could communicate with them they asked us to leave them alone and began to explain that they meant no harm to anyone and just wanted to get on with their lives. Many of them had died of chest infections after the war and they had decided to continue living together as they had been great friends and had no place left to go. By now, as they had been dead for so long, they had lost all concept of time.

We asked whether they wished to find a better location in which to live and to find lost families and friends and, to our surprise, they all agreed. They gathered up their belongings and over a two to three day period they all left the house. The room began to lighten and as one guest staying in the house exclaimed, 'It feels empty now.'

In war, when death is sudden and brutal, often away from home, and there is frequently no body to mourn, collective rituals of remembrance are an opportunity for earthbound souls to move on. Armistice Day, the day of remembrance for the war dead, is one such opportunity. Many of dead find their way to the ceremonies, still looking as they did during their time on Earth. When they see their comrades looking so old the penny can sometimes drop. For the first time they realize that the great shock which they felt at the time of their death did not just knock them out but actually killed them. Once they understand this they are ready to move on.

Rituals of remembrance and release can be particularly important in cases of civil war where family, tribal or cultural unity is dismantled by betrayal and violence, causing long-term suffering within the family tree. There is an argument that unless we can deal with the pain and sins of the forefathers there will be continuing difficulties for the descendants.

Many people throughout the world are working to help the earthbound, using compassion and understanding to help souls pass to the other side. There are Spiritualists who work in rescue circles, aboriginal elders who ceremoniously release the dead and shamans in Africa and South America who are using ancient techniques of healing and exorcism to clear earthbound spirits from land and buildings. In Germany and Poland many dowsers and occultists are working to release the souls still trapped in the Second World War concentration camps. As the world becomes a place where violent death through war, murder and accident is increasingly common, the psychic landscape is becoming even more cluttered with the lost souls and past memories of death, so the work of soul rescuers is becoming more essential.

THE MEXICAN DAY OF THE DEAD

El Dia de los Muertos, the Day of the Dead, is the homecoming of the spirits of the dead all over Mexico, a reunion of the dead and the living. The old ones say that when the spirits come back to the world of the living their path must be clear, the roadway must not be slippery with the wet flood of human tears.

In Mexico this is the most important festival of the year. No expense is spared to prepare the home altars for the arrival of the spirits of the dead ancestors. Icons of Jesus and Mary, photographs of loved ones who have died, candles and angels are displayed under wooden trellises covered with yellow marigolds, specially baked bread for the dead, sugar skulls, dough animals, fruit and corn. The night before, cemeteries glow with thousands of candles as the women and children chant and pray for the peace of the souls of the dead and ask for their blessings on the living. The sudden snuffing of a candle, a rustle of wind or knocking over of a glass are seen as proof that the spirits are present, and as the vigil draws to a close at dawn the sombre mood shifts into joy and release. Then a priest will come and give a general benediction and the families will return to their homes to feast, sing and dance.

Rituals and festivals of remembrance are profound ways of dealing with loss, but originally their aim was to help the dead themselves detach from their lives on Earth and move successfully into the spirit world.

These ancient ceremonies are the bridges which the soul can use to move forward on their journey instead of remaining bound to the Earth. The simple process of the living honouring their memory is enough to help them to feel safe enough to move on into the spirit world.

For many communities these festivals are an opportunity to restore spiritual balance as the living reconnect with the spirit of loved ones. They are not dark or mournful affairs, but rather to do with remembrance and healing. The spirits themselves are invited back for a celebration. From All Souls and Samhain in Western culture to Ch'ing Ming, the Festival of Brightness, in China and the Obun, the Feast of Lanterns, in Japan, special candles and lights welcome the dead back. All these ceremonies are linked to the light, both in the symbolic raising of the souls toward enlightenment or heaven and in lighting the way for their journey through the underworld into the ancestral realms.

Remembrance of the dead is particularly strong in cultures throughout the East, where veneration of the ancestors remains of great importance. In spring throughout China there is a flurry of festivals celebrating and invoking the ancestors. At the first moon of spring all work is supposed to cease as relationships with friends and family are renewed and dead ancestors and household gods are welcomed into the home with offerings and food.

In the autumn the Chinese have another ritual, this time for the release of general souls. Known as the Moon of the Hungry Ghosts, it lasts from one moon to the next and is a time when people in their millions pay reverence to all the lonely ghosts who have no descendants to care for them and who are therefore always hungry. Lotus flower lamps are carried through the streets and at dusk candles are stuck into tiny boats and floated down the streams. In Chinatowns around the world huge dumpling mountains are left outside the temples to feed all the hungry ghosts. Every day the mountains rise and every evening they are distributed among the poor. There is serious money involved as corporations as well as individual families contribute, believing that otherwise profit will suffer in the following year. For a full month children are not called by their name but are given the name of an animal as protection, for the hungry ghosts want to possess human beings, especially children. These superstitions run very deep, providing a backbone of culture which is rarely questioned.

In the West the traditional Catholic rites for the souls of the dead remain a powerful part of general worship. In November the Catholic feasts of All Saints, when the Catholics celebrate the deaths of the saints and martyrs, and All Souls remain two of the most important days of the Catholic calendar. On All Souls Day candles are lit and a requiem mass commemorates all the souls in Purgatory to help them attain the final cleansing and purification so that they may finally ascend to Heaven. Purgatory is a seen as a kind of waiting room where souls who are still blinded by self-importance and self-ishness wait to become sufficiently cleansed for them to be able to see God. As the living pray for them they begin to open up to divine consciousness.

These Catholic festivals replaced Samhain, which was celebrated as the most powerful festival of the Celtic year. It falls on the eve of 31 October, on the cusp of winter, and is a celebration of death and rebirth. As the old Celtic year dies to give way to the new, the veil between the living and the dead becomes as flimsy as gossamer. The spirits of the dead rise up and wander freely around the land. Offerings and gifts are left to honour the ancestors and faerie fold. Shades of this festival remain in the custom of ghoulish Halloween children playing tricks on the people who do not have any treats to give them.

In a symbolic rite which continued in remote parts of Ireland and Scotland until very recently, at Samhain everyone extinguished the fires in the hearth and rekindled them from huge communal bonfires lit by the Druids. Fire is a purifying force and the rekindling of new fires from the dying embers of the old was symbolic of the regenerative qualities of life and death. Today, in the current revival of pagan traditions, the festival of Samhain is becoming a healing rite of passage in which all the gain, losses, joy and pain of the previous year are given away to the flames of a fire.

Every year we hold a Sacred Healer retreat over this time and invariably it is the most powerful retreat that we hold. In 1998, on the cusp of the millennium, a healer who was working with us for a year suggested that we open the Samhain retreat with a ritual to honour departed loved ones with a bonfire and a feast. It was the first retreat that we had held in

Cornwall so it was also an opportunity to honour the spirits of the land and ask for their guidance in the healing. The healer wrote to our clients, asking them to write down names of all the dead they wanted to honour and remember. The response was overwhelming and in the end we must have had over 200 names.

It was a wild Cornish night as we found a sheltered fissure in the cliff opening to a shallow cave at the back where we could build a bonfire protected from the wind and the rain. The driving rain continued even as everyone made their way down to the beach with their gifts, letters, bottles of whiskey and tiny gargoyle nightlights to decorate the cliff. It looked as though it was going to be one of those moments when it would be hard for everyone to hold their focus with the rain running down their necks and freezing their fingers, but as we opened the ceremony the wind suddenly dropped and the rain disappeared. Each person in turn walked toward the fire and called out the names of the dead, sometimes silently, sometimes out loud. Some people said a few words about them, forgiving them for the past or asking them for permission to let them go and move on. They threw their names onto the fire and sealed the ritual by spraying whiskey onto the flames.

It was a potent ritual with a powerful intention and, as the clouds parted to reveal a crescent moon, we watched as each person gave up those beloved names to the flames and, like ghostly armies, we saw columns and columns of the dead walking through the flames and into the light. It was as if each ancestor called in this sacred way became a gateway for the rest of their lineage and as their name was given to the flames they were free to lead their people into the light.

Meanwhile I went down to the water's edge. Looking out over this place notorious for shipwrecks, smugglers and wreckers, I said a prayer to draw the ghosts out of the sea and into the light. As I watched, amazed, hundreds of souls came out of the sea and walked toward the fire, which had become an open doorway into the realms of the spirit world and eternity.

ANCESTRAL CONNECTION

CHAPTER THREE

The psyche is not of today. Its ancestry goes back many millions of years. Individual consciousness is only the flower and fruit of a season sprung from the perennial root beneath the earth.

Carl Jung

Our ancestors are our most intimate connection with the spirit world. The belief that we have an invisible connection with them is world-wide. Just as trees were thought to hold within their memory the vision and stability of the past, so when we look back down our own family tree and discover who has contributed to our spiritual or genetic inheritance we can feel the same sense of continuity. The family tree can be seen in the same symbolic light as the mythological tree of the world, its growth through the ages branching out into the world through life, death and experience. Some branches wither and die, while others become wider and stronger. Each family tree will bear its fruit.

It is often only when our grandparents or our parents die that it occurs to us to consider life after death and our need to continue to have a relationship with them. We do this in our thoughts, dreams and memories. Our connection with them does not stop when they die – instinctively we call out to them when we want help or advice and need to feel their presence around us.

The ancestors range in age from those who have just passed over to ancient elder guardian spirits. In many cultures they are officially regarded as the invisible guides, protectors and lawmakers for families, tribes and even nations. Belief in their power to draw both good or bad fortune to the family line inspires people throughout the world to honour and remember them with shrines and prayers, gifts and praise. They are consulted on everything from the smallest problem to the most important issues of marriage, property, education and most especially fertility and childbirth.

In the tribal traditions of many indigenous people a child is welcomed into the world as an ancestor returning to the family with special gifts and teachings. It comes from the ancestral realms of the spirit world, swinging through the gateway of birth, as other souls return through the gateway of death, completing the cycle of life.

THE ROLE OF THE ANCESTORS

The ancestors stand at the gateway of birth and death. In ancient Rome it was believed that each male child was born with a *genius*, a protecting spirit linked to them through family lineage, which would help direct their lives towards goodness and prosperity. The female equivalent was called a *Juno*.

We are all born into a bloodline which will give us the lessons, and the gifts, which will help us to perform our destiny in the world. We inherit a culture, religion, race and country as well as personal attributes and failings which will affect every step we take on our journey through life.

In Burkino Faso in Africa, when a child is born, the women of the village, chanting a litany of genealogy, surround the birthing mother. Each ancestor's name is sung so that the baby will be sure of its identity. The grandparents are the first to hold the baby because the newborn has just arrived from the ancestral realms where the elders are soon to return, so they share a special proximity to the world of spirit.

In our experience there is always an ancestor who connects with a newborn child in order to become a guardian spirit to help and guide them as they grow up. They come with the souls of children who are ready to become part of the family tree.

Some time ago, whilst staying in America, I visited a crystal healer in

A foundation for trust, inner strength or creativity can come from family, upbringing and lineage, but there can also be a darker side to one's heritage. As you trace your roots and find out more about your ancestors, you will find a continuum of characteristics, from the helpful to the harmful, that have come down through the generations to reside in you.

Denise Linn

Los Angeles. At the time I was unaware that I was pregnant with my son Ossian. I lay on a couch for treatment to help heal a digestive disorder brought on by stress. The healer, Frank Ozak, gently placed crystals across my body and around my head. The sensation of the stones created such a harmonious atmosphere that I fell asleep. During this time I saw a spirit standing over me. I assumed it was Frank's guide. Frank commented that when he was healing me he saw a man. He described his features and what he was wearing. The man told him that I was pregnant, that the child was one of his descendants and that he would guide him. I was rather shocked by his comments as we had no intention of having another child just yet and I did not think I was pregnant! A few days later I took a pregnancy test and it was positive! The spirit, by the description, was my father's father. It was the hat that gave it away!

We believe that our children carry a leaning towards different branches on our own family tree. Our eldest, Sequoia, is very much like Terry's family and she is guided by an ancestor spirit from his father's side; Ossian is guided by my father's Hungarian lineage and is very much like my father, both in his physical build and personality; whilst our youngest, who is newborn, is carrying the brown-eyed gene and is akin to my Spanish family.

There are so many stories from other families of the arrival of a newborn with a connecting ancestor. When my Irish friend Katherine came to see me for a reading, I could feel the presence of a man. He spoke to Katherine about her fears of being a mother and the reasons why she had not fallen pregnant much sooner than she had expected. One of the reasons was due to the fact that the spirit of the child was not ready to be born. He described himself and she recognized him as her maternal grandfather. A couple of months later whilst she was on holiday in Cuba she dreamt of her grandfather. He had brought her a present. A few weeks later she found out that she was pregnant with her daughter, who is now two years old and is a very wise little girl. Katherine still feels the presence of her grandfather guiding and supporting her role as a mother...

There are gifted children waiting to be born. The ancestors prepare them for their birth and they are aware of their destiny, so they are able to support them by their wisdom and guidance from the spirit realms. If a child were seeking to fulfil a business career or likewise had musical or creative gifts, their guiding ancestor would have the understanding that would help them fulfil their ambition. This inspiration would have been passed down from a talent source within the family tree. Earlier ancestors would have developed the initial ideas and these memories would be passed down the line to future generations for further development, to finally reach a child prepared to pursue that gift or role. Although the lineage in many cases can be traced back, sometimes the difficulty that comes with this level of genius is that the next generation may find it hard to follow in the parents' footsteps. They find it difficult to carry the banner of great success or fulfilment. The key for them is to seek their own destiny...

When we grow up and begin to work in the world, the ancestors continue to watch over our growth and development. In Africa, where people live with one eye on the physical world and the other on the spiritual dimension, they believe the ancestors are watching and guiding their actions, making the relationship a conscious one. Decisions are rarely made without consulting the ancestors and their influence is evident everywhere. Coincidences of nature, miracles and good luck are all seen as a result of the invisible guiding hand of a benign ancestral figure.

Malidoma Somé attributes his unprecedented success in the West as a shaman, healer and writer to his grandfather, who initiated him as a medicine man when he was alive and now guides him from beyond the grave:

I have an utterly co-dependent relationship with my grandfather. When I go to sleep I send a message to him. I tell him that I am going to do certain things and that I expect him to be there for me. The Western world is a treacherous place and it helps me that I have a buddy who has eyes for the past, the present and the future. 'Go this way,' he says. 'Say this.' He is constantly talking to me and guiding me. But I must be open and willing for it to work. I must listen to the guidance.

From a traditional standpoint, the ancestors are family. To us, death is not an end which separates the dead from the day-to-day affairs of the living. The ancestors like to interact with us, to dance with us, to work with us. There is a true relationship between them and us. We benefit from their help, their support and guidance, but equally their power is dependent on the people who have a physical presence.

Malidoma advises us to talk to the ancestors, shout if necessary, for our relationship is always on an equal basis.

From all the healing we have conducted with our clients it is very helpful when healing childhood trauma such as death, or sexual or emotional abuse by parents or family, that forgiveness is granted through communicating with them. After they have died many come to say they are sorry... They are eager for communication, especially if they have caused pain or discord when they were alive. They want to heal the mistakes which they made and for us it is often the only way to heal any unresolved issues, grieve freely and continue with our lives.

The ancestors are still keen to take care of their families. With our clients, we usually receive clear guidance from an ancestor from the spirit world who feels a sense of love and responsibility for their descendant. Whether the guiding spirit is an ancient ancestor from many generations down the line or a beloved grandmother from this life, they return again and again, telling us the areas which the client needs to address, problems with a lover or marriage, for example, offering guidance or just being there with some gentle support and understanding.

Our ancestors are more evident at times of great crisis or sickness, often appearing to us in dreams and visions. When Robin, Duke of Tavistock, was struck down by a severe stroke, the doctors believed it would leave him paralysed and unable to lead a normal life. He recalls that his mother appeared to him while he was in a coma, bringing comfort and helping him to overcome his fear. The experience, he says, has changed him immeasurably as he has slowly recovered. His mother is a tangible presence for him now and he is no longer afraid of dying because he knows that she is there for him.

The ancestors do finally help the soul make the transition into the spirit world. The dying often begin to see visions and apparitions of deceased family members as they drift in and out of consciousness in the transitional period before death and often die reaching out their arms towards some invisible presence.

Even in sudden death the ancestors are there ready to help the soul make the transition. With our dear friend Kadamba we saw a kind-looking gentleman come to take care of her just after her death. His manner was very caring and he was dressed in the clothes of the 1950s. It transpired that it was her father's father and that he had been a popular country doctor. Our description of him was accurate enough for the grandmother to identify him.

OUR RELATIONSHIP WITH OUR ANCESTORS

The word 'ghost' comes from the same root as 'guest'. They both derive from the word *Geist*, which is German for the spirit of a dead ancestor invited to join the family in great feasts and family ceremonies. In true tribal fashion the 'guests' of the otherworld needed to be honoured and welcomed; if they were not, the family could expect bad luck and misfortune in the coming year.

In cultures around the world, where religious and spiritual beliefs are connected to ancestor worship, people achieve their sense of life balance by constantly referring back to those who have walked the Earth before them. Such an attitude brings a strong foundation as well as a sense of continuity and protection. Ritual, prayer, visiting the ancestors' graves or silent communion are just some of the ways to cultivate a keen awareness of their presence in our lives.

THE GHOST DANCE

At the end of the nineteenth century there was a powerful spiritual movement in North America called the Ghost Dance. It was created through the vision of Wovoka, a Paiute holy man and the half-breed son of a shaman. At a time of an eclipse of the sun, he fell into a trance, which lasted for three days. Many of his people believed him dead and wanted to bury him, but on the insistence of his wife Mary, they let him be. She was proved right, because on the third day he came out of his trance, recalling visions of his ancestors in heaven. He said that no white people lived there and he had seen that the native peoples of America would once more inhabit the Earth as before the white man came. He firmly believed the ancestors would be revived and once more walk the Earth, bringing with them a return to the old ways.

Wovoka became a teacher and a mystical leader for many of the Plains tribes and taught them the Ghost Dance, a ritualistic dance to call up the spirits of the dead and to bring visions. He called upon the tribespeople to gather, to fast and to dance in a circle around a sacred tree. After the ceremony the dancers would often have visions, dreams of good hunting grounds and visits by dead brothers.

During the most powerful period of the Ghost Dance movement there were many documented incidents of the mystical powers of 'ghost shirts', which were worn by the ghost dancers to guard against any danger. Many believed themselves to be invisible to enemies and protected against bullet wounds when wearing such shirts.

Tribes who had fought each other for decades came together. The ghost dancers had visions and made contact with the ancestors who they believed lived in the 'happy hunting ground' of the dead. The US Government feared this mystical rite as it stirred up such a belief in the Plains tribes that they did not fear battle with the white man.

Ultimately, however, the movement proved futile, with the slaughter of 350 Native Americans led by the pacifist chief of the Hunkpapa Sioux, Chief Big Foot, at the famous massacre at Wounded Knee Creek in 1890.

===

Credo Mutwa, a South African shaman, writer, artist and healer, knows that the only hope for his people lies in their willingness to continue a spiritual relationship with their ancestors. Like the Ghost Dance movement of the Native Americans, he teaches that if they can be called to remember the strength, the freedom and the ancient wisdom of their own forebears then they will be able to retrieve their own pride and stability at a historic moment of momentous change and hardship.

Nicola, a friend who lived on Mount Tamalpais, a former home of the Miwok tribe, near San Francisco, California, for 11 years, went to see a Santeria priest as her life had become troubled and nothing was working for her. (Santeria is a Cuban combination of Catholicism and voodoo.) The priest told her that she needed to make contact with her ancestors, particularly her grandmother, and listen to their guidance. She was told to go to the woods and find a stick from which she would create an 'ancestral staff'. Every morning she was to go out to the hills and hit the ground with the staff seven times with her question or trouble firmly held in her mind. The next day as she was walking in the woods the perfect stick literally jumped out at her, so she took it home and decorated it with carvings, ribbons and little cat bells because the ancestors 'need to hear you because they cannot see you'. Every morning she followed the priest's advice, stamping the stick onto the ground and calling out to her ancestors, shouting her questions and troubles to the hills. Every day the answer or solution to her question was answered. She created a little shrine decorated with white cloth and flowers, with some water and other offerings for the ancestors, because 'they had wished to come and give me guidance'. At the end of seven days she had no more questions to ask and her life had turned a corner.

Our ancestors have an understanding about physical life as well as the vision and power of spirit. When we listen to their influence it can bring us a better perspective on how we are living our lives.

Malidoma Some believes that the West suffers spiritual hunger because we have neglected to cultivate a relationship with our ancestors. This means that we are alienated from the true cycles of life, birth and death. Immediate contact with the ancestors cultivates an intimate understanding of the world of spirit, which can support us in our endeavours and give us the keys to who we are and where our destiny lies. In 1984 Malidoma's homeland of the Upper Volta in Africa became Burkino Faso, which literally means 'The Land of the Proud Ancestors'. Malidoma attributes the current stability and peace there to the people's spiritual relationship with their ancestors and their profound understanding of the rituals which invoke and appease the ancestors. This creates a pervasive harmony in the lives of people and the agriculture of their land.

'The ancestors are not dead,' Sobonfu, Malidoma's wife, explains. 'They are still alive. They are in the stones, the trees, the newborn and the rain.'

LAND OF OUR MOTHERS AND FATHERS — THE POWER OF THE ANCESTORS

In a tale documented by the ethnologist Washington Matthews in the 1890s, a Navajo holy man told him the wind gave the first man and first woman life.

'It is the wind that comes out of our mouths now that give us life. When this ceases to blow we die.' The old man held his wrinkled hand to the light of the lamp and gazed at his fingertips. 'In the skin of our fathers we see trail of the wind. It shows us where the wind blew when our ancestors were created.'

If we let them, our ancestors can take us back to the very beginning of time, to the first man and the first woman who walked the earth. Cultures revere the ancestors because they are believed to hold the keys to many of the secrets of life; the more ancient they are, the closer to the source of creation.

Before the Industrial Revolution began to take people from the land in Europe this was the kind of sensibility which moved our own ancestors. They understood the land as the place where their ancestors had walked, tended, worshipped, given birth and died, and they too walked in their footsteps. The holy wells, shrines, venerated trees, standing stones and sacred groves were sacred because the ancestors had made them so. The gods and goddesses worshipped there were the most ancient ancestors, who by virtue of their lives in the earliest of days were given the power to govern creation. People were able to still hear their voices through these holy places.

In a modern world where we can often feel dislocated, a return to the land from which we emerged can be immensely healing, restoring a sense of self. It is the calling of our soul which takes us to certain places where we feel 'at home' and 'at one'. In the US, where roots can only go as deep as the Pilgrim Fathers for all but the indigenous population, there is a powerful urge to return to the land of their grandfathers and great grandfathers, build family trees and seek out the records of long dead relatives throughout the British Isles, Europe and the Middle East. For Black Americans, ripped so violently from their homelands to become slaves on the plantations, there is a deep hunger for knowledge, stories and understanding from the African continent to heal the wounds of dislocation. There is a calling which pulls us back to the land where our people once lived. It is a modern journey of pilgrimage.

Sophie is a freelance photographer living in Britain who jets around the world following rock bands from city to city, yet she only really feels at home when she is in America in the deserts of Colorado and Arizona. This is where she comes when she needs to restore her balance and strength. The land speaks to her. She calls it her 'soul home'. She has been drawn to visit the sacred sites of Native America, travelling to Mount Shasta and Native American burial grounds. In an interesting conflict of cultural and spiritual inheritance, she physically resembles the Native Americans to whom she is most drawn and yet the ancestors from her family tree were pioneers and railroaders who no doubt exploited the native people.

Sophie was not surprised to discover that she is guided by an ancient Navajo spirit guide, but has gratitude for her blood family who gave her most the immediate reason to return to the land of her forefathers.

Michelle, a successful make-up artist who is half-English, half-Burmese, attended one of our retreats and it was discovered that for all of her adult life she had been in conflict: the gentle, slightly subservient side of her Burmese culture and her go-getting, independent Englishness did not sit easily side by side. Her inner conflict was manifested in a series of allergies. She suffered from alopecia, hayfever and severe asthma, waking in the middle of the night being unable to breathe and sneezing for an hour every morning when she woke up. 'It got worse as I got older,' she said. 'On the one hand I felt like any normal middle-class English girl and on the other I knew that I was not and yet my Burmese side was an empty void.' We suggested that she needed to go to Burma to find her Burmese roots and meet the rest of her family.

Michelle took two months off work and insisted that her parents come with her to introduce her to her mother's homeland. The family showed her where her mother had grown up, where her parents had met, where they got married and their first home in Mandalay. She met aunts and uncles and cousins who looked like she did.

Michelle told us that her mother had advised her not to take the Chanel suits and designer wear that she loves and suggested that instead she wore traditional dress. It surprised her how much she enjoyed wearing sarongs and during her time in Burma she visited all the Buddhist temples and connected with her spiritual heritage.

When she came back she had changed:

I always used to feel as though I carried a burden, but now I can just be myself. All my allergies have disappeared. My body has calmed down and my work is going really well. It seems to have opened so many doors for me.

By going back into her culture Michelle recognized the aspects of herself which were uniquely Burmese and accepted them for what they were. She understood that what she had seen as subservient was actually just a natural generosity of spirit and humility which could sit happily beside inner strength. As she said, 'For the first time I am at peace with myself.'

━━━━━━━━━━━━━━━━━━━━━━━

This magnetic pull which draws us back to our homeland becomes stronger as we grow older. People who have lived abroad all their lives begin to feel a pull to return home as they near retirement, for there is a universal sense that to die in peace is to die where our ancestors died. This is why the Chinese will insist even if they cannot make it home to die that their ashes and ancestral tablets will eventually be taken back to China, and why Muslims and Hindus will similarly try to take the body or ashes home to be buried.

Aurora Sanchez, a psychotherapist who lives and works in Britain, recently married an Italian businessman. Her family are from Seville in

Spain. Although she regularly visits her mother she has not lived in Spain for over 20 years. Her husband recently suggested that they could move out of Britain and left the decision of where to go up to her. Aurora told him that it had to be southern Spain:

I am now in my early fifties and for the first time in my life I feel I need to go back home. Even though my husband is not Spanish, he is very happy for us to go to Spain. My sisters still live in Andalusia and I have many friends whom I still keep in contact with, but primarily my decision to return home is because I miss my language and my culture and the lifestyle.

In the land of our ancestors we tap into a spiritual lineage which runs alongside our human ancestry and links us back to a spiritual source through the land. There are shrines and sacred sites around the world to which people are drawn in pilgrimage. In this age of air travel and tourism we are able to indulge our desires to visit places which seem to speak to a deeper part of ourselves. Most often it is our soul which calls us back to some distant spiritual source of power and peace.

As the Jews returned to the land of Israel they returned as the sons and daughters of Abraham, connecting with an ancient spiritual lineage which made them feel safe. For certain Ethiopians it is their belief that they are the direct descendants of the Queen of Sheba and King Solomon, the original secular and spiritual leaders of their country, which gives them a sense of pride and national unity. Genghis Khan is regarded as the protector ancestor spirit of the Mongolian people and in Britain there are still some who look to King Arthur as the guiding ancestral force who unites the land in spiritual leadership.

HEALING THE PAST

I am thy father's spirit

Doomed for a certain term to walk the night

And for the day confined to fast in fires

Till the foul crimes done in my days of nature

Are burnt and purged away. But that I am forbid

To tell the secrets of my prisonhouse

I could a tale unfold whose lightest word

Would harrow up thy soul, freeze thy young blood

Make thy two eyes like stars start up from their spheres.

William Shakespeare, *Hamlet*

Janine is a drama teacher and her family are Jewish. Many of her ancestors were killed during the Holocaust. Recently she began questioning her own heritage:

Any ambivalence towards my Jewish background was released on the day I went to Bergen Belsen, a concentration camp in Germany. I knew I had to go to heal a wound deep within my soul. I went alone and stood by the Jewish Memorial in the middle of this 'hell'; there was torrential rainfall and I began to sing the Kaddish at the top of my voice and all I could hear was the rainfall, my voice and military gunfire, which came from a British military unit nearby! The experience was so powerful that I felt free for the first time in my life. An extraordinarily peaceful atmosphere came over me. It was very cathartic. As I wandered around the concentration camp I felt nothing could touch me. I was alive, and I felt free.

Three days later, I began to feel very sick, as if I had caught a stomach bug, but I knew I hadn't. I began to realize that I could feel a spirit presence. These souls did not feel free. I knew that I had brought them back from the camp and they had needed to be rescued. I called Terry to advise me on what to do. He suggested that we could release them together. As we rescued them, by calling their ancestors, using my voice singing traditional Jewish songs and prayers, I felt much lighter and uplifted. I was privileged that I could help in my own way to release the pain and suffering of my own people.

So many of our blood ancestors have died leaving their dreams and ambitions unfulfilled and their relationships with family and friends broken by arguments and misunderstanding. The trauma and unhappiness reverberate through the family tree. Whether these echoes manifest as unhappy ghosts, physical family illnesses and addictions, or the psychological problems of depression and other mental illness, the descendants are 'haunted' by the past. But there are ways to heal the past and break the cycle.

When we counsel clients we may have to look into the family tree to establish the root cause of a problem. While all of us have guardian spirits, some of us have well-meaning ancestors who can nevertheless carry with them a negative influence or debility. It is common for an ancestor who has a strong attachment to be connected to us by a cord which can be detected. Usually it is to be found in one of the psychic energy centres in the body. These are called the chakras.

Quite often ancestors have no malicious intentions, but many of them become too personally involved, too close to a situation. After a while it becomes impossible for them to detach themselves, not only from the issues but also from the physical body of their descendant. They become involuntarily enmeshed. This is can be termed as 'ancestral possession'.

What can happen in such cases is that the descendant will take on the physical or emotional impressions of the trapped ancestor. It begins just like a shadow cast over the personality or the physical body of the victim, but eventually develops into physical symptoms consistent with the ill health the deceased had in life.

For example, recently I removed an ancestor from a woman suffering serious back pain. She had been visiting an osteopath for six months, but was struggling to heal the problem. Since the removal of the ancestor, the osteopath expressed her surprise at how the condition had improved '90 per cent' and the patient only needed one more treatment.

When a person is either very similar to an ancestor or carries a compassionate nature, it is very common for an earthbound ancestor to chose not to move into the spirit realms but to remain attached to a family member.

In addition to physical ailments, such ancestors can also cause serious mental ill health, such as depression or psychosis. In extreme cases schizophrenia can stem from ancestral influences. Some psychiatric doctors are now suggesting that it is a hereditary condition. When a spirit is influencing the mind of a person it is like having two separate personalities in collision. The ancestor directs their own messages to the mind of the family member, which leads to confusion and an inability to make even simple decisions. This can lead to a nervous breakdown and chronic debilitating illnesses.

Sometimes we have to look back into the family tree to heal or release ancestral spirits who are influencing our clients. It is quite easy to see the positive and benevolent influences as well as the more negative and controlling ones. It is helpful to cut many of the invisible umbilical cords which tie the descendant to the more oppressive or negative characters dispersed through the family line and help them connect with the benevolent and positive influences.

We ask our clients to bring photographs of family members for as far back as they can find them and paste them on a board in the shape of a family tree. Beside each one they write about the life and the death of that person. What were they like? How did they live and die? What was their own relationship to them? How are they seen within the family mythology? This evokes the memory and presence of the ancestor so that it becomes clear which blocks or wounds the descendant needs to heal. The family trees are kept and then when the healing and release has taken place, they are thrown into a ritual fire to help release the memories and complete the healing process.

In the West psychotherapy is now the most usual way for people to heal the negative legacy which our parents, through no fault of their own, have imposed on us as children. Therapy is a healing tool for unravelling the negative habits and blocks which are usually given to us by our upbringing. But it is helpful to look much further back into the family tree to diagnose the effects of our ancestral heritage.

Medical tests now show that children are linked to the mother's subconscious mind, so from the moment they enter the womb they begin to learn about their family and draw off their ancestry.

These new insights from the psychotherapeutic world are no different from the ideas of cultures that believe that ancestors are reborn as new offspring. They are both suggesting that there is a powerful continuum of the family line, which can be seen in the strands which run through our historical lineage.

We have devised a system of meditation journeys to access the subconscious and help free any ancestral influences resting there. In one particularly powerful meditation journey a drumbeat was used to draw out ancestors who had been killed during the civil war in America. In surreal scenes clients saw them being drawn out by the sounds of the drum calling them out of their graves and walking to freedom. These sacred journeys can access the subconscious world and draw these trapped souls out into the open to be rescued. People often see them getting on a train, which symbolizes that they are taking a journey to the spirit realms.

The healing and release of ancestors is a responsibility chosen by the soul for a reason. Even before incarnation the soul will consider it its duty to release souls from its own ancestral heritage. Those who are strong enough to perform this task find their own liberation, but there are also those who cannot carry the weight of the responsibility.

Soizic's near death experience during an operation for cervical cancer was the catalyst which led her to explore alternative ways of healing. She was the first woman in her family to suffer cancer, but knows that she inherited it as a result of the suppressed anger passed down to her through the female line. She believes that the current prevalence of cancer among women, concentrated in the areas of feminine creativity and power, the breast and the womb, is the direct result of generations of suppression:

Rage and cancer are passed down through the generations and they are closely related, as they are both to do with repressed anger. We are the first generation of women who have known independence and power and we are breaking a pattern of many generations of women who were forced to suppress their inner natures through bearing so many children and being totally dependent on their husbands. Genetically, they have passed to us all their repressed rage, which often manifests as cancer.

Soizic does regular 'anger release' workshops where clients are invited to take out all their anger, because it is the release of anger which can begin the healing process:

Anger is like fire – it can sustain life or it can burn down the house. Anger is when the fires of power are out of control. I help people to release the rage of many generations and use this power in a positive way.

When the spirit is buttressed by many powerful negative emotions it is difficult for it to thrive and help the body overcome any physical illness. So these emotional legacies which are passed down through the generations are the keys which help us to begin to heal our line, our souls and ourselves.

A lineage can also be cursed by the 'sins' of the forefathers when one generation betrays the codes and laws of life. In many cases the lineage can suffer for generations as a result.

=================

Susanna believes that her lineage through her mother has been warped by a betrayal which took place before Cromwell's reign. A gift of land in Northern Ireland given to a Scottish ancestor by Cromwell for 'services rendered' raised her suspicions that her ancestors went against their own Scottish people by fighting for Parliament instead of the king. Betrayal in clannish Scotland would have necessitated emigration. She also believes her family were involved in a massacre.

She came to a workshop because she was overshadowed by low grade depression, a passive resentful negativity that she had fought for a long time. She had also come to the healing with a flaring of diverticular disease.

This feeling had hung around me from a long way back. I knew that it came from my mother's side of the family. She committed suicide when I was in my mid twenties, having fought this cyclical depression for years and years. Eventually she hung herself after years of frustration and gloom. My depression was like hers, though not nearly as bad, but I knew it was something which went deeper than that, something to do with 'bad blood' over which I had no control.

The mother's line had spiralled into depression and bankruptcy. The land had dwindled from generation to generation, thanks to strange family wills and a touch of alcoholism, until her grandfather had finally lost it all.

They lost their way and became poor bog Irishmen. The family started having more and more girls and today there are only two boys left with the family name and only one has a chance of having children. We lost the two most valuable things to an Irishman: land and male children.

During the ancestral workshop an ancient ancestor with a broad Scots accent came through and told Susanna how to heal her family legacy:

He was very specific. He told me that I had to go to Isle of Arran and take my son and that there I should do a ritual on behalf of the family group and pray to the ancestors of the land for forgiveness for my family's betrayal.

We went up there together and I was interested to find many sacred standing stones and circles, indicating that it had at one time been a focus for sacred ritual and celebration. We did our ritual and as we did so I felt a lift in myself as though something had been freed up inside me.

I honestly believe that what you do in this life you pay for and if you don't pay then subsequent generations will continue with unfinished business or bear the burdens of your mistakes. You realize that everything is interlinked and each action is like throwing a stone in a pond. The ripple goes across and comes back and goes across again.

Since the ritual Susanna's stomach disorder has completely cleared and she reports that her energy levels are higher, she is clearer, more optimistic and feels more balanced.

There are many souls who incarnate within families in order to heal them. They take on the responsibility of breaking the patterns which have trapped the lineage in unhappy cycles of loss and dysfunction. They are usually very strong and suffer from years of healing their own inheritance before coming to their own realization of the light which they have brought to the family.

Chloë is a successful theatre director and voice coach who suffered from a severe eating disorder which she had successfully hidden for years. She came from a long line of women who suffered from clinical depression. Her great grandmother, grandmother, mother, uncle and sister had all been immobilized by depression, while her cousins were also troubled by mental illness.

Chloë explains, 'I have always had a fundamental difficulty in distinguishing anger from madness, so I have always suppressed the anger by compulsive eating so that it would go away and everyone would get better.'

The madness in all these women was triggered by post-natal depression. Chloë remembers her discomfort when she saw her sister, just after the birth of her son, with her two-and-a-half-year-old daughter stroking her back saying, 'It will be alright, Mama, you just have to be strong.' Memories of herself as a five-year-old child making her younger sister's school lunch and comforting her depressed mother brought up such rage and fear that the terrible legacy should be continued into the next generation she decided that she was going to break the pattern and confront the sickness of her family line.

My turning point was at an ancestral workshop when I gathered together these photographs of them all. I faced them and their legacy and went into the pain of all that they had caused me. I realized that every day of my life had been lived in the shadow of my unhealthy ancestry. There were so many layers to peel off, but as I put the photographs together and threw them into the flames I really let them all go. I felt immeasurably lighter.

I can see myself now. And I can see this spirit within me which has nothing to do with the family. It is gentle, strong and beautiful, and as I continue to let go of my past I identify more strongly with that side of my nature.

Last Halloween in the torrential rain I went out onto the heath to do a ritual for my sister's daughter, who is now seven, intelligent, precocious and gorgeous. I took some offerings and I prayed that she would be spared the chaos which we had all suffered. I called on my great great great great grandmother, who I knew must sit way back in my family line, before the madness started. I know that she is good and strong and I asked her to protect my niece.

Chloë sees herself as the final gatekeeper for the dysfunction which has cruci-fied the females in her family for so long. She was born with this feeling. Now she understands that by healing herself and cutting the ties which bind her to the negative aspects of her bloodline, she can free her whole lineage.

Often children are born to families with this subconscious soul mission. They usually feel at odds with the rest of the family. This is where the myths of the changeling child spring from. They are the ugly ducklings of the fami-ly, the scapegoats for the family's anxieties and frustrations, or else they car-ry on their shoulders the dark unresolved actions of past generations.

The 'black sheep' in any family is often the one who is born either to take a spiritual path or to carry the sins or curses of the family's past actions. They are the ones who 'march to a different drummer' and, if the family will let them, they are often the ones who can change the course of the lineage and heal the past.

THE SCAPEGOAT

In one case the daughter of a well known English family, made wealthy through shipping and property, had an appalling relationship with her family. Her father was distant and cold, her mother fragile and addicted to pharmaceutical drugs, and her brother a manic depressive. She could hardly stand to be in the same room as any of them. In her late teens she found herself drawn more and more toward the Caribbean. She dated many black musicians, hung out at clubs, listened to black music, smoked pot and eventually moved to Jamaica, where she used her inheri-tance to set up a record company to promote local artists.

Her record company faltered, as all sorts of bad luck and bad choices took their toll, then she started to get really ill, with a disease for which no doctor could find a cure. By the time she came to us she had been to the Tropical Disease Centre twice and was now diagnosed as dangerously ill. She was underweight with a raging temperature of 104 and thought that she was dying.

In fact she had been cursed; her life force was being slowly eked away by some powerful black magic due to jealousy. The curse did not kill her – she fought it for three years, during which she was unable to sleep peacefully, as her dreams were haunted by the voice of the person she knew had cursed her, and she felt emotionally unstable most of the time.

Then quite by chance when talking to a cousin she discovered that her family had not made their fortune from shipping but from the slave trade. Based in Bristol 300 years before, they had traded in thousands of slaves, buying and selling them as commodities. When she understood this she realized that she was paying for the sins of her great great grandfather.

Family secrets always emerge in one way or another. Over the past few years, psychoanalysts have been studying the generation of the Holocaust. The children born to survivors usually live in the shadow of an unmentionable tragedy. They carry the burden of it within themselves. By the third generation the trauma is hidden in time, but the descendant now suffers from the ghost of this family memory.

Jessica's grandparents both died in the Holocaust. Her grandfather was marched to his death while her grandmother was gassed in the 'shower' at a concentration camp. For as long as she can remember Jessica has hated having showers and has to prepare herself mentally for one. She always felt that this was somewhat strange, but didn't really think anything of it. She also suffered dark depressions and dreams of war and dying soldiers. Talk of the Holocaust was taboo in her family, so Jessica grew up with only the vague notion of what had actually happened at that time.

Meanwhile her son, aged seven, who had no notion of his own legacy, became obsessed by the Nazis and the history of the Jews. He was terrified of dying and had powerful dreams of people dying around him. Jessica brought him to see us first and the shadow of the Holocaust lay like a heaviness across his aura. After his healing, his fear of death subsided. Then Jessica came to an ancestral retreat and the full force of her heritage emerged:

I can still remember the pain that I felt under my left shoulder, as though a knife was being turned in an old wound. It was as bad as giving birth. At that moment I could see my grandmother and I knew that this was all to do with her appalling death. After that I just felt this incredible sadness and mourning. I realized that I had been carrying her pain for my whole life.

Soon after the healing Jessica was admitted to hospital suffering from pneumonia and pleurisy. Attached to drips, moving in and out of consciousness, she experienced the same excruciating pain under her left shoulder. 'It was all to do with this poison in my lungs and the terrible sensation of not being able to breathe. It felt as though my lungs were exploding.' She was in hospital for two weeks, during which time she realized that she was haunted by memories of her grandmother's death. As she healed, these memories began to fade.

A tangible connection to her grandmother came in the form of some beautiful bedlinen, which was left to Jessica when her father died. The grandmother's initials were embroidered on it and Jessica immediately felt a powerful sense of connection. It was as if the linen had always been hers.

An Irish Catholic nurse was recommended to us by a therapist who had worked with her for years and found that he could not heal her. He told us that he suspected that she was cursed by ancestral influences. By the time she came to us she was on the verge of a nervous breakdown. Although she was just about able to hold down her job, she was beginning to display psychotic behaviour – she couldn't bear to be touched and she couldn't stand loud noises.

We helped alleviate the symptoms, but invariably they would return. Finally she emigrated to New Zealand, where miraculously the symptoms all disappeared. Seven years later she felt that she was probably safe to come back but three weeks after stepping off the plane all her nightmares had returned. She collected all her belongings and emigrated again, this time escaping the curse of her ancestors for good.

As we heal the old and face the curses which have brought death and misfortune to our ancestors, we liberate our own children, creating a fertile new branch on our family tree. Native American tribal tradition states that each generation will impact the next seven, so our efforts to clear the past and create a positive legacy will enhance the journey of the next seven generations to come. Similarly, the cycles of reincarnation mean that we will often be reborn into our family line as our own distant descendants, so we are in effect tilling the soil to benefit our own future.

RELEASING THE ANCESTORS

For many years my mother and I suffered from the same recurring dream in which we were blindfolded and able only to see through a crack in the bottom of the blindfold. Both of us felt enormous fear, although we didn't know why. This dream continued for many years until I went to visit my family in Galicia, Spain, and we began talking about the family history, particularly my grandfather, who had been a judge who had refused to comply with Franco. I knew that he had been shot in the Spanish Civil War. I didn't know that he had been wearing a blindfold at the time.

Terry and I decided to do a ritual for my grandfather. We went together to his grave, taking flowers and candles, and said prayers for him. As I prayed, I imagined that I was shedding light on his memory and helping to heal some of the pain he must have felt at leaving his wife and young children. Our family and many others in this part of Spain still carry the wounds of the civil war. My grandmother lost everything as a result of her husband's execution and had to send her daughters to Portugal, to her husband's sister's convent. My mother was separated from her for four years at only 18 months and remains affected by this trauma to this day.

In the months following our ritual the atmosphere within the family completely changed. My mother and I were not having the same dream any more. My aunt, the eldest daughter, began to talk openly about her relationship with her father. Ever since I was a child she had been a closed book, never referring to any personal grief or emotions in connection with her childhood. Something had lifted in the family as a result of the ritual when we had helped my grandfather to let go of his own pain.

My first experience of ancestral healing happened much earlier when I returned to Hungary, to my father's ancestral home. Every night I woke up with a heavy feeling on my chest as if someone were trying to suffocate me, although when I managed to move and open my eyes the feelings left. One night I decided to pray before I went to sleep and asked for my guardian spirits to let me see what was stealing my life force. I woke up as the feeling returned, but this time I pushed it away and as it floated toward the window I saw the face of a woman. She was in her mid fifties with fair hair and blue eyes and the round face and features which are common in that part of the country.

The next day I asked my aunt about any ancestors who may have died relatively young. It transpires that a great aunt had died after a very unhappy life. Her family had refused to accept her marriage to a gypsy and so she had left the village only to return after he had died. Within the year she too had died, a lonely and unhappy woman.

I again prayed before I went to bed and asked the guardian spirits to rescue her soul. That night I felt her enter the room but this time she did not sit on my chest, just floated in the shadow of the window. A peace then entered the room, which had not been there before, and then she vanished.

Souls such as this who are caught in an earthbound state due to the unhappiness or pain of their lives can really affect the living. Until they are released they cannot move on into the ancestral realms where they can guide and protect us.

One of the key features in a Druidic funeral rite is the release of the soul from the ancestral line so that it is free to find its own spiritual inheritance. Emma Restall Orr has organized many funerals. She explains:

We call to the ancestors and release the soul from the bloodline which that person has entered, lived within and is now leaving. We make the point that the bloodline is not critical to the soul line. The body is part of the bloodline, the soul is not. The rite ensures that the soul is released from its connection to the human and it also frees up the descendants to move on.

———————————————

Sue, a friend and godmother to our daughter Sequoia, asked us to help to release her ancestral spirits in the graveyard near her home. There had been negative issues surrounding her family which made her want to go back in time to see if there was some lurking sadness or conflict which was affecting them all. She took candles, gifts, whiskey and chocolates, and a copy of the family tree. She began to feel the effects of her intentions long before we reached the cemetery:

It took us ages to get there as we constantly took wrong turnings or came across heavy traffic, even though I was familiar with the route. I was feeling terrible by the time we arrived, really heavy in my heart, as though I had swallowed a stone, and foggy in my head.

Sue led us around the gravestones, finding herself drawn to the grave of her father's cousin Peter, who had been killed by a car on his twenty-first birthday when cycling home from university.

We stood by his grave and asked if he needed help. My whole body began shuddering and I felt a huge wave of sadness overcome me and I burst into tears. We called on the spirits to help, said prayers and asked Peter's ancestors to come and collect him. At that moment it was as if a great cloud lifted from the graveyard and it was obvious that the work was now done.

As we looked up a hawk which had been watching us from a gargoyle took off, circled the graveyard and flew off. I felt an extraordinary release after this healing and some balance returned to my relationships with my family.

Soon afterwards Sue's brother's wife became pregnant with their first child, who turned out to be a boy. Sue believes that Peter, released from the sadness of his unfulfilled life, was able to return to the family line to achieve a destiny which he had been unable to fulfil in his past life.

———

Most cultures retain a belief in the living influence of the dead through rituals, stories, dreams and spirit communication, which encourage each generation to look back into the past and understand the present in the context of a continuing human story. Each life is one link in a cycle of continuity which stretches into the future lives of our descendants and evolves from the lives of our ancestors. This perspective gives us a tangible link to a spiritual heritage and an understanding of the unseen world.

THE MARTYR'S SON

When Ken Wiwa's father was martyred in 1996 by the infamous Abachu regime in Nigeria, he went on a powerful journey of reconciliation which healed his relationship with his father, opened up the channels of communication between them and helped him to come to terms with his own personal destiny.

Ken had always lived in the shadow of his hugely charismatic and largely absent father, who had abandoned his family for his cause and relationships with other women. As his eldest son, Ken bore the full weight of ancestral responsibility and even though his father was being hailed around the world as a saint and a hero, all he felt was anger and guilt. In a recurring dream he would meet his father sitting down looking as though he had been in a really bad accident:

He was in really bad shape; he looked like a beggar with all his clothes hanging off him and cuts and bruises all over him. His hair was really strung out and his eyes were bloodshot. He looked as though he was in tears. I would come up to him and he would be lying down and I would ask him what the matter was and he would just kick the ground in frustration and turn his back on me and walk away. This just made me feel even worse.

Eventually Ken realized that there was no way that he could continue with his life until he had laid his father's ghost to rest. 'I was trying to run away from him and it was taking me close to a nervous breakdown. I was trapped in a cycle of anger and guilt.'

Soon after this he was he was listening to 'One' by U2 in the car and in that song he heard his silent conversation with his father. This triggered his grief:

I got out of the traffic and found myself in this park and I just broke down and cried and cried and cried. It was the first time that I had cried since my father had died – everything just came out, it was all the years of frustration, anger and guilt. Everything. Then I realized that I couldn't fight him anymore. I was at peace.

Recently he had another dream, which expressed the relationship he had wanted with his father: 'I was with my father and we were just talking together, me and him. We were laughing and discussing things. He was proud of me and I respected him.'

Then in one of his father's letters he discovered a message which, blinded by anger, he had completely overlooked. His father had said to him, 'I never want you to follow in my footsteps since my life has been far too dizzying. I have lived six or seven lives and what you should do is take one of these lives and take it on. I think that you should become a writer.'

Ken had worked as a journalist for many years and had wanted to be a writer since he was young, but had then found himself feeling as though he should follow his father into politics. As he began to write the story of his father's life and their relationship, the significance of a recurring dream which had haunted him when he first came to Britain as a child became clear:

I am walking down a dirt track to my village and then all of a sudden I see clouds coming and a great storm brewing. As I start running towards my village it just recedes in front of me as the storm comes closer and closer. Then I come to this bend in the road where it curves around a huge tree. The sky just suddenly goes black and lightning and thunder come out of the sky and smash the tree apart.

Ken Saro Wiwa's murder was a mortal blow for both his family and his people – the fatal wounding of both the family tree and the spiritual lineage of his people. But on his death he has been elevated to sainthood. The seeds of the tree which was smashed by lightning have been dispersed and find their roots in the stories told, some of them by Ken, to generations and generations of the Ogoni, offering them new inspiration and hope.

I am well aware that many will say that no one can possibly speak with spirits and angels so long as he lives in the body; and many will say that it is all a fantasy, others that I relate such things in order to gain credence, and others will make other objections. But by all this I am not deterred, for I have seen, I have heard, I have felt.

Emmanuel Swedenborg

In order for the ancestors to work with us, they need to be able to communicate in some way. Sometimes we need an intermediary for this, a bridge reaching into the spirit world. So we seek the advice of mediums, psychics, healers and clairvoyants who are able to communicate with the spirit world and offer evidence that our beloved ancestors, relatives and friends are still 'alive' and looking after us. Spirit communication has been an essential part of the human story and has been recorded by all cultures throughout history to the present day. In many tribes and cultures it is a cornerstone of religious observance. We ourselves began rekindling our connection with our own cultural roots by believing that there is a spiritual afterlife that affects the living, first dabbling in Spiritualism and more recently moving towards a belief in the ways of our Celtic and pagan ancestors.

Yvette Tamara, a famous international clairvoyant, explains the difference between communicating with the deceased and being a clairvoyant:

Being a medium means being a person who stands between two worlds, the spirit world and the Earth world, and giving messages to those we leave behind. Working as a clairvoyant is totally different from mediumship. As a clairvoyant, I work with my spirit guide. He transmits the information to me by either clairvoyance, seeing spirit, or clairaudience, hearing spirit. This is not a direct message from a relative or family member who has died, as in mediumship, but just pure clairvoyance: giving precise information about the future, reflecting on the past, highlighting events, people and recent happenings with uncanny accuracy.

I am able to quickly dispel doubts and a person soon finds themselves looking forward to knowing more. The elusive future takes on shape and meaning as the revelations begin to clarify its mysteries.

A clairvoyant will tell you about a relative who has come to give a 'message'. How do they hear these messages? In most cases they will 'hear' the deceased person talking to them telepathically. Telepathy can of course also take place between the living. It works best when two people are in love or very close, such as twins. Then the barriers come down and thoughts flow freely. The same is true of mothers and their newborn babies. Psychologists have done tests and found that if a sleeping baby is put into a soundproof room, in most cases the mother will know when the baby has woken up and started to cry, even though there is no way she could have heard her baby.

With psychics, generally it is assumed that they 'see' spirits but that is not always the case as many do not, they communicate with an 'inner ear', listening to what the spirit is saying. Psychics and clairvoyants believe that our thoughts are not limited to chemical processes in the brain but can travel outside ourselves, and just like a radio receiver and transmitter, a sensitive person can 'tune in' to these frequencies.

When working as a psychic or healing the land as in soul rescue each case is very different. Sometimes it is easy to see into and hear the spirit world, whilst on other occasions it is like trying to drive a car through a thick fog.

On one occasion I went to see a medium at the Spiritualist Association of Great Britain. I was sharing a session with a work colleague. My grandmother, who is Spanish, came to give me a message. She spoke to the clairvoyant in Spanish, not regarding the fact that she could only speak English. The clairvoyant asked me why she would be talking about a *gâteau* – was it because she baked cakes? I could not remember her baking cakes or relate it to a recent event. Then it occurred to me that *gâteau* sounds like *gato*, which is 'cat' in Spanish. I realized that she wanted to tell me that my cat saw her when she came to visit me. This language barrier is common. We forget that sometimes our relatives do not immediately change when they pass over and many hold onto their cultural and religious background.

Yvette explains how she manages to work in theatres and lecture halls where she communicates with large groups of people and delivers messages from the spirit world:

I feel the dead relative near me with their emotions and warmth. Their appearance is clear, just as though they were here alive today. The voice they speak with is in their dialect and is also very clear. I can feel and sense their personality; if they are shy it takes a little more encouragement for them to come forward. We still hold our personalities, even in death.

Once the link is made with the deceased, it is wonderful to see so much concrete evidence of life after death and that we do move on to a different way of life. Once I am on stage the messages come incessantly, the relative who has passed on talks to me to give proof of their existence, giving me dates and times of events that have just happened and then a message to help the family members in the audience.

One does not have to be a medium or clairvoyant, however, to communicate with their deceased families. Many people have told us how they have seen their loved ones both in dreams and as apparitions. Others talk of receiving symbols, such as a sweet smell of flowers or by a 'coincidence' that has the personality of the deceased written all over it.

One story I was told by friends was of their grandfather who loved playing cards. After he died his wife thought she had lost his favourite set of cards and she was very upset. That night she had a dream that he had put the cards in a drawer in a bedside table. In the morning she discovered the cards in the drawer. She believed he had come to find his lost cards and prove to her that he was still with her.

The dead can also communicate their presence through a sense of smell. When Englebert Humperdinck the well known British singer bought Jayne Mansfield's old Hollywood home shortly after her death he said, 'I am sure she lived with me in spirit for a time – I used to smell her rose petal perfume. Once I saw a figure in a long black dress in front of me. It was Jayne, but it wasn't frightening.

ANCESTRAL PERSONALITIES

The personalities of those who have passed into the otherworld seldom appear to have changed. This is because life after death does not miraculously bring perfection. People will remain themselves until they discover enlightenment within and conceive of a different way of being.

So, ancestors, close friends and relatives will still display their attitudes that they had in life when they appear to their families. They will show their disapproval on the behaviour of their descendants by making sure that their opinions are heard. Many communicate by poltergeist activity and physical manifestation such as moving objects, causing apparitions and in some cases haunting their living relatives. This is very much dependent on their personalities in life.

One of my college friends, Janet, had a grandmother who used to come and stay in their house after she died. The family felt safe when she was around, although many times she used to crash about and create poltergeist activity so they would know that she was there. She would also make it very clear when she was unhappy with something the family members were doing with their lives.

One day Janet brought me back home, together with a couple of other girlfriends from college and an old boyfriend of a close friend called Neil. It was a beautiful summer's afternoon and we were sitting in Janet's bedroom with the window open, deciding what we wanted to do that evening.

One of the girls, Rita, was a bit of a pot smoker. Not to appear antisocial, we allowed her to smoke a joint and we all joined in. The next moment an invisible hand opened the bedroom door, it was slammed shut behind itself, and then all the clothes were thrown out of the wardrobe. We had forgotten that Janet's grandmother really disapproved of smoking, smoking anything! Then Rita found herself pushed off her chair. My other friend could not stop laughing – she knew it was Janet's grandmother as she had already experienced her powers. Neil did not move or react and we are not sure to this day whether he noticed what was going on or just thought we were hysterical women. We asked Rita to put away her joint, explaining that Janet's grandmother disapproved. She left the house as quickly as she could, taking Neil with her, and never spoke about the incident again!

Aggie Richards, a practising medium from the Spiritualist Church, remembers experiencing a series of powerful dreams linked with a particular ancestor who in his lifetime enjoyed a tipple of rum. One night he told her to buy him a bottle so that he could have a drink when he fancied it. The dreams continued after Aggie had bought the rum and hid it in a cupboard for him. Then one night they stopped. Her dreamless nights continued for so long that she became alarmed. Then one night she saw the ancestor agitated and angry, claiming that his rum had been stolen. At this aggressive outburst she woke her husband, only to learn that he had discovered the rum and drunk it. The next day Aggie replaced the bottle, issuing a stern warning to her husband to leave it alone. Since then her ancestor has returned to her dreams to help guide her and her family.

HELPING THE GRIEVING

The loss of a loved one is one of the worst events that can happen to an individual or family. After the shock can come deep depression that can consume the mind and body. Mediums and clairvoyants can offer some form of comfort to those troubled by death by opening the door between worlds for the bereaved and for the spirits who wish to communicate with them.

The Spiritualist Church, which established itself during the nineteenth century, is still thriving as an important platform for a great many people who are grieving the death of a loved one. Spiritualists believe that death is just a passing from one dimension to the next, that there is a part of the person that cannot die. This is the spirit.

Spirits who wish to communicate with their living relatives will find ways to do so. There are many stories of apparitions of the newly dead appearing just after they have died when they are still hovering between this world and the next.

Many spirits come with the souls of children who are ready to be born into the family tree. A client in Scotland came to see me about the death of her sister. I felt the sister's presence; she had come with two young boys. I asked my client whether she knew the two boys and she said she didn't, but she had been dreaming about her sister coming to give her a message. A month later she found out she was pregnant with twin boys!

Spirits are also known to return around anniversaries or birthdays. Janet Cox, a medium and counsellor, told us a story about her brother who had died the year before on 3 August:

He was a wonderful man, always smiling and bringing humour to every situation. This year on 3 August, at midnight, I woke up in bed and saw him standing there in the bedroom doorway, leaning on the door, smiling. It unnerved me. He did not speak to me, but just stood there. The next minute he was gone.

Although unnerving, this incident convinced Janet and her family that her brother was safe and happy.

Janet has often seen how the bereaved heal their grief when their loved ones come from the spirit world to give them a message. She says,

Aggie Richards says, 'According to Spiritualism, we will always meet up with people we love in the afterlife. Love is eternal, so where strong love exists between people death cannot separate them. They will eventually be reunited.'

'It gives them the opportunity to get on with their lives knowing that their beloved is still there looking out for them and knowing the truth about how they felt about them, even though it may have been unspoken.'

Recently the parents of a six-month-old baby who had died of a 'cot death' had come to see Janet. The mother, Zoë Blake, said:

I didn't fully believe in life after death. I suppose you could say I sat on the fence until I had evidence for myself. I went along to a psychic fayre, taking my favourite photograph of my baby son, who had passed away last October. [Janet] saw that I had lost a beautiful baby boy at six months, although the photograph was of him at six weeks. He came to say that he was wearing his favourite blue woolly suit, hat, leggings and coat.

The spirit told her that she was having another baby. Zoë confirmed that she was in early pregnancy, a fact that Janet would not have known. She had been concerned that her son might not have been pleased about the pregnancy, but in the event she was thrilled because he said that the new baby could have his clothes and toys! This experience helped Zoë and her family to come to terms with the death of her baby.

Colin Fry, a physical medium who conducts trance state séances with spirits from the otherworld, also communicates with deceased relatives and friends. He says:

Mediums deal with sad, bereaved, and depressed people who are still grieving their loved ones. It is the evidence that you can bring into this world that heals people's pain.

One woman came to see me whose son, a plasterer, had died. He came through me and showed the cracks in his hands from working with plaster. This was sufficient for his mother to know it was him.

Another time, in Australia, I was giving a physical séance, which means that the spirits can manifest objects and even themselves to the audience or group in attendance. The deceased first wife of one of my clients appeared. She had promised him that she would give him a sign to prove to him that there was life after death. At the end of the séance, there were some tissues left on his chair. She used to do this when she was alive and this was enough to convince him it was her.

THE JOURNEY IS THE DESTINATION

Kathy was numb for several weeks after she received the call telling her of the murder of her son, Dan, a photojournalist who was stoned to death by an angry mob on his first assignment for Reuters in Somalia when he was only 22. It began a process of recovery which lasted several years. As Kathy said:

In the days, weeks and months after Dan's death, I felt pain I cannot now begin to describe. I learned lessons I never wanted to learn and discovered parts of me I was not aware existed. Sometimes I raged. Often I wept. At times I did not even wish to live.

Even in the first days after his death she realized that the only way that she could survive was by channelling her grief into something positive. Even as the pictures of Dan were flashed over newspapers all over the world she had set the wheels in motion for a Reuters exhibition which would celebrate his work and that of the other photographers who died with him.

I thought that it was really strange that Dan should be stoned in the twentieth century and I kept feeling that there was a meaning, a message to it. It was too strange. The whole thing was elevated into people's consciousness at the time. Four people stoned to death – you notice that. So out of this very visible death of a young man who had tried to live a good life we had to find a higher meaning and communicate that.

When a friend of Dan's phoned Kathy to tell her that a medium called Molly Martin had a message for her from Dan, at first she was sceptical. The friend had been visiting Molly on an entirely different matter when suddenly this young spirit, 'elfin and very funny', interrupted the reading tell them that he was fine and safe and that he hadn't suffered at all – one minute he had been there and the next he hadn't. He said he wanted to talk to her.

As much as she wanted to believe that her son's spirit was still around, Kathy was still careful. She booked to see Molly under a false name because Dan had been all over the papers and she said nothing about why she was there.

She was amazed when Molly immediately said to her: 'You have suffered something which is unfair, sudden and really, really terrible,' and described Dan's death. She went on to tell Kathy that not only was Dan's spirit around but that she had a strong role to play in communicating that fact. She told her that both Dan and his younger sister Amy were incredible children who would inspire many people whom they would never meet.

Then she saw me and my daughter Amy standing talking to hundreds of people surrounded by UN flags and travelling all over the world talking to heads of state and to powerful leaders in the communications industry. We were talking about the power of the human spirit and the fact that the soul does not die.

This was completely ludicrous to me. My 22-year-old son had just been killed in a place halfway across the world and my 18-year-old daughter was just about to drop out of college because she was finding it so difficult to deal with. And I was really struggling. I was as broken as it is possible to be.

Some time later Kathy received a call from a young friend of Dan's called Kwami, a half-Nigerian, half-American guy who had attended school with Dan in Kenya. He was nervous as he explained to her that he had gone to see a psychic about his love life when suddenly this young bright spirit came bounding into the reading:

It was Dan. He told me that I was two-timing my girlfriend and talked about the music we liked and the things we used to do. Then he said: 'Tell my mother to stop taking those pills.' I am really embarrassed to phone you, Mrs Eldon, and tell you this, but he is really worried about you.

Kathy had to laugh. Every night since Dan's death she had been taking sleeping pills and every time she took one she had inwardly apologized to Dan because in life he had hated pills. She threw the rest away and began to trust that her son's spirit was alive and wanted to communicate with her.

Some time after this she went to another medium who once again reported the presence of a vibrant, animated spirit. 'Stop manning me,' she said at one point during her reading, making Kathy roar with laughter as Dan was always saying, 'Hey, man.'

He told her to stop mourning over his baby pictures and remember him by the one which the press had picked up of him surrounded by smiling children. He also told her that he had died from a blow to the back of the head. The week before the autopsy had confirmed that he had died from a massive cerebral haemorrhage caused by a severe blow to the head.

Then he said to her, 'Most people live through their children, but I shall have to live through you.'

The psychic warned Kathy not to become addicted to communicating with Dan through psychics and mediums but to go for a reading once a year. 'Do not hang on to him, he has got work to do – just tune in.'

Kathy and Amy began working on various projects inspired by Dan and his death. There were projects for deprived kids in Los Angeles and Kenya, exhibitions of Dan's photographs and a book of his journals called *The Journey is the Destination*, which revealed him to be a prodigious and prolific talent with an offbeat sense of humour and a wise and compassionate approach to life. Amy completed a documentary with CNN called *Dying to Tell the Story* on photojournalists working in war zones and a Hollywood feature waits for release at Columbia.

Kathy learnt to operate on her intuition, tuning into the power, guidance and charisma of her son's spirit. She realized that by listening to this inner guidance the projects were helped along by extraordinary coincidences and synchronicity, always meeting the right person at the right time.

I became aware of the power and energy which is around us all the time if only we were open to it. If I don't know what to do then I just wait for the answers to come. Messages come in funny ways – in dreams, on billboards, in a conversation. Most of us don't listen, but when we are working with intuition we are connected to another dimension of thought. Call it what you will, but I believe that there is a certain energy which I can tune into and if I do everything flows. I have to suspend logic and act with this guidance and belief that Dan is as alive as I am, but just not as a physical presence.

Five years after Dan's death Kathy and Amy presented their documentary to thousands of delegates the General Assembly of the UN. As they were introduced by George Levine, the CEO of Time Warner, with the UN insignia all around the walls, Kathy remembered the words of the psychic all that time ago. She did what she has learnt to do whenever she needs inspiration: she cast her eyes to the ceiling, put her fears and insecurity aside and allows the words to come to her from the spiritual dimension:

It feels as though another presence enters the room. The whole atmosphere shifts slightly and the talks really have something extra. People listen, they really listen. I really don't take any credit and I almost always end up talking about the living spirit. My job is just to stay present, learn to walk my talk, be strong on integrity and humour and let this tremendous life force and energy move through me.

Through this sense of Dan's spirit I receive a tremendous sense of life and the reassurance that I am not alone. It does not lessen the grief of the physical loss, but it does make it easier to know that I am an ally of Dan's and that what has happened since his death is due to his influence.

Our planet has very little time and we have to start taking responsibility for ourselves and the people around us. If you can just suspend critical belief and say, 'Well, if it works then why the hell not?' Communicate with the person that you love and be open to a response. Your life can be much richer and the force of your being can be much greater and have much more power. And, besides, it's fun. The spirit world can only do good if they have people to work with them. They cannot do it on their own, so we have to get things moving. The world will change, but we have to start with ourselves – that is the essence of our message. Like I said, it is fun. We are surrounded by so much power, energy and love, and if we can tap into it then we can use it to focus on whatever we are doing. So you become like Superwoman or man – you are invested with a powerful energy.

Dan's death opened the gateway into the world of spirit for me.

DREAMING OF THE DEAD

The dead often return to us in dreams. They use the dreamtime to tell us that they are still around, that they are happy, to warn us about something or bring comfort. Many people who are not mediumistic or psychic dream of their dead loved ones.

Dawn, a successful artist and illustrator for the advertising industry, describes how after her mother died she felt the loneliness of not being able to just pick up the phone and have a chat. Her father had died several years before, so she and her mother had become very close. After her mother's death, she felt her presence around her, yet was too afraid to believe that life after death was a possibility until she dreamed that her mother had come to visit her in a green dress. Her hair was black and arranged as she would have worn it as a young married woman. In particular Dawn noticed her beautiful leather shoes. She was with Dawn's father and they looked so happy. She said, 'I have come to show you how happy I am now that I am reunited with your father. This was the time when we were the happiest in our lives together.'

Astounded by her dream, Dawn called her sister and described the dress and how her mother had looked. The sister searched through some old photographs and in one of them there was their mother in the green dress, with beads and a beautiful new pair of shoes.

Dreams are very personal and they offer the opportunity for us to feel safe with what we believe to be true and confirm our intuitive feelings about our ancestral family. In many cases people have told us that they know that their mother, father and grandparents are together in spirit, and in most cases it is true. If their relationship was negative or dysfunctional, then they tend not to be together, even though some do come and say that they have spent time with each other in spirit to heal the rift...

When ancestors come to visit or guide their families many use the intimate motifs of life to reassure the living that it is really them. They give clues to help us circumvent our own disbelief.

Anita, a film producer, laughs now when she recalls that after a 'grief moment' for her much loved mother who had died the year before she had a dream which was so much her mother that it made her laugh in the morning:

I just suddenly missed her terribly and went back into all those feelings of loneliness and heartbreak. I cried and cried and cried. Actually it felt good because I hadn't really thought of her for a while. I was longing for her. Then that night I had the funniest dream; She came to me and she gave me a hairdryer. The great thing was that was exactly the kind of thing she would have done and it was exactly that mumsy thing that I was missing. I felt great in the morning.

Gillian is a hospice carer who, despite her professionalism in helping others to die, found it extremely difficult to let go of her own mother when she died and was plunged into deep mourning for her.

Only days after her death her next-door neighbour called by to tell her that she had had a dream about her mother telling her to come and tell Gillian about the afterlife. At first Gillian was put out that her mother had chosen to appear to her next-door neighbour, but then she remembered that they had had a pact that whoever died first would try somehow to communicate to the others and the next-door neighbour explained that Gillian had been so distraught with grief her mother couldn't find a way of coming through to her.

In the dream the mother described the 'party' she was having with a few relatives and friends who had passed over. The next-door neighbour was able to give very specific descriptions of people whom Gillian had known in childhood. She is now under no doubt that an afterlife does exist.

Sometimes a relative comes not to convince the descendant that there is life after death but to encourage them in their spiritual life. Emma, a practising psychotherapist, has regular dreams about her grandmother. They had a unique bond and Emma is the only one in the family who receives the dreams. The grandmother often comes when Emma needs some advice and after the dream she is left feeling calm and centred:

Each time I wake with a feeling of joy, warmth and relief that this is not all there is. I am sure that it is her visiting me, not just a projection of my imagination. She changes each time I see her. One time she was wearing a funky green trouser suit, which she would never have worn while she was alive.

She always had this calm certainty about where she was going when she died and one time when she came to see me I asked, 'Hey, so how's heaven?' and she said to me with the most beautiful smile on her face, 'Better even than expected.'

More recently she came to me as a Native American, which was significant because all the women from her line, including myself, have a look from this culture. She still had this incredible stillness about her and she told me a story about love. She was more detached from me this time and I wondered if perhaps she had found her way home.

The

SPIRIT WORLD

PART TWO

In the beginning there was a river. The river became a road and the road branched out to the whole world. And because the road was once a river it was always hungry. In that land of beginnings spirits mingled with the unborn. We could assume numerous forms. Many of us were birds. We knew no boundaries. There was much feasting, playing and sorrowing. We feasted much because of the beautiful terrors of eternity. We played much because we were free. And we sorrowed much because there were always those amongst us who had just returned from the world of the Living. They had returned inconsolable for all the love they had left behind, all the suffering they hadn't redeemed, all that they hadn't understood, and for all that they had barely begun to learn before they were drawn back to the land of origins.

There was not one amongst us who looked forward to being born. We disliked the rigours of existence, the unfulfilled longings, the enshrined injustices of the world, the labyrinths of love, the ignorance of parents, the fact of dying, and the amazing indifference of the Living in the midst of the simple beauties of the universe. We feared the heartlessness of human beings, all of whom are born blind, few of whom ever learn to see.

Those of us who lingered in the world, seduced by the annunciation of wonderful events, went through life with beautiful and fated eyes, carrying within us the music of a lovely and tragic mythology. Our mouths utter obscure prophecies. Our minds are invaded by images of the future. We are the strange ones, with half of our beings always in the spirit world.

Ben Okri, The Famished Road (Vintage, 1991)

GHOSTS AND HAUNTINGS

CHAPTER FOUR

There are, in India, ghosts who take the form of fat, cold, pobbly corpses, and hide in trees near the roadside till a traveller passes. Then they drop upon his neck and remain. There are also terrible ghosts of women who have died in childbed. These wander along the pathway at dusk, or hide in the crops near a village, and call seductively. But to answer their call is death in this world and the next. Their feet are turned backwards that all sober men may recognise them. There are ghosts of little children who have been thrown into wells. These haunt well-curbs and the fringes of jungles, and wail under the stars, or catch women by the wrist and beg to be taken up and carried.

'My Own True Ghost Story' from *Wee Willie Winkie and Other Stories* by Rudyard Kipling, Macmillan and Co. Limited, 1929 edition.

Are all hauntings due to earthbound spirits or ancestral connections? Some, but by no means all. There is a very fine veil between the living and the kingdom of spirits and all sort of visitors from the otherworld can break through.

Spirits and ghosts are souls who can appear to the living. In general they are benign, not always seeking to harm the living. The difference between ancestors and ghosts is that many sightings in family homes tend to be ancestral or recently departed souls, whilst the sightings of other spirits and ghosts can be caused by events throughout history. They are a general paranormal occurrence rather than a personal or bloodline connection.

The term 'ghost' covers an astonishing variety of apparitions, from the traditional shackled skeleton clanking through a lonely graveyard to the spectral balls of light or fire smelling strongly of sulphur which have been reported on the sites of ancient battlefields. There are ghosts of vengeful monks, of weeping girls, of horses, dogs, and birds, of coaches, ships and even aeroplanes. There are headless ghosts and legless ghosts, invisible ghosts that can drag the living out of bed or cause blood to ooze from floorboards, ghosts that announce their presence by hoots, shrieks or groans, by footsteps or the touch of a clammy hand on the victim's skin.

SOME QUESTIONS...

HOW MANY PEOPLE HAVE REALLY EXPERIENCED GHOSTLY PHENOMENA?

Anyone who has may tell their story in a number of different ways, dependent on their level of sensitivity and natural psychic ability. It is the sensing of a ghost or spirit that creates an encounter. Some people are incredibly insensitive and disbelieving; most of these will never see a ghost as their natural thick skin will protect them from the encounter. In addition there are those who claim to see or feel a ghost but are having a psychotic vision. It is only by experience that you will know the difference.

WHAT CAUSES A HAUNTING OF A GHOST?

It is mainly due to the supernatural dimension using a physical energy to demonstrate its existence. It can achieve the ability to move objects, appear as an apparition projected onto the subconscious or manifest itself in its own visual form.

WHERE DO HAUNTINGS HAPPEN?

There are no rules governing the supernatural powers, therefore a haunting may happen at any time or place. There are collective sightings of ghosts, which means that more than one person sees the same ghost at the same time, though in general most phenomena are experienced when a person is on their own.

WHAT PHYSICAL ENERGY CAUSES HAUNTINGS?

In buildings, the bricks and mortar, the gas, electricity and running water are conductors of energy. They can be used to help manifest a haunting. Also the land may have a negative feature which underpins the building and this may cause a haunting. Such features range from historical events such as massacres and murder to powerful emotional scenes such as pubs and clubs. In general this is due to the emotional memory of a place, so if there has been a lot of activity this will be remembered in the atmosphere and will attract ghosts or spectres.

Paul Southcott told us that during the investigation of the London Dungeon, a German tourist claimed to see the spirits of two small children. At first he thought they were real children. He claimed that they told him that they were lost and then just disappeared. Judging by his description, the children's dress could be estimated to come from around the turn of the twentieth century. They were probably street children. This type of sighting is typical of spirit beings seen in a building or on a site with which they were probably connected when they lived. Though redevelopment changes the community, and each generation brings changes of fashion and lifestyle, it is still common for ancient echoes to pass down the years to the present day.

Back in 1920, Thomas Edison was working on equipment designed to permit communication with the dead, but it really wasn't until 1959 that it was discovered that magnetic tape registers electrical impulses which are unheard by the human ear. Electronic Voice Phenomena (EVP) is the modern term for such a recording. The technique was pioneered by an American called Sarah Estep.

Tina Laurent, an EVP investigator based in Wales, experienced her own breakthrough with EVP in March 1998. Tina picks up various entities that communicate via her machine. Some come on a daily basis and give her their names, former addresses and the names of relatives both living and dead. Tina has been able to look people up in the local phone book and has found that after a tactful probe, she has been able to tell them that she has messages for them 'from beyond'.

I recently investigated a case with a colleague concerning the recording of ghosts of dead RAF soldiers at a site in Wales. We went to look for the wreck of a Wellington bomber that had crashed in November 1944 on the peak of Carreg Goch in the Carmarthen Fans. The wreckage is strewn over a wide area, some parts of it still gleaming as when first new, shimmering side by side with the dozens of newly spun webs of the many spiders residing there alongside the ghosts of six airmen who died with their plane.

Using my equipment I discovered that I was getting the names Franz Joseph, like the Emperor! I kept recording. Slowly I made my way up towards the main bulk of the wreckage, stopping here and there to touch a piece of it or just to catch the air. As I got closer I remarked, 'Now I am thinking of the names Joseph and France. Let's take a look at the monument over there.'

Turning around, we read the beautiful stone memorial erected in the airmen's honour. Surprise, surprise! The first and third names were Joseph Burke and Joseph Allison and the other four obviously belonged to some of our courageous allies from France.

It is the natural psychics, the people who are sensitive, who will have an encounter with a ghost or experience a haunting. When someone claims not to be psychic and has seen a ghost, then the apparition tends to disappear as quickly as it has arrived. This can cause scepticism. It is when such a manifestation is physical, such as a door opening, or a spirit getting into bed with someone or pushing against them on the stairs, or knockings and voices that come from nowhere, that the manifestation is real for all concerned. These sightings usually take place in areas of high psychic activity such as a house or land that has a long history of recognized haunting caused by events that were charged with emotion – terror, death, and so on.

A few years ago I was out socializing with a group of young college students. We took a walk home from the pub down by the river. It had always been known as a haunted place, with famous sightings of the ghost of Queen Elizabeth I and other less well known personalities. The energy of water holds manifestations more profoundly than any other type of location.

We stopped by a small children's park. In the centre was a roundabout. Pushing the roundabout was a small child about seven years old, dressed in a Victorian nightshirt. He was unaware of the group watching him and just pushed the roundabout round and round. As this was about midnight there was very little chance that it was a living child playing by himself in a costume dress. What was interesting was that only one of our friends, a guy called Richard, did not see the ghost. He refused to believe us and marched over to the roundabout and sat on it whilst it was being pushed by the spirit of the child. It was only when he could feel the pushing sensation and the movement of the roundabout that he believed that we were seeing something supernatural.

Most of the time we are unaffected by the visitations and the habits of ghosts and earthbound spirits; however, there are a number of conditions in which the veil between the two worlds, the one of the living and the one of the dead, may be opened. Then the psychic influence of these spirits may begin to affect the way we feel, to influence our physical and mental balance, and in extreme cases affect the whole of our environment.

When these forces are concentrated, we will begin to be conscious of a feeling of malaise. A sense of fear or oppression is the surest sign of a haunting. What is actually happening is that the barrier between the conscious and the subconscious mind is being affected. People who have a less dense barrier are able to take on the negative or psychic effects of an earthbound spirit, a ghost or a negative psychic memory within the land or property.

Ted Hughes, the Poet Laureate, told the world of the hauntingly real visions of Sylvia Plath, his first wife, in the months after her suicide. He released a poem called *The Offers*, describing how on three occasions after Plath's death he saw manifestations of her. Two spoke to him. One day, two months after Plath gassed herself in February 1963, Hughes was on the London Underground when he saw her 'paler, almost yellowish, as you had been in the morgue' on the train and stared intently at her. 'My gaze leaned against you as a gaze might lean against its cheek on a hand,' he writes. The spectre remained silent and Hughes alighted. 'If you got out at Chalk Farm, I told myself, I would follow you home. I would speak.' He was left alone. Later Hughes had a vision of Plath 'young, untouched by death'. 'You told me the dream of your romantic life, that had lasted throughout our marriage, there in Paris,' he writes. But she leaves him 'gasping for air' and 'barely conscious'.

At the end of his poem he describes a third and chilling vision, Plath 'as if new made, half a wild rose, half a flawless thing' approached him from behind, catching him helpless as he was about to step into the bath. The vision said: 'This is the last time. This one. This time don't fail me.' His publishers and public were surprised at the openness of Hughes' poem and what is very interesting is that he was inspired to complete it just before he himself died in 1998.

==========

People who have a less dense barrier, for instance those who are sensitive to atmospheres, who have a keen sense of emotional and psychic energy, are those who may 'see' into the spirit world, but are not aware that they can. Sensitives see ghosts consciously with the naked eye, so the spirit looks real to them, as if the person was really there. Others see clairvoyantly. Then there are other ways of 'seeing' such as hearing, smelling, sensing and touch and dreaming. If a person has natural psychic powers that makes them magnetic to spirit and they draw them into the physical world. That is why there are more psychic phenomena in homes with people who are naturally sensitive.

==========

Janet Cox remembers a story from her childhood when their family home was a very old three-storey house.

The stairs were haunted by a spectre of a woman who used to pass us on the stairs in the evening. She only appeared after dark. Our mother used to tell us to ignore her and not to go up and down the stairs in the dark.

Janet disobeyed her and went to the stairs at night because she used to enjoy seeing the ghost. Her sister, who was really afraid of ghosts, used to lock herself in her bedroom and put the radio on full blast if she was on her own in the house, so she would not encounter her on the stairs.

On another occasion my two brothers, who used to share a bedroom, called out to our mother in the middle of the night, 'There's two men who are digging holes in the wall, and right into the old chest.' She told them to go back to sleep, and in the morning they found little holes in the wall and dust on the floor.

As a family we learned to live with ghosts and never found it difficult to live our lives alongside the occasional haunting and communication with the dead, particularly as both our parents were practising mediums.

===

As a child I lived in a block of flats in Mortlake, southwest London. For the six years we lived there, I had dreams and nightly encounters with ghosts who looked like monks, shabbily dressed characters with swollen and spotty faces. I dreamt of rats eating their flesh and the river Thames flooding over, taking with it all the dead that walked through the house. My family ignored it, thinking I was an imaginative girl, but a concerned family friend suggested looking up the local records and we found out that the block of flats was built right on top of a plague pit!

HAUNTINGS

What is a haunting? It is an influence or impression superimposed on this world from a supernatural dimension.

Sometimes hauntings are shadows of the past, such as the story of a crying child which for many years has been said to haunt a site of a Roman fortress. A number of babies' skeletons were discovered beneath the foundations, suggesting that the memory of an ancient tragedy or perhaps ritual sacrifice had lingered in the district for almost 2,000 years.

Sometimes hauntings are not due to wandering spirits, but to shadows of the past, such as those believed to come from the pits from the Great Plague that hit London in 1665. A fifth of the population was dying of the disease. What could they do with all the dead? When they ran out of burial sites, they began hasty burials in open spaces. Many of the dead were therefore not buried on hallowed ground but on common land – thrown in ditches, committed at night without any rite. The carts would empty their ghastly loads and flee precipitately from a sight that must have strained the strongest nerves. The hospitals were also over-flowing; there is evidence that they used to lock plague sufferers inside the building and leave them to die. Not surprisingly, the buildings now standing upon these sites have a tendency towards hauntings and nega-tive vibrations, contaminated by past memories and even earthbound spirits.

Most of the places where the victims of the plague were buried have been redeveloped as London has grown over the last 300 years. It would be the same for any other city in the world which has expanded over the last 1,000 years.

In ancient cities of past civilizations, including those of ancient Egypt and the Incas of Peru, the memories of those who lived and died there still permeate the atmosphere. Every area of any size in the world has places which have a bad 'feel' or are connected with a tragic history. In the USA and in South Africa houses that have been built on tribal cere-monial land have been disturbed by echoes of the ceremonies of the past. Sometimes, too, a house is built over an underground stream. This will also affect the house or land. Running water is a great conductor of psy-chic energy. All these provide a good gathering-place for ghosts – if a place has one ghost it is quite likely to have two or more.

I have seen the grey ladies around graveyards and stately homes. They are usually unconscious and pass through walls of the living, or go by without recognition. They have no attachment to life or spirit. They exist as fleeting memories, a negative imprint or shadow on the ether. These spectre or phantom sightings are common; these floating essences are not steeled with any intelligence or conscious intent. They are like shadows – we can see them but they do not look back. As the sun which causes a shadow is very real, so the person who was once the owner of that body was real, but now all that is left is a shadow of the former self.

Such apparitions can be recorded on the atmosphere due to an event that has released a huge amount of emotion, such as war or murder. It is not surprising that sightings of the ghosts of warriors are common. In Hawaii, for example, at Manunaloa, the site of a famous battle, on certain nights the spirits of those killed during the battle are said to return to the scene and wander about searching for friends.

Sightings of monks are much more complex. Some monks are so dedicated to their vocation that after death they simply stay on in the monastery, conducting rites of mercy and acting as mediators to those who have recently passed over and become lost. Often long after a monastery has been demolished, the brotherhood is still there, continuing its work. This idea also applies to the sisterhood of nuns.

Once, in an investigation of the haunting of a shop and flat, I was drawn to the cellars of the front part of the building, which appeared to have been part of an old church or hallowed ground. Later on this was found to be true. I had the impression that there were monks there, a dozen or more dressed in brown habits. There must have been a Christian order which at some time resided close to the site of this shop.

In a psychic image, there appeared a scene of monks chanting and singing. Possibly, it was their presence which had attracted the other spirits to the site. This is also common; where you get one ghost you will find two or three others, all fallen into each other's company. In this case the monks would rescue the lost souls. So when the area was redeveloped, particularly after the bombings of the Second World War, they had drawn a number of spirits to this site and many felt held there until they were able to move on to their ancestors and the otherworld. Even after I rescued the souls that were ready to move on, the monks remained on site; the feeling they gave was one of benevolence and protection.

In another of my investigations I came across two ghosts who had suffered as a result of the English Civil War.

A REUNION IN PLUCKLEY

It was at Jack's invitation that I went to Pluckley. The newspaper he worked for had commissioned him to write an article on ghosts so he had asked me to accompany him as his 'professional' advisor. Jack and I have been friends for years, so the idea of spending a warm June day together deep in the Kent countryside with the promise of an expense account pub lunch seemed too good an opportunity to miss.

So why Pluckley? Well, Jack figured that if you're writing an article about ghosts you need to go to where the ghosts are and Pluckley has the reputation of being the most haunted village in England. In fact its reputation is so widespread that there are even guided coach tours of the village, and more than once the police have had to deal with kids going over the top, dancing and drinking in the local cemetery over the Halloween weekend.

It's hard to explain why some places are more psychically charged than others. Maybe it's due to the rich mineral deposits in the earth or more likely to excessive amounts of trapped water underground. Whatever the reason, I felt a 'presence' as soon as we walked into the graveyard at St Nicholas' church. It was the spirit of a sad woman in white. The vicar of the church confirmed that she had been sighted many times. It seems she was the wife of a local squire who, after her death, was so distraught that he buried her body in a lead-lined coffin, thus hoping to preserve her beauty. Sadly all he managed to achieve was to trap her soul and consequently she has haunted the local area for the last 400 years.

Jack has many qualities, but being psychically aware is not one of them. However hard I tried to enable him, he was completely shut off to any psychic activity. Realizing that it was useless to help him see any spirits himself, I spent the rest of the morning helping him instead to research the story and posing for photos: standing behind a gravestone; smiling in front of a Jacobean manor; talking to a local villager about the 'headless' coachman. Even though I wasn't being professionally challenged, I was being paid to spend a wonderful day in the country – how could I complain?

We had lunch in the Black Swan, a former Tudor roadhouse inn. As with most pubs in small rural villages, it proved to be a source of much gossip and rumour. Once the word had got around that Jack was a journalist seeking out ghost stories, our table was swamped by the locals and their tales. From the brickmaker who fell down a clayhole and whose fading scream could still be heard to the schoolmaster who had hanged himself and whose silhouette could be seen on moonlit nights swinging to and fro from the tree where his body had been found, we heard them all.

After a couple of pints I excused myself and made my way to the gents'. As soon as I closed the bar door behind me, all the chatter, music and laughter of the smoked-filled room died away. It was against this newfound stillness that I became aware of a quiet voice calling. It seemed very distant and yet oddly desperate. I looked around the corridor that led to the toilets but I couldn't see anyone. Where could the voice be coming from? Concentrating hard, I was able to gradually identify vague words: 'me', 'please', 'where', 'please', 'talk', 'so'. I listened intently, trying to trace where the voice was coming from. Slowly I inched my way carefully along the corridor away from the main saloon and the toilets towards a set of stairs that I assumed led up to the landlord's private living area. I began to climb the stairs, but almost immediately the voice began to diminish.

Turning round, I noticed a door to the left of the stairs. I held my breath as I stepped back down. Putting my ear to the door, I closed my eyes, hoping that it would help me to hear better. Yes, I could hear the voice clearly. I realized that it was crying mournfully as it pleaded:

'Simon, Simon, it's me. Please, please, where are you? It's Matilda. Please, talk to me – it's been too long, please!'

Returning to the bar I asked the landlord if any ghosts had ever been seen or heard in the pub itself. 'Oh yes,' he said without hesitation, 'we've got Matilda!' He stopped polishing a pint glass as he added, 'The story is she's haunting the pub looking for her husband, who was arrested on a charge of treason by Cromwell's Roundheads. It seems they took him away to Rochester Castle where they tortured him. It took him three days to die, poor bugger! And it wasn't much better for her, they say. Apparently she put up a real struggle as they were carrying him away and some of the soldiers took her down to the cellar where they raped her!'

I didn't really need to ask but I asked anyway. 'Where's the door to your cellar?'

Holding up his dishtowel, he pointed in the direction of the toilets. 'At the bottom of the stairs!' he said.

The light at the top of the cellar stairs wasn't very bright but I managed to see my way down the uneven stone steps to the floor of the cellar. I sat down on an old cask, letting my eyes get used to the dim light. I only had to wait a few minutes before Matilda's disembodied form appeared. I was expecting a young woman, so I was surprised when Matilda turned out to be in her sixties. At first she was disappointed that I wasn't Simon, but I reassured her that I could help find him. Before doing anything I had to find out whether her love for her husband was strong enough to justify my trying to reunite them. After hearing how she had never remarried and had died broken-hearted, I knew that at least her love was genuine. The next step was to see if I could contact her long-lost husband.

I always compare calling up a spirit to fly-fishing for trout or salmon. Both of them require immense persistence. Sometimes the trout is not tempted by a particular fly and sometimes the fisherman keeps on casting in the wrong part of a pool. So too the soul rescuer has to adapt his tools and intuition to the needs of a particular situation.

Luckily Simon wanted to be called forward. As Matilda had been searching for him, so he too had been looking for her. I only had to chant for a matter of minutes before he began to appear. At first he appeared as a small sphere of pulsating light, circling and spinning below the low beams of the cellar. As he became used to my presence he seemed to unfurl into a cloud of mist that over a minute or so recognizably took on the shape of a man. When I finally saw him I was shocked by the cuts and bruises that covered his whole form. He was in such a confused state that I'm not even sure he knew he was dead. Over the three days of his ordeal he must have often passed between life and death to the point where the two are almost indistinguishable.

Even though Simon and Matilda were in the cellar with me they were unable to see each other because they were in separate time zones; Matilda had died over 40 years after Simon. One of the most important skills of a true psychic is the ability to see past, present and future as one reality. Having perfected this skill, they need then to know how to travel freely in time. Once they have learnt to do this it is a simple step to be able when necessary to include other spirits on these journeys.

In Simon and Matilda's case it was their overpowering love that reunited them. All I had to do was ask each of them to focus and visualise on an important event in their lives and then to trust in each other's love. Both chose their wedding day as their particular important event. All three of us then prayed for their reunion.

I was so happy for them, reunited on their wedding day and then able to move into the spirit realms.

POLTERGEISTS

Poltergeist is a German word meaning 'noisy ghost' and this is usually a very accurate description. Poltergeists can make crashing and banging noises and even anomalous voices through tape recorders, CD players and TVs. They are also very physical – they can lift, move and throw objects, sometimes quite beyond the capacity of any normal person. The bad news is for the person who becomes the victim of poltergeist activity is that the house will need some serious redecoration!

If the haunting is even more physical, with outbreaks of fire, the movement of furniture and the manifestation of objects, then the forces behind it may not be human but elemental. These forces are from the Earth's own energy field and are much harder to dispel. However, with poltergeist activity, the possibility of a natural or physical explanation must be explored, even if a supernatural element appears most likely.

These types of hauntings can easily be mistaken for malevolent ghosts. Poltergeist activity can be caused by a spirit, but sometimes it is the continued manifestation of some sinister activity which took place a long time ago. In one such case at a small estate on the Brecon Beacons in Wales, the owners experienced such severe poltergeist activity that it ruined their business and affected the couple so much that the wife, Sandra, had a nervous breakdown.

In this case the property had been impregnated with energies left behind when a black magic group had performed ceremonies on the land, causing a young man to meet a mysterious death there during the 1800s. This left a doorway open to the unseen world.

Sandra and Paul are Christians and not practising psychics, but somehow the poltergeist could access their world. On one occasion they had called the local vicar to bless the property. He arrived by car, playing a tape of Gregorian chants. After he parked the car, the music was turned off by an invisible hand and the Rolling Stones' song 'Sympathy for the Devil' came blasting out from the car's stereo.

After the vicar had blessed the property, the manifestations of poltergeist activity became more dramatic. It was only when the couple called in a local land dowser and psychic that they were able to diagnose where the interference was coming from. The dowser was able to determine that the interference was not just a normal haunting but a force that had been called upon by occultists or black magicians, as the spirit form was not human. They found a spot in the old barn where the young man had been murdered. The local records identified him as a farm worker. Following the dowser's diagnosis and advice in healing the land, peace resumed and Sandra and Paul were able to sell up and leave. The new owners are perfectly happy with the property and have not experienced any paranormal activity.

HAUNTED OBJECTS

There are occasions when ghosts attach themselves not to particular places but to objects, even if they are moved considerable distances. Such objects can be haunted by the person who made the object or by a person who once owned it. Some objects are cursed, often those connected with religious ceremonies, murders, weapons, military regalia and relics plundered from temples or burial sites.

In a number of cultures, when someone dies, all their personal and intimate possessions are either destroyed or buried with them, as it is believed that the deceased may need them on the journey into the afterworld. It is also believed that a person's intimate possessions have been imbued with their energy and emotions. So they can act as chains preventing the dead person from completing their journey into the otherworld.

With antiques, it is common for each piece to emit an emanation, for unlike modern items, each piece would have been moulded by human hand. Until recently this was still the case in many less developed countries. In making any object, either for household use, ornamental or for religious purposes, the creator puts a little of their soul into each item. So, a handcrafted item will carry residual memories of its former owners, including its maker. If previous owners have a strong emotional connection to that item, they may still wish to connect with it, and return from the spirit world from time to time to see it. In rare cases they may even be possessed by it, like the 'genie in the lamp', so when someone sensitive rubs it, out pops the genie and the person begins to feel a ghost or presence around them.

Antique beds are another type of object that may be haunted, not usually by ghosts in this case, but by the energy of the person who once slept in them. This may seem strange, but consider that we spend a third of our life sleeping and this is when the subconscious mind is open to dreams, ideas, feelings, and so on. For this reason, it may take months for the new owner to become accustomed to the vibration of an antique bed, while at other times the bed is conducive to the new owner's personality and vibrations. If hotel guests find sleep difficult or have dreams more traumatic than normal, it could be just the energy of the last guest. If someone had died in the bed, their residue could be left, as with someone who had just given birth. The power and emotion of a spirit moving either into life or out of life can linger in the atmosphere for a long time.

In haunted objects sometimes curses are not delivered intentionally; feelings of anger and resentment can be planted quite accidentally. Rings can often be repositories and transmitters of psychic energy. Engagement and wedding rings will possess the whole energy of that person's relationship. In addition, if the person is sensitive to psychic influences this will add to the emotion transmitted by the ring. Most pieces of jewellery would do the same. Because they are metal objects, they transmit electrical impulses into the skin of the wearer. If a piece of jewellery is emitting negative energy, it is always best to cleanse it by burying it in sea salt.

Susan Grant, a friend living in Cape Town, told us the story of a friend of hers who had been given a ring by an aunt who had passed away:

Clarissa wore this ring all the time, but gradually found herself becoming depressed and angry, which was unlike her true personality. Her husband noticed the change and suggested that she went to a healer. It transpires that the ring was feeding her these bad feelings. The healer was also a psychic and he asked to hold her ring. He found that the energy it gave off was tremendous; it was as if he were holding hot coals. He saw that a deceased relative had given her the ring and that this person had had an unhappy life. Clarissa confirmed that the ring had been given to her by an aunt whose husband had been an alcoholic and had made her life intolerable.

Lucky for Clarissa, the healer knew what to do. He told her to bury the ring in sea salt for 24 hours to 'ground' the energies in it.

Susan confirmed that Clarissa's condition disappeared almost immediately, probably due to the memory of her aunt's pain rather than the haunting of her spirit.

An Indian friend of ours used to work for British Airways. She had a colleague, Rachel, who was working on long-haul flights to Delhi and had been given a small ornamental elephant by a local she had met on a sightseeing tour. As soon as she brought it home, the family started having terrible problems. There were accidents and flooding in the home and even their car was destroyed by a drunk driver when parked outside the house. The house was burgled, her husband lost his job and poltergeist activity started. The phone used to ring and then when they answered it no one was there, toilets flushed by themselves and their electricity bill increased to almost double the normal cost for no apparent reason.

One day Rachel was on duty at check out when a woman in her sixties came up to her and said that she was a medium and she could see that she was having trouble at home that was caused by an ornamental elephant. Rachel had to get rid of it immediately, but not give it away or destroy it. The only way to break the spell was by leaving the elephant outside the house for someone else to find. 'Let God choose what happens to it.' Rachel was so shocked by this woman's vision that when she got home she immediately put the elephant on her front garden wall. Next morning it had gone.

At once the family and home life returned to normal and Rachel's husband managed to find himself a job within the week. What was in the elephant was not known and nobody will ever know what happened to the person who took it away with them!

STATELY HOMES AND ESTATES

Many people go away on holiday and stay in hotels or rent a cottage only to be tormented by some unseen nuisance, while others claim to have seen a ghost. Some owners of stately homes use their haunted history to attract tourists. It is great entertainment for the public to be able to feel themselves back in time and let themselves be touched by the atmosphere of past events. But it is less gracious when owners allow unsuspecting visitors to stay in or buy their haunted homes.

I have spoken to a number of owners of stately homes and castles in the British Isles about releasing ghosts from their estates and in most cases they wish to keep them, as they have become familiar with the haunting. Most are ancient family members, but ghosts do add to the mystery of the properties.

Sir Humphrey from Northumberland, for instance, confirmed to me that although he was happy for investigators to check out his ghosts, he personally did not want to get rid of them. This was a typical British castle haunting, in which the history and atmosphere were powerful enough to draw spectres and ghosts from the past.

In many cases the owners of these estates welcome their ghosts as they help the castle or estate to attract visitors and paying guests. Some people have grown to love their ghosts and do not consider it necessary for them to leave.

In most cases the ghosts in these properties perform the same task or job over and over again as if in a time warp. There is a theory that suggests walls and soil act like videotape; when humans emit tremendous amounts of energy, for example during a violent death or a traumatic event, that energy is somehow stored and subsequently trapped in the physical surroundings.

The reason why some estates are haunted and others are not is because everything on Earth has a natural energy field and sometimes patches of energy are left, either by people who have died or by living persons who have moved on. It is like an echo that goes on being repeated after the original sound has been made. The spectres, the visible ghosts, occur when the energy field has created a kind of hologram – the place has been imprinted with a photograph that comes into view from time to time. Often when there's a particular atmospheric condition, I simply 'ground the energy' and clear the psychic interference. There is no need to be afraid – most of these types of ghosts cannot do anybody any harm. They may be a nuisance, a distraction, but they cannot physically hurt the living.

Barbara Erskine is one of Britain's best-selling novelists. Her *Lady of Hay* and *House of Echoes* sold million of copies. She lives in a deeply haunted manor house on some of the highest ground in Essex. The house is next to the church and the foundations are pre-Roman. The house itself dates back at least to the 1500s and the earliest rectors at the church are from the 1100s. Barbara often finds ancient fragments of pottery in her garden. The house has never been the ancestral home of one family. The last Lord Rivers bequeathed all proceeds of the house to Guy's Hospital in London and the family finally sold it on after the war. Barbara moved into the house in December 1991.

It was a move from hell. We were burgled the day we moved in and when we turned on the water we found approximately 37 leaks in the house. So on our first day the house was full of removal men, police and plumbers. When I met a woman on the first landing wearing a long dress and a white apron, I didn't even think about it. Even when she disappeared I thought she had just gone into another room. I was highly stressed and thought she was just one of the many people in the house. She was as real as you or I, totally solid and not like a ghost at all. We had eye contact and she smiled. She had pink rosy cheeks. It was only when I asked my new cleaning lady downstairs if she had brought anyone with her that I began to think.

Then sometime later this same woman woke me up. It felt as though she was shaking me awake. I was in a total panic and I woke to see her face two feet above mine. Then she disappeared. I was a total wreck for the rest of the night.

There is also a young man who stands in the kitchen doorway dressed in dark colours. We call him the boot boy because we think he was in love with one of the kitchen maids. We often see him in the evening and our dogs have seen him. They rush to go to talk to him and when he disappears they are left looking rather confused and a little silly.

Their hackles used to go up on the main staircase, the one place in the house where there were a lot of incidents, which I think may be related to the housemaid. The soul rescue people who came told us that there was a little girl here who had had a very unfortunate life, because she was epileptic and was therefore a disgrace with her father. We would see this white blur rushing up the stairs. She would push people and knock people on the stairs, so it was becoming a little frightening and I asked my friend to come in and clear her. She thought she must be Victorian. We have tried to match her in the churchyard but we couldn't find her. Ever since then the maid has also disappeared, although the boot boy is still around. We definitely think that the housemaid was here to be with the little girl.

None of these phenomena have ever scared us. Guests are usually rather thrilled when they see a ghost, though when we had a lunch party of 80 guests about four years ago and several of them saw a grey lady on the lawn, one chap did actually leave. He was very upset indeed. Sometimes my sons enjoy winding up their friends when they come and visit.

You tend to see the ghosts when your mind has gone off somewhat, slipped, which my mind does all the time. If I am mentally exhausted and I have done a lot of writing, that is usually when I switch off and I see them.

The burglar alarm used to always go off at 2 a.m. if it wasn't set. The Chubb man couldn't find anything wrong with it and then asked us if we had any ghosts, as he had just had a similar situation in another house and he believed it was due to the ghost. We found out that the alarm would go off because of a sudden drop of temperature, which would happen at this time every night.

There is a place in the barn which for no apparent reason at all that I can explain absolutely gives me the creeps. I can't even stand there. I get colder and colder and start to shake and that really is terrifying, yet I have never seen anything there. One or two other people have mentioned that same kind of feeling about the place.

The soul rescue people gave me a great crystal which spins the energy around it and mentioned something about a huge energy surge and something being all bottled up and fizzing and ready to go. The land has its own negative energy and somehow the crystal helps to modify it.

======

HAUNTED LAND SITES

It is important to realize that the land is a living organism and in its deepest cellular structure it retains the memories of every event since the beginning of time. These memories can remain dormant for a very long time, locked in subterranean levels, yet the Earth can shift and the memories rise up. Natural forces such as tidal waves, storms and earthquakes can draw memories from the land, as can the heat from modern technology, roads and buildings.

Most cities of the world have mass graves and memories of murder

It is not our part to master all the tides of the world, but to do what is in us for the succour of those years wherein we are set, uprooting the evil in the fields that we know, so that those who live after may have a clean earth to till...

J. R. R. Tolkien, *The Lord of the Rings*

and disease. But even in places that are less populated such as prehistoric sites in Australia and South America, there are burial sites and ceremonial places where the memories can seep back through the porous materials of brick and wood constructions.

Throughout the land, ley lines feature as arteries, maintaining a flow of energy just as the blood streams around the human body. Should too much pressure be put on a major artery, it will cause a dysfunction in its flow. In the same way the energy of the land can be disrupted and the land itself fall sick. Almost any landscape can fall prey to this kind of disturbance. Building a town can affect the whole surrounding area, if it is built on a main ley line. Livestock or bloodstock may be affected, crops may not grow and even the trees may die.

LETHBRIDGE AND DOWSING

The noted archaeologist Tom Lethbridge, an important figure in the investigation of power places in the land, used dowsing to 'pick up' electrical fields of objects and reactions to them. He believed that spirits were not conscious entities but energy fields.

Lethbridge was an honorary keeper of Anglo Saxon collections at the University Museum of Archaeology and Ethnology at Cambridge. His first supernatural experience took place when he was an 18-year-old youth, out walking with his mother in a wood. Both simultaneously felt a 'horrible feeling of gloom and depression'. They hurried out of the wood. A few days later the body of a man who had committed suicide was found close to the spot where they had been overcome by the 'horrible feeling'.

Lethbridge's research led him into strange, bewildering realms where all his scientific ideas seemed to be turned upside-down. He compared himself to a man walking on ice, when it suddenly collapses and he finds himself floundering in freezing water. Of this sudden immersion in new ideas he said, 'From living a normal life in a three-dimensional world, I seem to have suddenly fallen through into one where there are more dimensions. The three-dimensional life goes on as usual, but one has to adjust one's thinking to the other.'

Lethbridge explored various types of field forces connected with water, wood, mountains and open spaces. Out of these experiments he argued that the ghosthunter and the dowser should walk hand in hand. He believed that dowsing and psychometry would reveal pictures of past events sparked off by touch. He was convinced that nature was full of 'tape recordings' that date back millions of years and that our brains possess the equipment to play them back. Nature, he felt, was alive, not only in trees, plants and flowers, but in water and rocks too. He believed that the physical world was only one level of reality. And as I too have discovered, the quartz crystal used as a pendulum must be alive to be able to detect living things and discover points within the Earth that are dead or negative.

In the dowsing technique that I personally conduct, I use a quartz crystal primed to work as a radar on selected frequencies. To a psychic, and maybe to a non-psychic, it can induce telescopic vision.

A ghost can be seen as a visual being whilst being drawn by the crystal into the human aura or etheric web. Once the ghost is located by the crystal, it functions as a fishing line, which has caught a large fish, drawing it at first slowly, then faster, into my aura, which acts as a fishing net. Once caught, there is no way out for the ghost as it is held firm in the aura. This in turn is held firm by the Earth's gravitational pull, so the ghost cannot move with any amount of freedom. Once it has been trapped in this way, it may be removed from its geographical location and relocated in a more suitable environment.

One of my cases of land clearance concerned an estate in Bedfordshire where there was a tied cottage which had been left derelict for 25 years. The locals claimed a madwoman haunted it. Since she had died, nobody had gone to the cottage for fear of being chased off by her demented spirit. The owners had let it fall into neglect because of its history and the legend, and it was only when an accident occurred and two dogs from the estate were drowned in an old well close by that the property was opened up for investigation.

I arrived at the cottage to find it surrounded by thick undergrowth, briars and ferns having long since strangled the garden out of its earlier beauty. There was a strange feel to the place, but it felt moody rather than malevolent. I soon discovered that the house was split into halves, with two main doors, one into each side, and stairs leading to an upper floor. Going up the first set of stairs, as I turned into the front bedroom I saw the skeleton of a fledgling bird on the floor. This is a good sign when investigating a site, one of innocence. In the other side of the house, again from the stairwell, I set foot into the corresponding bedroom only to see a bat skeleton completely covered in fur. It looked as if it had been stuffed. This was not a good sign and suggested that there were two separate influences, one benevolent and the other sinister. It made me believe that there must have been a reason behind the person going insane and the death of the two dogs.

Armed with my faithful quartz pendulum, I wandered around the building, dowsing the land using the crystal as a sensor, an extension of my body. My sensory perception takes me in the general direction I need to go to detect certain negative or haunted spots in the house or land, while the pendulum detects the precise spot, which will vibrate at a different frequency from the surrounding area. As I have used pendulums for many years, healing people and houses as well as land sites, I am experienced enough to be able to estimate the extent of a problem and determine the necessary remedial action, which can vary with each individual case.

On this investigation I discovered a black stream in the land. This is a disease within the Earth that may be caused by a number of environmental problems. Dowsers and diviners will often pick up on this kind of condition and diagnose it in their own way. As I advanced along the black stream I crossed two fields. One was yielding good crops, the other was in decline. When I reached the top of this particular field, I looked into the distance and immediately noticed a dead tree standing on a direct line with the black stream, leading back to the house. The black stream running through its roots would have caused its death.

Using my pendulum again, I picked up the direction in which the stream was running. Much to my surprise it entered the adjacent field. The crops in this field had grown and should have been flourishing at this time of year, but every plant was dead. Following the line further, I skirted into the next field, which led into woodland. This field had endured, except for the corner through which the black stream ran. That part was dead. It took me some time to unlock the main vortex of negative energy that had centred on this black stream.

When I completed the investigation I spoke to the owners about my diagnosis. They were fortunately open minded. Some clients are not interested in the paranormal, just in whether I can solve their particular problems. In this case, one of the owners confirmed this area had been a battleground at the time of Hereward the Wake and that part of the land was an old burial ground. We cleansed the site and realigned the energy. This provided the support the land needed to return to its optimum function.

The traditional solution to such problems was the erection of a small shrine where regular ceremonies or exorcism rituals could be performed to clear a site. Unfortunately in a land where disbelief or planning laws prevent this, alternative means have to be used. These are the major application of a modern harmonizer and the reorientation of the site, including a private ritual in appeasing of the local spirits to ensure their support.

In common with shamans and healers that work with the land, it is understood that the forces of the Earth need to replenish lost energy, ground and heal, because we are at a point of overuse and degradation of the land. It is important to realize that the Earth is magnetic and holds the memories of everything that has occurred over the millions of years that life has existed here. It holds these memories in its deepest cellular structure. Modern technology, roads and buildings generate heat and they begin to draw memories out of the land which have been held in abeyance for generations. That is why when there is building development, archaeological sites dug up and so on, there can be a knock-on effect, which disturbs the land, and the memory, which can cause chaos or the release of malevolent forces onto the surface, affecting the building, the people and the community.

In *feng shui*, the ancient Chinese method of geomancy, buildings should never be erected in yin areas. Yin is associated with graveyards, churches, hospitals and police stations, because such buildings contain the dead or dying, either spiritually or physically.

Special devices are set up as protected gateways in many cultures. The Chinese believe that spirits travel in straight lines and combat them by making winding paths to prevent demons from approaching temple doors. For additional protection, a 'spirit wall' is constructed in front of the entrance, creating a corner un-negotiable by straight line flying spirits. The Shinto shrines in Japan are protected by *torii*, gates of entry similar to the Stonehenge trilithons. These entrances serve the magical function of excluding evil. They guard the entrance to the mountain sanctuary of Inari, near Kyoto.

If you are experiencing problems and the land's history features plague pits, mental asylums, death camps, battlegrounds, burial grounds, churches, church graveyards, ancient sites or even bomb sites from the Second World War, then you will need an expert to investigate and clear the area because the problem will not go away.

Barbara Erskine has had many encounters with ghosts and spirits.

Our best and most favourite ghost was that of a Roman soldier who was on duty in my herb garden for many years. A friend who is able to speak to ghosts came to interview him and was told that he could not leave his post because he had not been given permission to do so. She tried to dismiss him and then resorted to persuasion, but he refused to go. Then we realized that it was probably because he was unlikely to be dismissed by a woman. I phoned another friend who was a ghurka officer and asked him if he could help. The next day he came over, having learned some Latin for the occasion, and honourably dismissed him. It was really quite simple. We never saw him again. I miss him.

═══════════════════════

Barbara Erskine has offered top tips to help anyone who feels they may be bothered by spirits. These simple methods of communication and ritual will enable anyone with sensitivity and common sense to clear their home and remain confident in their encounters with the spirit realms:

Talk to them.
Start by talking. Just talking can be reassuring to both parties.

Watch the pets.
Animals can let you know if there are any spirits around – say, if a dog or cat is scared and leaves the house full tilt!

Smudging.
Smudging is a method of burning incense to create a sacred space in the land or in the home. It is derived from Native American traditions and in the Americas they tend to use sage. The herbs are wrapped around with string and then lit, the flame is blown out and the stick is moved in a sweeping movement around the space, beginning at the four corners of a room or area of land.

Bells.

Bells can get the atmosphere really ringing. They are good for clearing trapped thought forms.

The sign of the cross.

I do use the sign of the cross a lot as I think signs stay hanging in the air like the symbols used in Reiki healing. The cross is an easy symbol for us to use because it comes easily in our culture.

A psychic spring clean.

It is important to create a psychic cleanliness in the house and keep the vibrations raised by using the above methods and recognizing when an atmosphere is becoming cloudy and heavy.

A diary.

It can be useful to keep a diary to see if there is a pattern of events. It can be that the atmosphere makes it easier or more difficult for ghosts to show themselves to us. They are light bodies trying to show themselves in very dense atmospheres.

Emma Restall Orr has some recommendations on what to do if you have a haunting:

First locate the room where the spirit is and then take anything out of that room which you value and see if the spirit is attached to that and moves with it.

Light a candle in the room.

Go into the room feeling strong and ask the spirit to leave, telling them why you feel that they should go. If you do not have a good reason, then you shouldn't be asking them to go anyway. They have as much right to be there as you do.

Clear the room, open the windows and make it spotlessly clean.
If they are still there, then you have to call the professionals.

SOUL RESCUE

CHAPTER FIVE

The myths and religions of most peoples have an area set aside for demons, goblins, and other spirit beings. They form a pantheon as it were of their own with powers covering the whole range of man's dialogue with the supernatural. Man has tended to conceive of these spirits as animate beings...

They may be benevolent; on the other hand they may take the form of dangerous demons who have to be ritually placated. All kinds of natural phenomena, including sickness and death, are attributed to them. In magical rites man invokes spirit powers against his enemies; the shaman summons up good spirits to drive out the demons of illness.

Alexander Eliot, in conjunction with Joseph Campbell and Mircea Eliade,

Demons and Spirits in Myths (McGraw Hill, 1977)

THE CALLING OF THE SOUL RESCUER

In order to undertake soul rescue, the novice must be toughened up and made acutely aware of the physical, mental and spiritual demands that are made on a soul rescuer. To be able to release spirits or dark forces successfully there must be an awareness of two realities: the world of spirit and the conscious reality of the physical dimension. The soul rescuer will understand their own inner spirit, they will know that it is separate from the human world and will be conscious of the separate reality. In achieving these skills soul rescuers become aware of their own limitations in the human domain, but are able to call upon the powers which uphold their own vision and faith in immortality and the human soul.

Usually they will undergo a deep experience, which may take them to the doors of death and back. Some appear to suffer from an acute illness, only to recover rapidly once they have accepted their encounter with the otherworld. Also, some go into the dark side of their personality only to realize they wish to use their power in a positive and compassionate way. They begin to recognize their gift comes from God, the world of spirit.

BORN WITH THE GIFT – THE INNOCENT

There are souls who communicate with the spirit world from childhood when the magic of innocence has not yet left and the corruption of the world has not disturbed the relationship with the spirit. As we grow older and mature many of us keep this secret world to ourselves, not finding anyone to understand that we have this magical world into which we delve to find our visions, our creativity, our love and our magic. The lucky ones find teachers, soul mates and opportunities to use their wonderful and mysterious gifts of communication with the other worlds.

Terry and I have three children. Our middle child, Ossian, has always been imaginative and creative in his relationship with the world and yet he feels in touch with spirit. His first drawings were of ghosts, eyes covered in sheets and floating through the air. As a very small child, he dreamt of magical beasts and ghostly hauntings. It was common to find a little hand pressing against my face in the middle of the night and Ossian asking to come into our bed. A relationship with spirits has always been a part of our own lives and it does not surprise us that at least one of our children would have been born with the gift of second sight.

During one of our shamanic retreats, Nikkita, one of our students, had to remain behind after one of the daily workshops and had the opportunity to play with our children. Ossian had met her before and had a soft spot for her. Later that night he came to sit on my lap and told me that Nikkita had looked at him in a peculiar manner. Cocking his head to one side and twisting his mouth to show me how she had looked, he said she had told him that her brother had died. As I did not recall her having a brother, especially a dead one, I asked Ossian again about what she had said to him. He repeated word for word what he had told me.

The following day I managed to find a quiet moment to talk to Nikkita. She told me that she had never mentioned anything about a brother to Ossian and that she only had one sister. Then all of a sudden she said, 'My sister's best friend from college has just committed suicide. My sister is devastated by his death.'

What had happened? Did Ossian see the face of the boy overshadow Nikkita's or was he feeling something that was on Nikkita's mind? Fortunately as a result of this conversation we were able to advise Nikkita what to do to help this young man move away from his sad death and into the realms of his ancestors. As Nikkita was attending the funeral the following week, it was an ideal time to give her the tools to help.

In folklore there is a belief that children born during the hour after midnight, at twilight or at dawn have the privileged gift of seeing spirits. Terry was born at midnight, Ossian was born at twilight and I was born at dawn. Among tribal traditions it is believed that spirits are visible to some people and not to others, and many of the tribal elders can tell even before a child is born whether they have the gift.

Many find that they are carrying a hereditary gift which sometimes misses a generation. For instance with our friend Jenny Waite it was her grandmother who was a medium whilst her mother had no interest in the paranormal.

CHILDHOOD

People who later in life develop a talent as a psychic often seem to have had imaginary friends during their childhood.

Aggie Richards recalls how as a child she had imaginary friends:

I thought that everyone had these friends. They used to help me with my homework. I used to go for long walks and pick buttercups and daisies in the local fields. But most of all I used to enjoy my own company, sitting quietly daydreaming and meditating. This all started when my mother, a very spiritual woman, used to sit and pray, going into a meditative state, sometimes even going into trance. She would then relate to me where she had been and what she had seen on her journey. Getting tired of waiting for her to return from her trance, I would begin to meditate for myself. I used to practise this regularly until I became accustomed to being able to take myself into the same state.

LEARNING FROM THE FAMILY

Many gifted psychics, healers, shamans and witchdoctors come to their profession through the guidance of their own families. Malidoma Some was initiated by his grandfather.

My grandfather had always been my confidant and guide since the day I could walk. The first few years of a male child are usually spent with the grandfather while the other members go on with their family responsibilities. There is an unspoken closeness between one who has freshly entered from the otherworld and one who is close to returning to that otherworld. Eventually, it is the role of the grandfather to direct the grandson.

PUBERTY – UNCONTROLLED PSYCHICS

Natural born psychics do not always begin their 'sight' in childhood; some start during puberty.

Liz, a good friend, describes the opening of her psychic gifts:

I was at boarding school and 12 years old. I woke up at 2 o'clock in the morning, having heard a bang. No one else was awake. When I looked at the clock on my dressing table I saw that a little carved duck I had been given by my parents had fallen over. I couldn't think why when everyone was asleep, but thought perhaps it had been knocked over earlier. For the next five nights I was woken up by a bang and each time saw that it was exactly 2 o'clock and that my duck had fallen over. I checked the duck before I fell asleep and I moved it to different parts of my dressing table. It didn't make any difference. The last time it happened its head fell off! All of this was fairly easy to dismiss, even though it started to frighten me a little.

The next term I moved to a new dormitory of six. That term I was 13. Every night in that new dormitory I was scared. I used to wake up in the middle of the night petrified and didn't know why. After a while, I would creep out of bed after lights out and put the light on in the hairdressing room, which shone through the window next to where I was sleeping. Then I swapped my bed for a very unpopular place in the middle of the dormitory. I thought I'd feel better surrounded by everyone.

One night I woke up feeling very uncomfortable and saw a woman standing at the end of my bed looking down at me. Then in front of my eyes, she disappeared. I screamed the place down. Everyone woke up and told me to shut up.

After that almost every night I was woken up by the woman spirit, then a little boy and then a strange man, all staring down at me in bed. The little boy was standing in mid-air, on the same level as my bed. At first I woke up the whole dormitory. Then my friends decided I was making this all up to get attention and sent me to Coventry. I used to wake up, watch the person or spirit until they disappeared and then spend the rest of the night in the toilets with the lights on. None of the spirits or ghosts ever tried to talk to me, but they all seemed to want my attention. All this time, I wasn't sure if I was seeing 'ghosts' or whether I had something wrong with my brain. The figures were so solid and real, and ghosts to me were supposed to be see through.

Other things started happening at that time. One afternoon a few of us were in the dormitory chatting. None of us were near my dressing table but it suddenly moved two feet and hit the bed next to it with a bang. The weird thing is that one of the other girls blamed me, even though I was nowhere near the table. Somehow they all knew I had quite a lot to do with it. Another time we were all chatting by another's girl dressing table when a coin flew across the room and hit the mirror in front of us.

After a while I got so used to seeing people at night that I would just wait for them to go away and then fall asleep, praying frantically.

At the end of term I told my mother that I had a problem with my brain and should see a doctor. Luckily she was sensitive enough to tell me she thought that I was psychic. She explained that my great grandmother had been and that she and my father had always thought I was too because funny things had happened around me when I was young. I used to talk about things I couldn't have known about and I used to sleepwalk, but they had decided not to talk to me about it because they didn't want to scare me.

As I got older the psychic phenomena got less and less. Sometimes I didn't see the spirit people at all, though I saw strange lights above my bed. Then when I was about 17, I was in bed in the old gatehouse of the school, in a room I shared with one other girl, when I woke up to see a very tall man with a black hat and cloak staring down at me. The girl in the next bed started screaming and as the man disappeared she told me she had seen him staring down at me and thought it was a burglar, describing him even down to his cloak. At last someone else was a witness. It was only then that I fully realized that I was seeing 'ghosts' and wasn't just mad. I could have hugged her, but she was far too scared for that. She left the light on all night and I felt like a real pro, not being as scared as she was!

Incidentally, quite a few years later I went back to the school and went to see the bedroom where it had all started. It had a very strange and nasty energy and I wouldn't have spent one night there given the choice.

INITIATIONS

Initiations into soul rescue can take many forms. Credo Mutwa, a great Zulu elder and witch doctor, or *sangoma*, saw visions during his initiation:

Strange vistas opened my mind. I was no longer afraid of the fearsome visions that I saw; rather, I worked with them and saw them as useful guides which greatly strengthened and broadened my perception, not only of the world in which I lived, but also of the entire cosmos.

On the other side of the world, in the mystical priesthood of the Venezuelan rainforest, a young man is being initiated. He is given hallucinogenic drugs which expand his attention to include the spirit world. So his vision is opened to the realities of this world and he is subjected to psychic attack by elemental influences, which are prevalent in the region. In the ensuing battle to overcome these forces, drained by a week of fasting and hallucinating, the initiate is expected to stay awake and keep his body alive. He is assisted by experienced shamen, one of whom, in the event of possession, ensures that the spirit does not wander too far from his body, while the others exorcize the possession to keep the initiate on the correct path. If the possessed initiate were to wander too far from his body, he would be drawn into the forest and held by elemental forces. This would result in bodily death. Once the initiate has faced the demons of the forest and mastered them, he is acknowledged as a shaman.

Soul Rescuers

In Shinto, the Japanese folk religion, they follow the way of the *kami*, the native gods who are the focus of anything vivid or powerful in nature. By tradition women are the special conduits of the spirits. As well as communicating with the spirits and deities, they divine the future, offer prayers for the sick and purify new buildings.

The initiates or novices undergo training disciplines such as cold water ablution, purification, fasting, abstinence and the observance of various taboos. They are taught the techniques of trance, of communication with super-human beings or spirits of the dead, of divination, prayer and incantation; they learn the melody and intonation used in the chanting of prayers, magic formulas and liturgies and the narratives and ballads of local custom. After three to five years' training, they become full-fledged shamanesses through the completion of initiatory ordeals and an initiation ceremony, which includes the use of symbols of death and resurrection. It is believed that woman have more yin energy so they are better equipped to communicate with the spirit world.

INITIATION RITES IN THE WESTERN WORLD

In the Western world, the person being initiated into shamanic mysteries commonly suffers a debilitating illness during which they have the first meaningful encounter with spirits, who use the delirium or coma to introduce the initiate to the shamanic state of consciousness. When the initiate recovers from the illness they may have no conscious memory of the journey and may suffer considerable memory loss about what occurred in ordinary reality.

Some initiates refuse to take up the 'calling' and some who refuse become unhappy, losing the interest in life that they once had. Some may die shortly afterwards. Such individuals suffer great psychic damage in their attempts to repress their psychic or shamanic energy, to the point of becoming haunted by it.

Western thought induces fear – fear of failing, of feeling ill, of dying, of being diseased, being insecure, failing in a career, failing to be married, to have children. We must fit into the community. This attitude does not lend itself to the courage that is expected of someone who desires to be initiated in the ways of true spirituality and develop the qualities that one needs to become an initiate.

Courage is needed because the place where the force of evil will test or enter into combat with an initiate is in their own fear of evil. Through their own corruption their weaknesses are highlighted. This is why when a person becomes a priest, a lama, a shaman or healer and so on, life will bring its tests. But by being able to go through the darkest point within the soul, the initiate will be given vision, compassion and wisdom.

This is true of all traditions, but in the comfort zone of the Western world we are not equipped or prepared to cope with the powerful initiation rites of the otherworld. So many healers remain superficial and ineffectual in moments of great darkness or evil. They become either unwilling to recognize the intensity of the encounter and ignore the message or they run away from the confrontation. This disempowers their skills as an initiate and the lesson will come around again if they are still on the path of being a soul rescuer!

Emma Restall Orr has been working in shamanic paganism and druidry all her adult life and has experienced ghosts and earthbound spirits for as long as she can remember. She endured an initiation of sorts when she was 17 years old and living in Tokyo. The archetypal rebel, she found herself hanging out with Vietnam vets in a heavy scene which included opium, pornography and alcoholism:

It was a sordid scene and very dark. All of them had various disabilities, both mental and physical. They were deeply scarred by what they had experienced in Vietnam and were trying one form of escapism after another. I became their totem. I was not a normal kid and I understood their physical pain because I was in pain with rheumatism in my spine. I was innocent but rough enough to deal with them and make them feel good about themselves.

As well as psychological scars the vets were also carrying the spirits of the dead:

The guy I was closest to was a musician and he had been out there playing to the troops. They would sit and listen to him, laughing and crying and getting pretty hysterical as the music would open them up emotionally. Then they would go into the field and die. Because of that connection, that emotional link just before they died, their spirits would become attached to him.

Emma found that this man wanted to be with her all the time because she made him feel better, even if he didn't know why. Meanwhile she knew she was passing these spirits on, but did not have a clear idea of how or where they were actually going:

I found myself threatened by the spirits hanging on to these people, so it was in self-defence that I began learning about spirit possession and exorcism ... I was dealing with spirits who had died a violent death and who had died on morphine, which stays in the soul memory and can cause attachment in the same way that emotion can, so they were pretty hysterical and psychopathic.

I tried all kinds of things for protection – calling in the light, calling for guides to help me – but nothing was working. This taught me that guiding a spirit into the light is totally dependent on that person and their beliefs. It works if they believe that heaven is light or comes from light or through light, but if they don't, they will not buy into that kind of religious symbology. For those vets, all of that had been shattered because of all the horror when they died. For them, light did not exist, so they would not relate to it.

This enabled Emma to recognize the dark realities that can hold a spirit to the earthly plane. Many of these spirits are aware that they are dead but do not wish to take the responsibility of moving on into the higher realms. They prefer to hold on to human life and deliberately continue their habits and emotional anxieties through another person.

In the end I kind of gave up into laughter, laughing with them at the ludicrousness of what was going on and I found that when laughter reaches a pure gentle place it works as a positive guiding force. So I learnt about laughter and how to laugh because to show fear does not work. That was my greatest lesson.

=====

RITES OF PASSAGE – DEATH AND RESURRECTION

Initiation always signifies death and resurrection. This is a true rite of passage marking the entry to a new phase of life. The former life must be destroyed and erased.

The period of initiation strips the healer or shaman of all their social and mental habits as well as their religious and philosophical ideas. To use a more graphic expression, they are chopped up into pieces until there is nothing left but their bones. Eskimo shamans must see themselves as no more than a skeleton before they accept the powers that are offered from the otherworld. Tibetan yogis are said to meditate upon death in charnel grounds or cemeteries until they experience a decomposition of their bodies and perceive themselves as skeletons. This is why so many shamans, witch doctors and *curanderos* use bones, including human bones and skulls, as ritual objects and the skirts of Siberian shamans are embroidered with a skeleton.

In the legends of many cultural traditions, including European, the spirits of the underworld not only take the body of the initiate apart in the most gruesome way, but also put it back together, albeit in a curious manner which endows the person with superhuman powers.

Credo Mutwa's own call to become a *sangoma* began with an illness within his mind as well as body:

A shaman has walked up to the gates of his or her personal hell and then walked in. The self-created demons of fear, insanity, loneliness, self-importance and addiction have been confronted and conquered by the shaman who has gone through the gamut of Shaman's Deaths. The quality that always shines in a true shaman is compassion for the paths that others must walk. This comes from the fact that the shaman has also walked through the underworld of the shadow and knows first hand the pain involved in breaking the stranglehold of inner darkness.

Jamie Sams, Native American teacher and writer

I had a sickness then, which was one of the reasons why my mother recommended that I take my grandfather's profession. It was a very weird sickness which
medical doctors did not understand. I felt strange to myself. I was not who I was.
Sometimes I had visions of myself being torn apart by great cannibals and sometimes leopards. I could see through solid objects... Since then I have been cursed
with a very strange gift, the gift of seeing things before they happen, which I've
been trying to get rid of, but I cannot.

The initiation of shamans and witch doctors takes them into a near death
experience, offering a journey in to the otherworld, and when they return
they are different. Their vision, gifts and whole perception of life have
changed.

The experience of near death, when the consciousness separates from
the body and journeys down the tunnel through the cosmic web into the
world of spirit, often brings the power of communication with the spirit
world. Such an experience reinforces the idea that life after death does not
need to be feared and strengthens the initiate's connection with the universe.

ADEPTHOOD — BECOMING THE MASTER

It is a world-wide tradition that to become a great master, the initiate
must first understand their own evil and then move through the dark night
of the soul, death and resurrection, to cleanse the evil from body and soul.

Adepthood occurs when the soul rescuer qualifies their natural abilities. It can occur in the moment of challenge with a paranormal force or
encounter when the soul rescuer knows that they have understood their
own evil. When evil touches them it challenges their beliefs and their own
ability to win.

It is in the overcoming that the initiate turns from being an innocent
enthusiast or pauses on their own journey. If they do not wish to take the
qualification of adepthood, they remain working on the level they have

He who desires the soul,
who plays with the soul,
who makes love with the
soul, who attains ecstasy
in the soul, becomes his
own master and wanders
at will through the worlds.
But they who know other-
wise are dependent. They
dwell in perishable worlds
and cannot wander at will.

Upanishad

reached. Others are inspired to seek a greater vision and their challenges are chosen for them by God.

=====================

The traditional stories of Tibetan culture tell of a man who was called Milarepa. He was born in rural Tibet where the people lived in their own communities and worked the land for food, kept livestock and hunted. The fates conspired against Milarepa, or so he thought, and in this self-deceptive belief he learned the craft of black magic, which he eventually turned on local farmers, destroying land, families and kinship with the potency of his spells. His reputation spread and he became the most feared and hated man in Tibet. He lost all his friends, his family disowned him and eventually he became tortured by his own evil. This was the turning-point. Milarepa had cursed the people and cursed the land, so now the curse had found its way back to him.

Far away there was a saint called Naropa. Milarepa sought his guidance and help; he began his own resurrection with the arduous pilgrimage to the place where Naropa lived. When he arrived Naropa instructed him to build a house, then to take it down again, brick by brick, until it was dismantled. Then he had to build it up and take it down again. So it went on. Milarepa had destroyed so much in his life that the action of building and destruction was the only way he would be able to understand the effect of his evil ways.

This method of discipline enabled Milarepa to exorcize his demons from his mind and body. Finally he could see neither good nor evil in his work; it had become sacred. He became a famous master and is still celebrated today in Tibetan Buddhist culture.

=====================

When the soul rescuer deals with evil it is the recognition of what they are dealing with in their work that is the mastery and whether they are in the position to challenge that force.

Sudhir Kakar, an Indian trained in Western psychoanalysis, describes his encounter with an 87-year-old Muslim Pir, or wise elder, in North Africa:

The core of his efficacy was that he believed in the soul force, the power of the divine that he was able to transmit. This only comes to a Pir after years of service to a guru and devotion to God. He stated that he as the healer had finally started racing toward Allah and Allah had started pulling him heavenward. When the two forces combine, one has the connection that makes the Pir an effective healer and exorcist.

The dividing line that may be drawn to separate the soul rescuer from the exorcist or shaman is that the soul rescuer will seek to help trapped earthbound spirits who need comfort and encouragement, whilst the exorcist, shaman or adept is involved in healing the sick from mental and physical problems that are related to soul loss, disease and malevolent forces. They also rescue trapped or lost spirits of the dead, but in addition delve into the sphere of dark forces and demonic beings.

FROM INITIATE TO ADEPT

It started with a garbled phone call from a frightened lady. I tried as best I could to calm her down, but I could feel that she was gripped by panic and thus unable to convey to me what it was that was so frightening her. Luckily, with some degree of patience, I managed to get her address and promised to visit her.

It was a time early on in my career when to be honest I was a little too confident. I had been a successful initiate for some time and as yet I had never felt myself truly tested. I remember that as I travelled northeast on the train to my appointment I became fascinated by all the fledgling birds who, proud of their newfound ability to fly, were boastfully

Lillian Too, the international *feng shui* expert, talks about her master, an adept in the craft of exorcism of evil spirits:

I personally have never experienced, nor been in the presence of evil forces, mainly because I avoid such places. But my *feng shui* master Yap Cheng Hai is a specialist in exorcizing spirits. He uses both his knowledge of exorcism as well as *feng shui* to cleanse an environment of evil spirits. Not everyone is able to withstand the onslaught of evil spirits. And unless one is specially trained and is armed with special protection, it is foolish to attempt to do so. My master in this field has been doing this work for many years. He is very strongly protected, but even he has shown me the places on his body which bear the scars of battle with these spirits.

circling and playing in the early summer sky as if they had owned it. I too felt that I was capable of anything.

I make this point because if I had been a little less cocky, I would have been more aware of the sudden chill I felt as I walked down the suburban street where my new client lived. If I had been a little wiser I would have taken more notice of the sticky grey mist, textured like honeycomb, which had wrapped itself around the little bungalow that was my destination.

My client, Joan, who was in her early sixties, was very pleased to see me. Initially I felt that her over-attentiveness, the freshly cut flowers from the garden that she brought with the tea and the offer of something stronger if I wanted, was a reaction to loneliness, but I soon realized that she was merely trying to avoid talking about her reasons for calling me. Eventually I took her by the hand and calmly asked, 'Joan, what's wrong?'

At first she was embarrassed, persuading herself that I would laugh at her story. But gradually I was able to convince her that I would listen and that I would try to help.

Joan's husband Bill had died suddenly from a heart attack a year earlier. It had been hard enough for her to cope with the grief of her loss, let alone with the poltergeist activity that subsequently occurred. At first it was small things like kitchen utensils disappearing from the kitchen and then reappearing in her bedroom. This could easily have been Bill's earthbound spirit playing pranks on his wife. But then Joan was physically attacked by a force. She had been woken in the middle of the night by a noise that was like a strong wind coming through an open window. As she had put on the light, she had been pushed to the ground by an invisible force that rolled her round and round the floor. Scared for her life, all she could do was curl up and scream.

This physical attack worried me. Bill, as a discarnate spirit, should by now have been reunited with his ancestors and friends. If he was trapped, why was he trapped? And why was he attacking his wife? And if it wasn't

Bill, who *was* attacking Joan? To answer these questions I made my way to Joan's bedroom. The chill hit me as soon as I opened the door. But all was still and quiet. Joan had not been back to the room since the attack, so it was still untidy with bedlinen, pillows and clothes thrown about the place. I caught my breath as I spotted dried blood smeared across the dressing-table mirror. Walking over to the window, I rubbed my fingers along the fresh gouges and scratches that scarred the woodwork. I knew then that for the first time in my career I was witnessing the work of some feral beast – indeed, a demonic presence. I'm not ashamed to say that I was frightened.

Before I could do anything else I was aware of three spirits in the room, eddies of wind that flitted around the room chanting, 'We've got Bill, we've got Bill! He is paying!' I recognized them as mere scouts of a bigger force and my physical presence alone was enough to diminish them. However I knew that they would be missed and that a greater force would return to search for them.

I didn't have much time. I had to have an idea of what I was up against. I went back and found Joan hiding behind the living-room door. 'Why have they got Bill?' I asked. 'What did he do? Why does he have to pay?'

Joan didn't really understand what I was asking, but little by little from what she told me I was able to piece together some sort of story. For 35 years Bill had been in the purchasing department of the local council offices. He had begun at the bottom of the ladder but over the years he had, by his diligence and hard work, reached the top of his department. Bill and Joan had had no children, so even though Bill's salary was no more than that of a middle manager they were able to maintain a good standard of living without Joan having to go out to work. However, when Bill was 55, without discussing it with his wife, he quite suddenly gave up his job and began a new career. It was impossible to get out of Joan what exactly this career change was, as Bill had refused to talk about it. What she could tell me, though, was that for seven years the money had rolled in. They had bought a new bungalow in a nicer part of town, they had new cars every two years and holidays abroad.

The night Bill died he had arrived back late from work. Joan noticed how anxious he seemed and was surprised that he, a confirmed teetotaller, poured himself three large Scotches. For an hour or so he had stood by the hallway window, looking out across the road. Eventually he left the house. The last words he said to Joan were: 'I don't know when I'll be back. They're after me!' His body was found on the local common the following morning.

It was obvious to me from Joan's information about Bill, combined with the demonic activity that I had witnessed in her bedroom, that Bill had made some sort of pact with a Satanic sect. Whether contacts from his previous career had tempted him or whether they were brand new acquaintances I couldn't tell. But what was also clear to me was that Bill had reneged on the pact. Why else were they holding him and making him pay?

The only hope for Bill was that I could weaken the demonic force holding him long enough to enable a spirit guide to lead him away. I approached the task in hand with foreboding. Having made sure that Joan was safe, I returned to her bedroom.

As always it was the change in temperature which made me aware that an evil presence was approaching. I could feel the coldness and heaviness of the atmosphere. After a while it was like being trapped in an underground tomb. My breathing becoming laboured. The evil presence circled me for a while, playing with my fear. I stood my ground, praying for help from my spiritual elder.

The attack, when it came, was sudden and violent. First I was gripped by a vice of steel around my upper body and then I was thrown around the room in a helter skelter of turmoil. My only weapon was my faith – and like a man standing tall in the face of some hurricane my faith held firm. At the very worst moment, when I felt as if my whole body would implode under the suffocating pressure and violent crushing, I caught a glimpse of my spirit elder. I realized that I was being tested and that when I survived this encounter I would no longer be an initiate, I would be an adept.

I don't know how long I was attacked, maybe a few minutes, maybe a few hours, but I always knew I would win – my faith and my strength of resolve were too strong for any other option. Then quite suddenly it was as if the floor had opened up and I fell into a black hole. The force field around me broke and the pressure abated. The last thing I saw was my guardian leading some indescribable entity away. It did not look entirely human.

By now the warmth of the sun was glowing through the curtains and the grey pallor seemed to fade away. The contract on the soul of Bill had been lifted and he was able to return to his ancestors.

With the train gently rocking me from side to side on my journey home, I couldn't help but think about the playful fledgling birds that I had seen that very morning. It was a world I could never be a part of again. I was now truly a man and moreover an adept. I fell asleep, proud in the knowledge of my achievement and confident of my role in life in the future.

SOUL RESCUE — WORLD TRADITIONS

In all traditional cultures healing and exorcism are practised by priests, healers, witch doctors and shamans. These exorcism rituals work in a different way from those of Spiritualists and Church exorcists. In tribal cultures in Africa and Australia, the belief that death comes from beyond the physical dimension is commonly accepted and rituals are practised to heal the sick, cleanse the soul of evil spirits and cast away spells.

This tradition is world-wide, but each country has a different name

Each human being has his own *jinn*, who is born with him and stays with him until he dies. When the angels come to take away the soul of a good man, they kill the *jinn*. This is the reason why we Muslims bury a dead body and the Hindus cremate it – it is to ensure the death of a man's *jinn*. Sometimes, however, especially in the case of a sinful man, it happens that the *jinn* escapes by hiding in the organs of elimination, which are impure and cannot be reached by the angels. He then becomes a demon or *bala* and is on the lookout for a victim in whose body he can find a home and whose blood he can drink.

Sudhir Kakar, quoting the Muslim Pir, *Shamans, Prophets and Sages* (Macmillan, 1974)

and a different way of displaying these gifts. For instance a South African witch doctor is called a *sangoma*. *Sangomas* have the skills to heal the sick, divine the future and communicate with spirits. They conduct rituals and ceremonies for their tribe; they understand the power and use of herbs, and the exorcism of evil projections or possession by evil spirits. They heal physical and mental conditions caused by soul loss; this is when someone loses a part of their soul through shock or trauma or other people capture parts of the soul or damage it by magic or hatred. When a person has lost a part of their soul they become vulnerable to disease, so the *sangoma* heals the soul first before healing the body.

It is the belief of these peoples that all sickness is caused by malevolent manifestation which shows up in the body as an illness. Being a spirit form it may be exorcized by natural herbal remedies and incantation rituals. Similar rites are still carried out by Aborigines of Australia and numerous tribes in New Guinea. Like our ancestors the Druids, living close to the earth, such tribes treat spells and witchcraft as common occurrences. Life is seen as both dark and light and their belief is that all sickness is based on soul loss or possession.

Among the Navajo of North America, a hand trembler is able to determine the cause of an ailment and recommend a ceremonial cure, which is performed by a chanter. It is said the hand trembler's diagnostic abilities arise from the joining of his forces with the force of the Gila monster, who causes his arm and hand to shake and thereby locate an illness, or spirit possession, much as a divining rod is said to indicate the location of water.

China also retains shamanic features from its folklore traditions. The Taoist priests seem to have been popular exorcists, but the ritual materials they employed show the influence of the Confucian beliefs of the yin and yang dualism of the world. The yin forces are associated with the dark, passive and feminine, the yang forces with the light, active and masculine. One of the ways a person could fall into a state of possession that necessitated exorcism was by having the yin forces overpower the yang. Consequently the ritual of exorcism was replete with yang symbols such as firecrackers, peach wood, cash or coins, swords, invocations, burning candles or incense sticks, gongs and freshly killed cocks. These elements opposed the yin side of reality and so were able to bring the patient back to a balance that would oust the possessing forces. The function of the priest was to confront these forces and cast them out by his superior will-power and the force of the symbols he wielded. People feared demonic possession and needed an impressive exorcism ritual.

Sheila Simpson lived in Zimbabwe as a child and she remembers a story of the *Tokoloshi*. This is a Matabele and Shona word for an earthbound spirit, which is normally found near burial grounds.

Our first house was built on a burial ground and the household men wouldn't go into a certain part of the house because of the *Tokoloshi*. There are women witch doctors like spirit mediums who go into trance, make live chicken sacrifices and perform community rituals and ceremonies. They even choose the chief of the tribe. These are the people who come along and clear spirits with their incantations and trance communication. It is fascinating to watch.

Traditional African religion is hard to typify, but most African cultures are sensitive to the spiritual realms. They know when people are possessed by spirits or attacked by negative energy and they understand the powers of the mind. African protection rituals are based on appeasing the spirits and their ancestors. Being haunted by the spirits of the dead is considered common. Many people go to the witch doctors and healers to cure themselves of physical problems that the undead may have caused.

In Africa it is accepted among tribal people that if a man is in perfect health, then one day starts to ail, becoming a shadow of his former self, and in some cases dies, he is suffering from a sorcerer's spell. No modern medicine can avail against such a disease, it can only be exorcized by a more potent sorcerer or perhaps by religious faith or the sorcerer who cast the spell. These spells are more common than we would care to believe in the Western world.

One of my clients, Peter, is the head of a charitable organization in Ethiopia and had been having an affair with an Ethiopian woman for a number of years. She also worked for the charity and lived with him when he stayed out in Ethiopia. After a time, Peter met a Frenchwoman in London and decided that he wanted to marry her, so he returned to explain to his Ethiopian girlfriend that their relationship was over:

Unbeknown to me she had gone to see a local witch doctor, taken a photograph of me and asked that I would be cursed so I would leave my current girlfriend and return to her. Later that year, when I returned to Ethiopia for my normal three-month trip, I began to get excruciating headaches. I had to make a long trip in to the hills and when I arrived I collapsed with a possible brain tumour. I thought I was dying. They flew me back to the city by helicopter and then I managed to get a flight back to the UK, but the doctors couldn't find anything wrong with me even after CAT scans and all the general investigations. I felt exhausted. I couldn't work or function.

I went for a healing session with Terry to investigate the problem on a psychic level and he detected the possibility that I had been cursed by someone in Africa. Then my head administrator rang to tell me that he had found an effigy and other magical items under my bed in Ethiopia. I was mortified. He found out it was my old girlfriend who had done it. He managed to get her to return the curse to the local sorcerer and it was lifted. But it took me a few months to recover.

Similar cases of psychic attack have been documented throughout the ages. Psychic attack is based on wilful intent and may be conducted by magic or spells. It is often used in the black arts and spell binding, and is similar to curses, or hexes, as they are called by occultists.

The doorways to psychic attack are telepathic hypnotic suggestion or the employment of some physical substance as a point of contact or magnetic link with the victim, for example photographs or hair or a personal object such as jewellery or clothing that the victim would have worn.

VOODOO

The voodoo priest or priestess generally inherits a calling, but to become active they must serve an apprenticeship and to become influential must both demonstrate leadership in the community by superior wisdom and be able to heal the sick and lift curses.

When religious celebrations reach a peak the gods, ancestors, or tribal guardians may enter into the living and 'ride' them. It is considered good fortune to be possessed in this way; it is termed as being blessed by the Loa, or gods. Possession is most likely to occur at the moment of sacrifice. The possessed is known as the horse, or *cheval*, and their gestures, expressions and voice become those of the Loa or other occupying spirit, who is thus able to communicate with the living.

According to voodoo belief a person has two souls. There is a *gros-bon-ange*, or personal soul, and there is a Loa *mait-tâte*, this is the Loa that enters a person the first time they are possessed. After the first possession the Loa *mait-tâte* and the person are joined together for life. Only death can separate them. On death the Loa *mait-tâte* will return to its home in the waters which flow deep under the Earth.

In Cuba the voodoo rituals of the Santeria cult are conducted by priests or priestesses called *mayomberos*. They may concoct evil spells or *brujeria*, which means 'witchcraft' in Spanish, so the people also use the *babalawo*, the diviners and herbalists, for help and protection.

Tana is Nigerian but has lived in Britain all her life and feels as British as she does African. Although her mother is Christian she did not grow up in any kind of spiritual tradition, but she was always drawn to Brazil, so in her year off from her studies she decided to go there.

Almost immediately she felt as though she had come home and begun exploring the spiritual lives of the Brazilians. One night she attended a ceremony of drumming and trance and she felt herself taken over by one of the spirit deities. What was strange was that the whole religion has its roots in Nigeria, in Tana's ancestry, the Yoruba tribe. The deities, or *orishas*, the language of the litany, everything is in Yoruba.

I had travelled in the opposite direction to Africa and come to a direct contact with my roots. They called me a *macumba*, which is someone who works with spirits and possession in a pagan way, and it felt so much as though it was a part of myself even though it was difficult and frightening when I got back to Britain.

What was interesting was my mother's reaction when I told her that I thought that I might have been possessed. It completely freaked her out. She just didn't want to know and began accusing me of having a nervous break-down. I found out later that my great grandmother was also *macumba*. My mother had turned her back on that tradition for some powerful reasons and now here was her daughter pitching up telling her about spirits and offerings and possession. It was her worst nightmare.

Tana also discovered something else. All her life she had suffered from an irra-tional and obsessive fear of being hit, although it had never happened to her. She asked her mother how her great grandmother had died and found that she had died in an ambush, being hit by fists and sticks.

Tana's African culture will tell her that her great grandmother has been born again in her; the transgenerational therapists of the West will say that these are hidden strands of the family culture which had to emerge again in the psyche of the next generation. Whatever the theory, Tana's discovery that her great grandmother carried the same gifts makes her feel safe with her own.

Later Tana found a different atmosphere in Cuba. They practise the same form of religion there but Tana realized that there were not the same levels of responsibility as in Brazil:

In Cuba the political situation permeates everything. Everybody wants something from you. In Brazil I felt as though I would be looked after. In Cuba nobody trusts you and you can trust no one.

She found this out to her cost. She was brought to a state of possession by a medium and began channelling a spirit whom she calls Queenie:

Suddenly there I am sitting bolt upright, with my eyebrows raised and eyes peering at everyone in this impossibly regal way. The next moment I start bossing everyone around: 'Do this, do that, sweep the floor, get me a drink.' It was embarrassing. When I asked the woman who had brought this on to depossess me, she refused. That would never happen in Brazil. But she just left me like that. For days I couldn't sleep. I was not myself.

Before leaving London a psychic had given Tana a cryptic warning that she should not drink anything given to her by a man. She had assumed that meant a boyfriend, so when the landlord of the guest house offered her a drink she did not think to refuse, despite the fact that he had been trying to persuade her not to go on to Brazil but to stay in Cuba. For two weeks after accepting the drink she could hardly move. She could not rouse herself to any kind of action, felt claustrophobic, wanted to commit suicide and became convinced that she was going to die. Somebody suggested that she should go and have a 'coronation', a simple exorcism in which a small bird would be killed in front of her.

I had no choice, I was desperate, and although it did make me feel a bit better, it was expensive and it felt like when you take another drug to nullify the effects of a drug which is making you feel bad. It was just all getting worse.

Finally she flew to Brazil as scheduled and found her way to a *baba lou*, a spirit communicator. By this stage she was getting possessed at any time of the day. Unless she concentrated on holding it together her body would go into convulsions. She was sleeping three hours a night. The *baba lou* told her that the uncontrolled possession was the spirits wanting her to become initiated, but he did not recommend that she do it so young. He explained that it was a battle of wills and that she had to learn that she could control the spirits instead of having them control her.

An alternative view was offered by the eminent anthropologist she was staying with in Rio. He told her that all her talk of spirits and possession was that of 'uneducated people' and that she was 'just' having a nervous breakdown! In despair, Tana called her mother and asked for a ticket home.

In the UK her symptoms continued but she was too afraid to talk to anyone.

I was still shaking and I couldn't sleep. For three weeks I thought that I was going crazy. Nightclubs were the only place where I felt OK. I kept thinking, 'I am going to die, I am going to die.' I couldn't stop crying. I really wanted to end it all.'

Finally, during a heady night at the Blue Note in Hoxton Square in London, she confessed to a friend what was going on. The friend knew all about such matters, thanks to an aunt who was a Ugandan mystic living in Birmingham. They phoned her immediately, at 2 o'clock in the morning, and the aunt told them that she had been waiting for their call. She advised Tana to put two pound coins in each of her hands and make her way to Birmingham.

All the way to Birmingham this thing wanted me to kill myself. I really had to concentrate on not throwing myself onto the tracks. It is not pain exactly, but such severe physical discomfort that you cannot breathe and you just want it to stop.

I found myself in a market in downtown Birmingham with a woman practising hardcore witchcraft. She took 'it' out of my body and put it in a brown bag. She said she would 'smoke him out' later and then started giving me all this advice. On a Wednesday I had to put on all my gold and wear beautiful ethnic Nigerian dress and I had to go and buy a gold necklace with a cross. She told me to stop smoking weed and said that my spirit did not want to be initiated and that I would probably be initiated when I was in my late forties. I immediately felt better. It had all gone and I was back to myself.

Many of the recommended formulas for the ritual of exorcism or soul rescue include prayers and incantations, mantras and religious symbols. Each tradition has its own methods. In the Western world the traditional Christian priesthood and the Spiritualist Church are the main vehicles for the craft of exorcism or soul rescue.

THE CHRISTIAN PRIESTHOOD

Jesus of Nazareth was perhaps the most publicized exorcist the Western world has ever known. There are many stories in the Bible of Jesus commanding a demon to leave a person. Luke 4:39, for example, reports that Jesus healed Peter's mother-in-law: 'Then He stood over her and rebuked the Fever Demon and it left her.' These forms of exorcism reflect a ritual similar to those of shamans and witch doctors.

Despite the fact that exorcism and healing were the mainstay of the ministry of Jesus and his disciples, the Church is careful to keep talk of demons and ghosts very quiet. None the less each diocese has a trained exorcist. The most common requirement is for them to come and bless a home with holy water.

The Christian priesthood are well known for their active participation in exorcism as each diocese has a clergyman who specialises in exorcisms and in the Roman Catholic Church every Roman Catholic diocese is supposed to have at least one priest qualified in exorcism. Under the rituals currently enforced the priest lays his hands on the head of the possessed person whilst reciting the words *Exorcitio te*. He then calls out '*Excruciem Domini*' while wrapping the hem of his stole round the neck of the possessed and keeping his right hand on his or her head. Exorcists say that the evil spirits emerge 'sometimes a bit at a time, and sometimes in one big convulsion'.

The Times, January 1999

A particular order of ecclesiastical order of exorcists does not appear to have existed in the Christian Church until the close of the third century. Yet in the Old Testament King Solomon learned the skill of expelling demons with incantations and this method is used even today by modern rabbis, particularly to avert the influence of Satan's wife Lilis, who is believed to visit women who have just given birth to rob them of their children.

In Christian deliverance, which is a Church of England form of exorcism, a variety of demonic spirits are identified in a power hierarchy behind Satan, from the extremely powerful spirits, identified as Beelzebub, Pasuzo and the Anti-Christ, to the lesser spirits who, according to author Francis MacNutt, 'identify themselves by such names as lust, hatred, murder and envy. These names are not exactly personal names but they represent the sins or weaknesses that the spirits seem to induce and, in some mysterious way, feed on.'

Victoria and her father, a Church of England minister, recently moved into a property that was obviously haunted. They discovered that a young woman had committed suicide there a few years earlier and it appeared that her spirit was still haunting the property. The Church of England has no official rite for the exorcism of earthbound spirits or ghosts, only evil forces, so Victoria's father blessed the house using the Lord's Prayer. Although this lifted the atmosphere in the house, it did not release the spirit of the young woman. As Victoria explains:

The Church of England does not believe that a spirit could possibly be earthbound, so there are no prayers within the Church of England's exorcism rites to banish or release a spirit of the dead. My father bases his prayers for a house blessing on the New Zealand prayer book...

In general the Church does not believe ghosts to be spirits of people who have died, only malevolent energy left behind by an act of murder or death. The reason for this is that the Church believes all spirits go to the place of the

Last Judgement before being guided to heaven or hell, therefore there should be no earthbound spirits.

———————

The Roman Catholic Church announced in January 1999 that it no longer considered Satan or the Devil to be the cause of an embodiment of evil, casting aside those beliefs in favour of definitions more compatible with modern concepts of 'psychological disturbance'. So priests now are conducting exorcisms dealing with evil as a psychological force 'lurking within all individuals' rather than as a force, traditionally embodied as Satan, threatening from without. Yet Catholic definitions of 'demonic possession' and the rituals for dealing with it have largely remained unaltered since Pope Paul V in 1605.

SPIRITUALIST RESCUE CIRCLES

In the Spiritualist Church soul rescue is occasionally conducted by certain rescue groups. But this does require complete harmony between the sitters and that fear be at a minimum level. If this is not the case, serious damage can be inflicted within the group through possession or psychic disruption, which can cause physical or psychological damage to the sitters. For this reason, a Spiritualist rescue circle's main work is releasing earthbound spirits rather than dealing with black magic curses and malevolent forces. The work carried out by these groups is of a healing nature, bringing relief to many disembodied spirits who have passed on from the physical world with no understanding of the afterlife. The spirit workers or guides who help these groups are the equivalent of social workers on Earth or policemen who show people the way.

Most confused disembodied spirits are collected from a rescue group by their relatives due to the collective consciousness of the group being raised to a level equal to that of the Summerland, the spirit land where it is believed by Spiritualists that spirits go after death.

The advantage of these rescue groups is shown by a personal experience of mine during my years with development groups and rescue circles. Some years before I started this work, I had a German penfriend called Helga, with whom I had long since lost touch. When I had first joined a development group (which was not a rescue circle), the group leader explained to us that a spirit had just arrived. She was in a state of hysteria and fear, and the medium could not understand what she was saying, as she was speaking in German. The only thing he could understand was her name. I then knew who she was and he was able to describe her to me. I realized that she must have died and later learned that she had been killed in a car crash at the age of 26. About a year after this communication, she came to a teacher of mine who was also a medium and spoke to me. By now she had recovered her English and had come to thank me for the help I had given her earlier. She explained the reason why she couldn't speak English earlier, although in life she had been fluent, was that the shock of her death had closed off her ability to do so. She had since rehabilitated at a sanatorium and was recovering well.

In many cases this work is safe and problem free. But sometimes work at this level can be dangerous. It is possible to attract malignant energies if a group takes on more than it can handle or if helpers in the spirit world inadvertently draw dark forces to the group. In addition if the main medium's energy is not protected or if they are exhausted from too much psychic work and the site is not correctly cleansed, malevolent spirits may break through and cause chaos. Rescue groups should limit their length of existence to 12 months to ensure that they have the space to clear the site of the rescue work and eliminate any spirits who may have attached themselves.

Once I was conducting a rescue circle and a group of malevolent spirits kept coming through to disrupt everything. They were like a gang of bullies. Somehow they had managed to break through the protection that had been set up within the spirit world. We ended up closing the circle for a few months and resuming the group at a different location, giving the original site time to be cleansed and to settle down.

HOW DOES IT WORK?

The séance, or circle, as it is more commonly called, is where two or more people are gathered together to communicate with spirit. It is an open invitation to the world of spirit. These circles are varied; some worship in a Christian tradition, whilst others are non-conformist and non-denominational. A circle in most cases is led by one member of the group. In general this will be a channelling medium. Usually the gathering commences with a prayer, followed by a meditation, leading into a period of absent healing from a list of names of people who are sick or troubled. This follows on to a period of psychic phenomena, such as channelling information from the main medium, that answers questions from the group.

Janet Cox, a medium and clairvoyant, describes setting the scene for the séances that she conducts in her home:

We clean the room thoroughly, no one wears perfume, we all wear clean clothes and the room is darkened. There is a faint light or candlelight and we play music to lift the atmosphere ... After the people assemble and engage in a preliminary talk, we sit down in a circle, the main medium being one of us. There is a trumpet in the centre of the room. This moves around when the spirits come. Sometimes lovely coloured lights appear and our own loved ones come to give messages. Songs help, as the spirits respond to the music, particularly wartime songs. The singing continues until the medium is in deep trance.

The care and time taken to create the right atmosphere and to ensure there are no negative energies allows the whole experience to be safe, enlightening and supportive for both the spirits who come to communicate and those sitters in the group.

Quite often a group will prepare the setting, beginning with prayer and ritual and building the power in the séance through song, music, and prayer, while the channelling medium is left to prepare themselves to sustain the communication for approximately an hour. In general most séances are conducive to communication. They are anchored by the person sitting opposite the medium. This person has to have a strong character and understand the circle's purpose, whilst continuing to maintain the balance of power.

DANGERS

When communicating with spirits, there are spiritual laws that need to be upheld, rules to follow. Anyone breaking these laws can leave a doorway open into the spirit world through which ghosts or earthbound spirits can come to haunt the sitters, the house where the séance was conducted and the main medium.

This is more common when a group gathers to communicate with the dead through a ouija board, as the spirits that you attract through this medium tend to be of a lower astral form. This method of communication is usually very negative. The board works on the principle of what you want you can have. Perhaps the curiosity involved in calling upon a deceased person is what draws these lower forms to the sessions. The ouija board is mainly a tool that the non-initiated use to conduct psychic experiments.

Psychics and mediums who have not trained may also communicate with spirits in pubs and clubs. They do not realize the danger to both themselves and others when they do this.

Eileen Quirke, a natural psychic, offers her own personal encounters as warnings for those who have not the experience to stop spirit communications in unsuitable places:

My first experience happened one evening after having a few drinks with friends. I was sitting on my bed with a girlfriend, Lynn, and we were talking about life in general when I saw an old woman hovering at the end of my bed. She identified herself as Lynn's grandmother. She wasn't very nice and appeared to be very bossy. She kept trying to enter Lynn's body, and Lynn started to cough and choke. I was on top of Lynn, stopping the spirit getting to her. I asked her to leave, but she wouldn't. I then felt her trying to possess me and I blanked out for a while. I woke up and saw her hovering above the bed. Finally, with all the strength I could muster, I shouted at her to leave and she hit me on the head with her walking stick. It physically hurt and then she left, laughing.

Thereafter, when I would be out socializing, spirits would appear to me. At first I would try to figure out if they had any messages, but I found it very draining and people would laugh at me and say that I was mad. So gradually I learnt to keep quiet. I explained some things to some people and they were so shocked that afterwards they did not believe what I said, so I stopped...

Now I am learning how to communicate properly and under instruction. When I do see spirits I ask them to leave me alone if I am tired and I have learnt never to open up to them if I have been drinking.

======================

There are also those enthusiastic psychics who wish to organize development circles and psychic groups without knowledge and experience. Andrew, a practising medium from Yorkshire, remembers an experience which he believes taught him such a great lesson:

Many years ago, just a few weeks after attending a psychic development course, I invited two brothers who were Malaysian students to sit in a group and communicate with the spirits and see what we might get. Within three minutes of sitting in the group, one of the brothers went into complete trance state. I freaked out and began screaming at the spirit to get out of his body, unable to know what to do, what kind of spirit was in his body, whether it was malevolent, a relative or otherwise. Eventually we got him to break the trance and release the spirit. I never allowed myself to conduct a group again without further experience and knowledge.

It is so important to be aware of where you study psychic development and what kind of environment you are in when you communicate with the spirit realms. The group you may be developing with may be at different levels with different types of personality; above all the atmosphere has to be safe and conducive. The main protection is to know yourself well enough to understand when you are unhappy about the spirit communication. Although many spirits who come are benevolent, some are not and you have to be so sure of what messages you are receiving. This is why many success-ful mediums take a long time before they practise, groups and séances are protected and prepared for the communication, and the mediums under-stand their relationship with the spirit world can be a dangerous one.

There have been occasions when a medium may also be misguided, for there are spirits called 'hungry ghosts' who are not what they seem. Personal instinct will protect mediums against the deceptive ghosts and more malevolent spirits.

The well known medium Jessie Nason claimed to public audiences that from time to time she was troubled by discarnate spirits who haunt-ed her. Having spent many years communicating with all kinds of spirit she would say, 'I've been to see someone to get them sorted out.' She believed other mediums also experienced troubling times with bad spirits but 'most of them won't admit it'.

DANGEROUS POSSESSION IN A RESCUE CIRCLE
Most mediums and psychics have such faith and trust in the spirit guides who work with them that they are willing to forego the opportunity to expound their own feelings and ideas during communication. They willing-

ly invite their own spirit to leave the conscious state, permitting a discarnate being to transfer its energy into the empty body in the same way that drivers exchange controls in a car. After the communication has been completed the discarnate spirit exchanges places with the regular occupier and the conscious state is resumed.

Total change can be evident while the trance is in operation – change in voice, bodily movements, expression and temperament. This form of channelling can be the most dangerous, for a wilful or malevolent spirit can occupy a body against the will of its owner.

I experienced this type of event once whilst working with a medium who had branched away from the Spiritualist Church and set up her own rescue circle. Such groups generally emerge out of Spiritualism. Whilst some may be affiliated to a Spiritualist church, in the main they are unapproved. The reason for this is that the majority of Spiritualist mediums deal with dead relatives or friends who communicate with the living in a rational way because they know they are dead. Rescue circles deal with spirits who are unaware that they are dead and these may include evil spirits who can infiltrate a circle and cause problems.

A rescue circle invariably consists of a main channel who permits the discarnate entity or spirit to take possession of their body on a temporary basis, similar to a trance medium. Each week, the same members of the group attend and each person is chosen for different purposes – one for their psychic abilities, another for their counselling skills, another for their healing gift, another for their compassion, and so on. The main channel is the most gifted medium within the group, as trance is the most dangerous form of channelling. This is because once in a trance the medium has no control of actions that take place within their body.

A so-called 'deep control medium', who can consciously monitor the communication which is taking place through them, is best, as in that case a discarnate being will not be able to gain complete control of the mental faculty unless the medium permits them to do so or is unable to stop it. This would take the medium into full trance, which means a state of possession. It is as though the invading spirit has taken over the driving seat in your car – once they have done this, they have full control over the way it works. It is because of these dangers that many Spiritualists and psychic development groups will not entertain these types of groups and séances.

As a group you are relying on spirit guides to ensure the safety of the main channel and the rest of the group by bringing in only those spirits who are ready to move on to the otherworld. To do this they have to accept that they are discarnate and not want to live anymore in the physical world.

In this particular rescue group Mary was our main channel. She was a very talented trance medium who would leave her body to be taken over by a guide, who would discuss with the group the character or spirit he was allowing to come and talk to us. But on one occasion the guide allowed in a very negative spirit, who immediately became abusive. It had full possession of Mary's body and started to rip off her clothes. It took three male group members to pin Mary to the floor, possessed and screaming. This gave the guide and his rescue team the opportunity to take the bad spirit out of her body. This being done, the guide entered Mary's body to settle it down and shortly afterwards Mary's own spirit came back to her body. She had absolutely no recollection of the events and sat dumbfounded when she realized that her blouse was ripped and buttons had been torn off. She claimed no side effects and the following week she was back as usual to continue the work unfazed.

THE SOUL RESCUE OF EARTHBOUND SPIRITS

Most psychics, exorcists and healers believe hauntings by earthbound spirits are the result of spirits' misunderstanding of the process of dying and the afterlife, including the restlessness they suffer if they have not been given a 'proper' burial and grieved by their family or community.

There are many reasons why the world is so polluted with the spirits of the dead.

Soon after death the spirits who have failed to move on must learn to shift for themselves or wait for someone to come and rescue them. We had an incident in an old cottage in Scotland where we discovered an earthbound spirit who used to wander around the living room and kitchen giving off a cold gusty energy. When we managed to attract his attention, which took several days, it transpired that he had died in the house and did not know where he was or what to do after death. We managed to convince him to be rescued and taken by our spirit guardians to a better place. He agreed and the following morning we felt him come and say goodbye. The image we had of him was that he had packed a small bag and was dressed in his best suit.

==========

Janet Cox is frequently asked to bless people's homes and rescue any unruly ghost or earthbound spirit there. She recalls a story which is typical of the attitude of many earthbound spirits.

I see the spirits, they appear as a mist and then disappear as a mist.

On one occasion a family had just moved house and they had a male spirit who would slam doors and blow on their faces at night to wake them up. When I arrived at the house, I saw an old swing in the front garden and thought how I would not allow a child to sit on it. Then the family let me in.

As soon as I entered the front room I could hear the old man. He was furious. 'I had to pay for her bloody funeral and this is my house so I am not going!' He told me about the property and the land and how it had been sold and that the new family had altered the kitchen and he did not like what they were doing to his house. What surprised me was when he said, 'They have taken my bloody swing down. That's hers, the one in the front.' The family confirmed many

It is one thing when you are dealing with Aunt Marjory who is stuck and traumatized but wants to leave and you have the name, the wording and by the environment which she sees around her. Then you can work out the symbolism or language which she needs to move on. There is no point using a language which she does not understand. Earthbound spirits are stuck in a language and within the culture in which they died. It is very different dealing with someone from the eighteenth century, say, or an Egyptian mummy. What is their concept of heaven? And what is their fear of death? Is there anyone who will come to the other side to draw them through or don't they believe they exist?

Emma Restall Orr

of his opinions about the property and in particular about the swing. They said that their daughter would not move unless they brought her old swing.

The old man refused to be guided into the light and all the prayers would not move his spirit from his home. In the end he stayed and stopped bothering the family as much, just occasionally blowing on their faces during the night.

What Janet has found is that if the soul does not want to move on, even if it can see the light calling it, it will not go:

This is free will. In addition, I have found that if the spirit is against an orthodox religion and the family call in a priest to exorcize the spirit this can make matters worse. We learn by trial and error.

To be aware of the spirit's expectations is essential; to understand their temperament or religious leanings, if any, helps. Failure to understand may result in a spirit not trusting those who are trying to help it move on.

═══════════════════

Another method of rescuing earthbound spirits is through astral travel during dreamtime. As a child I used to dream of flying over mountains to places where they were suffering mass death due to war and or natural disaster. I used to dream that I saw myself carrying the souls of the dead to a higher sphere within the spirit realms, which looked like Earth but were lighter, more transparent. I was always met by spirit guardians, who used to appear to me as people, but much taller and larger than physical reality.

═══════════════════

Denise Linn talked to us about her own experiences of rescuing earthbound spirits:

I am sure that rescuing spirits which have become earthbound is a part of the ancient and native cultures, but the way that I entered into it was through my own dreamstate. Although my dreams are usually filled with personal messages, there were times when they had a unique and luminous quality which was beyond the bounds of the psychic reworkings of my day. I understood that a part of me – my spirit or soul – was journeying at night to help other souls, particularly souls who had become earthbound.

If I find myself where I feel there is a problem then I will help to release any souls left behind, but it is normally something which occurs in the night hours. The first thing I do is communicate with them; most earthbounds do not know that they are dead. Often just that initial communication is enough to help them realize that they are dead and move on to embrace the light. If it is difficult getting them to move on then I will call in their guides and guardians and other workers on the other side who help beings move on. If necessary I will do a clearing of the land with blessings and prayers to clear any harm or negativity which has lingered there.

There are workers on the other side who have an understanding of the Earth plane and who find it easier to relate to an earthbound because they have been earthbound themselves – they are the real workers, they are like counsellors who know how it feels so they have a real sense of compassion and real acceptance for someone who is earthbound.

Usually I find that being earthbound is the result of traumatic circumstances, say, where someone dies so suddenly that they do not have time to integrate this world and the next, or else it is to do with a powerful connection to the Earth plane, a connection to a relative or even to an event or part of their lives which they keep replaying again and again because their identity is so closely related to the Earth that they have difficulty releasing themselves.

EARTHBOUND SPIRITS AND POSSESSION

Earthbound spirits in states of illness, insanity and mental aberration may either temporarily or more permanently transfer their condition to the living through an obsessional desire to hold on to a physical body. Sometimes obsessional spirits labour under the delusion that the body of a living person *is* their own. Frequently these disturbed or tormenting spirits have failed to recognize they have become disembodied.

Spirits can enter in at many points in people's lives. It is common for them to enter children simply because their soul skin is not yet sealed. Spirit possession can also happen at any moment of unconsciousness. Often it happens through drugs, alcohol and anaesthesia, which is why hospitals and pubs are filled with spirits looking to possess bodies for a sensory experience. It can also happen during moments of trauma.

Not so long ago, Nick O'Reilly, an unemployed builder in his mid thirties, contacted me. He had recently been told he was suffering from symptoms of schizophrenia, brought on by domestic troubles which had become stress-related. On a bad day, he seemed to be going insane – he was volatile, angry and very aggressive. I expected him to swing a punch or kick out whilst I was trying to heal him. It was difficult for him to switch off or find any means to peace and relaxation. All he could hear were voices in his head, followed by breathing sounds in his ear, both day and night. He had been prescribed various types of medication, none of which alleviated his condition. By the time he began his series of sessions with me, it was very clear that he was at breaking point. He had become so neurotic that he was hardly able to communicate, but with a little patience and gentleness he was able to tell me his story.

Irish by birth, Nick had been brought up a traditional Roman Catholic, though by now his religious faith had long since lapsed. However, when this condition began to seriously affect him, he went to see a priest, who agreed to exorcize the demons that were making him ill. When the ritual was being performed, Nick let out an almighty howl, more animal than human. This noise was repeated time and time again, resonating around the church and beyond into the night. It was more than the priest could cope with. He started to shout and scream at Nick and halfway through the ritual he decided to discontinue the exorcism. Nick was returned to the streets.

I saw Nick on three occasions and discovered that the source of his troubles was an ancestor spirit who had been killed many years ago by an accidental explosion at work. He had come over to Nick seeking help. Ancestors often resort to seeking help from the family when they are lost as earthbound spirits. They generally mean no harm; they are seeking guidance and the opportunity to be rescued. The ancestor would have expected the Catholic priest to help, not call him a demon. This would have most certainly provoked him into screaming out, for he would have believed he was about to be sent to hell. After the ancestor was released Nick slept well and heard no more voices.

In Tibet, it is believed that earthbound spirits can possess family members, leading into obsession and problems within the family group. Often they will cause the person who has become possessed to pick up the same disease and personality traits that they had when they were alive. Tibetan lamas travel around the countryside visiting families performing exorcism rituals to move the spirits of the dead out of family homes and land. The spirit is then drawn out of the magnetic pull of the Earth and taken to a safety zone where it can recover before going to what they call the Second Heaven.

Some cases of possession that I have personally encountered include physical problems which have arisen after a member of the family has died and remained earthbound. The departing spirit attaches itself to the auric field of another family member and an illness or psychological condition begins to occur; the victim is slowly taking on the condition of the dead person. This tends to happen only with the earthbound spirits of relatives.

In cases like this it will often be assumed that the illness runs in the family. Sometimes this is true, but sometimes it is a case of possession or being overshadowed by a dead relative.

In *Healing the Family Tree* (Sheldon Press, SPCK, 1982), Dr Kenneth McAll describes the symptoms which are common when someone is possessed by an ancestral spirit:

A victim of ancestral control may feel himself taken over by a force that is indescribable save as a 'foul smell', a 'weight on the back', a 'black cloud' or a 'directing voice'. During such periods, his words are not his own and his actions are not of his own volition.

He gives a humorous account of the case of a 73-year-old woman. When she felt possessed she would have violent outbursts of temper, displaying unprovoked aggression towards her younger sister, with whom she lived. After each attack she would be genuinely remorseful, but unable to offer any explanation. Her sister sought Dr McAll's help and commanded 'Satan' to leave in the name of Jesus Christ. However, her sister then slapped her across the face with great force, screaming, 'It's Great Aunt Agnes! It's Great Aunt Agnes!' It was subsequently discovered that for the past six generations the eldest woman in each generation had developed a tendency towards violent temper tantrums, influenced by Great Aunt Agnes!

In *Song of the Stars* (Station Hill Openings, 1996) Credo Mutwa tells of exorcizing an ancestor spirit:

As a *sangoma* I have participated in many expulsions of evil spirits from people, and I tell you I still don't like it.

There was a man who had a very peculiar and evil habit: he had been arrested for mauling children by chewing on their hands. In several cases he had quite badly hurt the children by trying to eat their hands. I was called to work with this person, along with other *sangomas*.

We discovered that he was possessed by one of his own ancestors, a cannibal spirit from several generations back. It was this wicked creature that was causing all the problems, because he still desired to feast on human flesh. Seven *sangomas* and I did a ceremony. We built fires all around and we brought the ancestor forth so we could see who was there, and then we expelled him. A dark cloud and a terrible stink came forth from the man and we sent him on his way, and after that the man was quite normal.

Not all cases of possession are caused by ancestors and earthbound spirits. Many of these conditions may be caused by psychological disturbance and psychiatric problems. These conditions cannot always be remedied by soul rescue or shamanic healing.

===========

POSSESSION

Spirit possession is regarded with either disbelief or horror in the West but in the East, Africa and the West Indies, the power of possession, both good and bad, is encouraged. Religious communities do not assume that each possessing spirit is evil. Someone who finds themselves host to another spirit, good or bad, angel or demon, becomes the focus for the community and their religious rituals. The gift of being an oracle for a community is believed to be a gift from the gods. Those who are possessed by good spirits, those trained to pass between the spirit and the physical planes, the oracles, shamans and witch doctors, are the natural enemies of the darker forces. Sometimes, however, the darker forces themselves will try to take possession.

In cases of mental illness and pathological disorders, medical and psychiatric remedies should be tried before possession is seriously considered,

There is an understanding in the Craft that possession is not necessarily a bad thing; it is just a relationship between the spirit and the body. Ultimately everybody is possessed by spirits, it is just some are guiding and some are not. Even when you talk about soul animals ... that is also possession. In therapeutic or Jungian terms you would talk about the different facets of behaviour and personality. So as in therapy it is purely a matter of working out which spirits you want to work with and which you do not.

Emma Restall Orr

but at the same time it is important, particularly in the West, to look into the possibility of such conditions being caused by the powers of spirits. In tribal traditions the world over, including Africa and South America, extraordinary cures have been brought about though shamanic traditions that heal the person's soul and likewise heal their mind. In many cases the victims have been ill for many, many years.

Although in the West we rarely permit ourselves to accept that people can become sick or die through the forces of evil, spirit interference and what is termed 'soul loss' in the shamanic tradition, these powers certainly do exist and the folk beliefs on which our culture is based do acknowledge that they can cause disturbances in the mind, body and emotions of a living person.

How can you tell when someone is truly possessed by a spirit? Possession is when a person is so completely under the control of a separate power that the spirit is able to sit within their body. The soul of the living person is subservient to the will of the possessing spirit, so that sometimes even their voice and appearance may change.

There are two forms of possession: voluntary and involuntary. An involuntary possession is when a spirit possesses a person without invitation. On the whole a fully trained and experienced soul rescuer will easily diagnose such a possession and the subsequent exorcism should be a straightforward task. A voluntary possession, however, is a more difficult case to deal with, for though 'voluntary' suggests 'with volition', it is usually a 'volition' made not by a client's conscious self but by their subconscious self, i.e., for whatever psychological reason a person's subconscious self invites the possession. This could be due to an inability to grieve, a need for companionship or just simple curiosity. Whatever the reason, it is a subject which perfectly highlights the co-operative relationship that is increasingly developing between psychotherapists and psychic healers.

But are all possessions simply symptoms of mental illness or vice versa? In Western medical practice, the treatment of mental illness and

It is my earnest desire that it will not be long before there is a general acceptance that spirit possession exists and that it can be treated. After the invading spirits are exorcised the value to the victim is substantial. When the worth of an exorcist becomes more widely recognized, as with hypnotism, I am certain that this process will be accepted and will do as much to alleviate the suffering of many of our fellow humans.

The Reverend Eugene Murray, *Exorcism* (Whitford Press, 1988)

medical theories of possession are based on the diagnosis and treatment of delusions. In a psychotic state there is the belief that what one is seeing or feeling to be true is beyond the common reality. For instance there may be strong ideas based on cultural archetypes, so if a patient is Christian, they may believe themselves to be possessed by the Devil or that they are Jesus or God. There is a fine line between mental disorders and visionary experiences and the conditions conjured by an overactive imagination.

Dr Wickland's *Thirty Years among the Dead* (The Spiritualist Press, 1952) has become a classic of abnormal psychology. Wickland was a pioneer psychiatrist whose conclusions and methods were based upon his wide experience of treating mental disorders and his understanding of the spirit realms. He worked with many people who suffered from obsession and possession by earthbound spirits.

The theme of the book was the rescue work conducted by Dr Wickland and his psychic wife Anna. They uncovered many attitudes in discarnate spirits and investigated in depth why so many earthbound spirits infest the living. Wickland claimed that spirit obsession was a fact, believing it to be the perversion of natural law. He and his wife proved how earthbound spirits in states of illness, insanity and mental aberration, either temporarily or more permanently, transferred their condition to the living, whether a relative, a friend or stranger, by the obsessional desire to hold on to a physical body which was not their own. These spirits' understood that they no longer had a physical body, but they desired to continue living as they always had, even to the physical or mental cost of somebody else.

A good example of a voluntary possession is reflected by a case I had recently with a client called Colin. On the whole he considered himself to be an amiable, quiet, friendly man with a positive view on life. However there were two aspects of his life which were causing him and his wife concern. First he was consistently suffering from frightening nightmares which he couldn't remember in the morning. Secondly and more worryingly, he was unable to remember long periods of either his childhood or adolescence; in particular he had no memories of his twin brother who had died when he was still young. This was a sure sign that Colin's subconscious self was protecting him from memories that his conscious self could not deal with.

With the intention of regaining his memory Colin undertook a course of hypnotherapy. Sadly for Colin, this treatment revealed a history of terrible childhood abuse and trauma. Amongst other things he recalled that he and his brother had been tied up and sexually abused by his parents and their friends and that they had both been involved in black magic rituals which may even have involved the murder of a young woman. Worst of all, though, Colin was able to remember that after his twin brother's sudden death, his parents made him lie with his dead brother in the coffin.

It takes a psychologically strong person to deal with trauma. Colin was not and so his subconscious self put up barriers to protect him. Primarily, having just rediscovered a shared existence with a twin brother, he could not at the same time accept the death of that twin brother. The obvious way to keep his brother alive was for Colin's subconscious mind to invent his continued existence and then to invite that psychological invention to possess him.

With time and good grief counselling Colin may slowly have been able to attain the confidence to let go of his invented brother; however, the revelations of his traumatic childhood filled him with an enormous anger, which manifested itself in violent attacks on his wife. Colin was deeply ashamed of these attacks and his conscious self could not rationalize them. Unable to make sense of or take responsibility for his own actions, he blamed his violent outbursts on his twin brother, claiming he had possessed him. It was at this point that I was consulted.

It was immediately obvious to me that Colin's possession was a voluntary one. As such I understood that his problem was primarily psychiatric and so I worked closely with his therapist. We both agreed that Colin needed to confirm the reality of his memories. Maybe then he would be convinced that his childhood had indeed been so traumatic that it was completely valid for him to a) be angry and b) hide from that anger by psychological invention, i.e., possession by his brother.

To this end I accompanied Colin to his childhood home. The young couple who now owned the house were very kind and understanding and graciously allowed Colin to go round the house. I could see how moved he was as he went from room to room. At one point in the dining room he was overcome by the power of his sad memories and I held him closely. Afterwards we went to the local police station where they confirmed that there had indeed been a murder in Colin's childhood home some 25 years previously and that a black magic group and paedophile ring had been involved.

There is no easy way for people like Colin. Only years of therapy and understanding will reconcile him to the reality of his experiences and only then will he release himself from his brother's possession.

In the case of Colin's voluntary possession, psychiatric therapy proved to be the correct and most beneficial remedial treatment. However it must be stressed that psychiatrists are not qualified to deal with cases of 'uninvited' possession. An uninvited possession is precisely that: the hijacking of a person's psyche and physical being by an uninvited exterior spirit or demon. No amount of psychiatric treatment will exorcise such a spirit from a patient's body. Moreover, the longer a possessed person's true condition is undiagnosed, the worse their physical and mental health becomes.

My healing of Eva perfectly illustrates this point. After moving into a new home, she began to have aches and pains in her arms and legs. Quite rightly her doctor gave her the necessary medical tests, but when the results failed to show any physical illness, instead of exploring Eva's personal circumstances, the doctor merely attributed her problems to a slight depression that may have been triggered by the stress of moving house.

Subsequently Eva's condition rapidly worsened. She became constantly tired and prone to tears, she gave up work, she lost interest in her appearance and finally she stopped eating. Her doctor's reaction to this was simply to prescribe her anti-depressants.

Sadly, in our modern society, the diagnosis of 'depression' has become an all-pervasive easy explanation for our ills and unhappiness. True depression, though, is usually caused by something, whether it be childhood trauma, as with Colin, money problems, career stresses or whatever. In Eva's case there were no identifiable reasons for the supposed depression: she ran a successful interior decorating business, she was happily married to an international lawyer, she had a healthy young son and she had just moved into a large home in one of the most exclusive districts of London. Those are not the circumstances of a depressed personality.

Luckily for Eva, a friend of hers identified the fact that Eva's illness coincided with her moving to her new house and that therefore her problems might be due not to the stresses of moving but to a negative influence from or in the house itself. It was this friend who asked me to help.

By the time I met Eva she was too weak and detached to communicate with me effectively. Instead I had a long discussion with her husband, who convinced me that there were no underlying emotional reasons for Eva's illness. He also told me that for the first three nights that they had slept in the house, Eva had experienced nightmares in which she had been chased around the house by a screaming girl dressed in black and white, and that on the fourth night she had kicked and flayed out her arms wildly as she slept, shouting out, 'You're suffocating me! You're suffocating me!' Armed with this information I began to explore the possibility that Eva had been possessed.

The first thing I did was to explore the house, which for the most part had been redecorated in bright refreshing colours. However the basement, where the kitchen and servants' quarters would originally have been, was still like a building site. I clearly sensed that a spirit had been residing there.

I then called the previous owners of the house. Though they had never experienced any psychic activity themselves, they told me that when they first bought the house in the early sixties they had been warned by their neighbours that it was famously haunted by a deranged servant girl.

It did not worry me that the last owners had not been haunted by the servant girl. It just suggested that they were closed to psychic activity. If anything it explains why Eva was so quickly possessed: after 30 years of being unable to haunt, the servant ghost would have been immediately drawn to a psychically sensitive person, as Eva obviously was. The life light emanating from Eva would have been too great for the ghost not to be tempted. The trouble is that having possessed Eva, the ghost inevitably fed on Eva's light and subsequently weakened her to such an extent that she became ill.

It was my duty as a psychic healer to provide the life light necessary to outshine Eva's, a light that would tempt the ghost away from Eva's weakening body. This I did with a ritual of chanting and prayers. When the servant ghost did appear I realized why she had had such a profound physical effect on Eva: she was consumed by madness.

In Victorian and Edwardian England the insane were usually committed to vast, often cruel asylums; in this young girl's case I supposed that her employers had kindly allowed her to live in the house, probably locking her away in one of the basement rooms. Being insane, she was probably very confused when she died and therefore unable to register that she had died. Once I had been able to quieten her, I was able to explain to her that she was dead. I then called down a spirit guide to help her to finally move on from her Earth existence to the next leg of her soul journey.

Because of Eva's susceptibility to psychic activity I spent a good deal of time securing the house from further spirit intrusion. I first placed quartz and tourmaline crystals in vulnerable parts of the home and then I smudged the whole property with herbal incense once a day for three weeks. I was pleased to see that when Eva returned from a well-earned holiday with her family she had completely recovered her good health and radiance.

MALEVOLENT SPIRITS – POSSESSION

The gift of being human is the power of the will. That is why many cases of possession are a battle of the wills; the will of the person and the will of the spirit. If a person is used to being dominated or enjoys the experience, then the spirit will overshadow them, whilst if they have a strong will, they certainly have power over the spirit and will eventually override any conditions inflicted by any spirit forms.

When someone has an encounter with a malevolent ghost it creates a shock to the nervous system. Sometimes this freezes the body, panic sets in and then they are unable to control the events that follow, mainly due to the state of fear. Sometimes when these psychic phenomena happen during sleep, people wake up and feel paralysed. It takes all the will in the world to break the paralysis and then they may find themselves able to move, but feeling as though they have a heavy weight on their chest and are suffocating. These kind of symptoms can be due to vampire spirits trying to draw energy from the body whilst the spirit is away during sleep.

Eileen has had an interest in psychic phenomena since childhood and is a natural psychic. She recalls a recent event that placed her in a vulnerable position:

I should have known something was going to happen during my trip to Humberside earlier this year. For about three weeks before we had to leave, I couldn't sleep well and was irritable even with my partner. The minute I walked into the house, I could feel spirits everywhere, but dismissed it as the others in the group had arrived. I knew, though, that my feeling was a common one amongst the group.

The estate dated back to the seventeenth century and the house we booked was one of the oldest there. It had been a part of the fishing community and was filled with memorabilia from that era; an antique dealer could make a fortune from some of the objects in that house. Even the beds and bathrooms were ancient. We all had the feeling that we could be living back in the 1700s. There was no television and no modern appliances except for a cooker and fridge. This encouraged the gothic atmosphere.

By the time we had completed the day's workshop, I was so tired that I wasn't bothered about which room I stayed in. I got to sleep straightaway. I then started to 'dream'. In my dream I knew there was something in the wall to my right-hand side. I was shouting in my dream for David (one of the other members of the group staying at the house) not to open my door, as the 'thing' would come out. As soon as the door did 'open' the 'thing' came flying out of the wall and onto the bed. It had me pinned down on the bed and was hissing in my ear. It was dressed in black and had a large hat on. I asked it to show its face but it wouldn't. I tried to get up at this point, as I had woken up, but I could not move. I felt paralysed. I finally swore at it and then it did move away. I tried to find the light and couldn't. It was then I started to realize what had happened and got into a panic. I told myself to calm down and turned the light on and found it was 5.45 a.m., an unearthly hour for me. But I could not go back to sleep, as I was very, very scared.

As I had to stay for the week, I moved into the other girl's room. Her name was Freddie. I was still scared, but I felt a little more comfortable. During the night, I got woken up again and thought, 'Here we go again.' As I looked round to Freddie, I saw that she was asleep but that something was trying to get into her body. I couldn't move to help her. The following day she also felt terrible.

We called Terry to assist us with this haunting and he kindly came to investigate the problem. He found that although the house was haunted by a number of spirits who had probably lived there or nearby in recent times, the problem was caused by a dark malevolent spirit. It appeared that its only intent was to control the earthbound spirits in the house and 'vampire' the energy or life force of the living people there. So when tenants came into the house, it immediately went to the most sensitive of the group or family and drew from their energy source. As I am a natural psychic it decided to pick on me first and then Freddie, who is also very sensitive. Terry managed to banish the malevolent spirit, which did not appear human. As it was being released it appeared to us as a very dark shadow with a horrible emotional atmosphere. The other spirits who had been trapped in the house were also released over the week we were there. The house appeared to become much lighter and calmer and both Freddie and I were aware that something horrible had gone.

This was my first experience with a malevolent spirit. It was a good lesson for me as I could see that it could not kill me or attack me, as I am a strong-willed person, but the idea that these kind of forms exist was very enlightening.

POSSESSION BY VAMPIRE SPIRITS

Sometimes these vampire-type spirits are really feeding off the living because of their need to survive within the limbo land of the astral, or the earthbound dimension, as it is traditionally known.

In India there is a strong vampire tradition similar to the beliefs of the gypsies. The *bhuta* is a vampire-like creature known in western India. This is the soul of a man who has died an untimely death. In life he was either insane or deformed. It is believed that he wanders between midnight and the early hours of the morning, which is the most common time for this kind of haunting. *Bhutas* often appear as dark shadows, flickering lights or misty apparitions. They have been known to enter men's bodies, causing them great sickness and even death.

In gypsy tradition, the vampire spirit is especially horrible in appearance, apparently having undergone some dreadful change in the grave. It has been known to have hair so long that it touches the ground, as is the case among certain groups of Indian gypsies. It may have yellow or even flaming hair. The colour of the vampire itself may be that of congealed blood, while his mouth may have fangs or tusks. It is believed that the vampire is visible only to a few. In some instances only those he has the intention of attacking may be able to see him. If true this may be the reason why it can be very difficult for people who are being haunted to make their families or friends believe them.

THE ELEMENTAL POSSESSION

Many years ago, I was approached by an old student of mine in connection with a 13-year-old boy, Ben. His mother, Mary, had noticed a dramatic change in her son's personality. He had become very moody, aggressive and unresponsive. He started to lose interest in his studies, was finding it difficult to sleep at night, complained of hearing noises in his room and appeared to be afraid of the dark.

The family put his behaviour down to pubescent mood swings, but one night there was an almighty crash as all the books in the study were thrown off the shelves, the lights went on and off in the hallway and they heard screaming coming from Ben's room. The mother entered his bedroom and found him petrified in the corner of the room, looking up towards the ceiling. There she saw a small red spirit, not much taller than her son, with very bright eyes. As she had had training as a medium, she was not afraid and tried to communicate with the spirit, asking it why it was there and what it wanted from her son. It did not reply, began to throw things around the room and then disappeared.

Ben admitted that he and a few of his schoolfriends had been playing about with a ouija board in the house. The last time they had played with it, the red spirit had appeared and all the lights in the house had gone out. That was when Ben had started to feel unwell.

This poltergeist was an elemental fire spirit who had become attached to Ben and was slowly possessing him by drawing his energy to keep itself in the living world. It required some assistance in returning to the earth kingdom whence it had been called and the door to that part of the spirit world had to be closed to prevent future repercussions. After this was done, Ben returned to his usual cheerful self.

LAND RESCUE WORK

For the first few nights after the birth of our second child, Ossian, in the wilds of the West Highlands of Scotland, very close to the Celtic festival of Samhain, I felt an uncomfortable presence in the bedroom as soon as night fell. I assumed it was exhaustion due to lack of sleep, something which can cause anyone to feel sensitive to an invisible presence and have mild hallucinations! But one night the physical sensation of a force pushing against the base of my spine and entering my solar plexus, paralysing me, was enough to convince me that it was real. Ossian was lying next to me in the bed. Through love and the motherly instinct for my child, I managed to call upon the angels to protect me and break out from this psychic paralysis. I felt the force of a spirit leave my body and the bedroom and, I assumed, the house. Yet the following night I had the same experience again. Now I was beginning to worry about the effect on the baby, who had become colicky and temperamental. I knew that something was coming in to affect us.

The next evening, before dusk, we held a ceremony and called upon the guardian spirits of the location, lit candles and a fire, left food out for the spirits and asked the soul to come in and show itself to us and explain what it wanted. About midnight the energy in the bedroom changed. The spirit of a child had entered. Terry drew it towards his energy field, away from me and the baby. We called the guardians to come and rescue this soul and move him on to his own family.

The next day we went down to the archivist's office in town and checked the records on our property, which dated back to the 1740s. We found out during the 1800s a family had lived there whose only child has died when he was about nine or ten. I realized that the spirit had not been attempting to attack, but calling out for help. What could have drawn him out of the memory of the house was the spiritual activity that can occur when a child is born. I am very sensitive to these things, in fact many women are very psychic at the time of giving birth. It was quite a relief to rescue this soul and afterwards we no longer felt any paranormal activity in the house.

The veil between this world and the spirit world opens at the birth of a child and remains open for the first six weeks of the child's life. This is why in many cultures the first 42 days are the most sensitive for both mother and child and many tribal customs include taboos, talismans and protective rituals to prevent the spirit of the child being taken away at this time. It is believed that when a baby dies, as in a cot death for example, the stealing of the spirit was caused by otherworldly forces.

Sometimes spirits are themselves in thrall to darker forces, as we found in the case of a traumatic land clearance that took place in Greece.

PIRATES OF AN AEGEAN CRYPT

We both felt a spirit presence from the moment we arrived on the island. But it wasn't until the second night of our stay that we actually saw a ghost. It was Natalia who first heard the sound, a sad weeping that followed us as we crossed the courtyard to our client's house. Stopping and turning to look behind us, we saw the ghost. She was a woman in her early twenties, with light brown hair that hung down to her waist. She knew that we were aware of her presence – indeed, we felt that she was looking to us for help. We tried to communicate with her, to ask why she was so sad and troubled, but we were unable to make ourselves heard above the constant cries of her lamentation.

I was surprised by the young woman's presence. From the details of psychic disturbance and phenomena given to us by our client we had been expecting to encounter some sort of malevolent force and yet here was a soul clearly earthbound by some personal tragedy who could not possibly have been responsible for the events that we had been asked to investigate.

Our client was a Greek shipping tycoon whose large estate dominated the island. In recent years his son had been killed in a freak accident, his wife had been taken seriously ill, his business had struggled and the crops on the estate had failed. His only explanation for all this bad luck was that maybe the family had been cursed.

It was two incidents that followed each other in quick succession that finally persuaded him to ask for help. First, hundreds of dead squid had been found rotting in one of the outbuildings behind the house. Now and again dead squid were found washed up on the beach, but this was hundreds of them in a building over two miles from the sea. Secondly, faeces and blood were smeared haphazardly on the walls that surrounded the courtyard which separated the main house from the guest cottages. To say the least our client and his family were very, very worried.

No expense was spared in getting us to the island. Our tickets were waiting for us at Heathrow and a private helicopter flew us from Athens across the Aegean to the family home. Set on the side of a mountain, the main house overlooked a whitewashed fishing village built around a small bay. Large as the estate was, I was still surprised to find a domed medieval Orthodox church within its grounds. It was in the crypt of the church that I was later to find the source of the family's troubles.

It turned out that sightings of the ghostly crying lady had been well documented. Apparently she was the only daughter of an admiral who had waged successful campaigns against the Turkish pirates who marauded the Aegean Sea in the fifteenth and sixteenth centuries. On the very night of her wedding, whilst her father remained on board his ship celebrating her marriage, pirates landed quietly on the island and in an act of revenge murdered the 'crying lady' and her new husband. In his grief the admiral built the church in the grounds of my client's estate and buried his lost daughter in its crypt.

As I said before, I knew that our 'crying lady' could not have been responsible for the malevolent energy which had so frightened our clients, so in the days after our arrival Natalia and I set to work to find out who or what was responsible. Whilst I went round the estate and surrounding countryside with the estate manager, looking for elemental land disturbances, Natalia tried to find out more about the local history and folklore. Time and time again, she unearthed stories of how in the years after the fall of the Byzantine Empire in 1453, Turkish pirates had habitually raided and pillaged the island. Surely it was in the violence of those pirate years that we would find the source of our problem.

The breakthrough came when the estate manager told me that during recent renovation work the crypt had been flooded, even though there was no running water near the church. I knew then that the building work must have disturbed souls of the dead and that it was these souls who were responsible for my client's problems. Needless to say, I wasn't surprised when I discovered that two of the coffins in the crypt were engraved with the skull and crossbones.

With the manager's help we were able to slide off the coffin lids. As I had expected, inside the coffins we saw the spirits of the dead pirates attached to their bones. We were quite safe from them because they were 'night walkers' – only at night would they be able to detach themselves from their skeletons and wander freely around the estate.

Looking at my watch I saw that we still had a few hours of daylight in which to prepare for the night ahead. First we walked around the circumference of the main house and church and placed at measured intervals crystals and black tourmaline. These would provide a strong energetic boundary within which to trap the ghosts. Not only would this barrier stop the ghosts from escaping to haunt another part of the island, but it would also restrict the area in which I would have to hunt for them if they chose to make themselves invisible to me. To improve my trap I placed iron pyrite in strategic spots around the estate, thus focusing the strong psychic energy within the ground.

It was only when there was total darkness that we made our move. First I returned to the crypt. While Natalia held a candle behind us, the estate manager and I once more opened the coffins. As I had hoped, they were empty of any energy or spirit life; the night walkers had gone for the evening. I took this opportunity to complete the trap by putting jasper arrows amongst the bones in the two coffins. Jasper is an opaque crypto-crystalline quartz which when shaped like an arrowhead keeps spirits away from the treated location. The night walkers now had nowhere left to hide.

Sometimes when spirits feel threatened they make themselves invisible to a soul rescuer. But these two pirates were arrogant. Far from hiding from me, they attacked me immediately, trying to terrify me, as they had terrified the 'crying lady' for so long. All night long they attacked me, convulsing me and punishing me with violent dreams. I could feel the full weight of them on my chest, suffocating me and wringing the strength from my body.

This kind of power struggle is common with darker, more controlling spirits. They know that this is the final frontier where they have to move on and lose control, so of course they resist. The soul rescuer has to wear down their resistance by withstanding their attack. I knew that ultimately the power struggle was taking far more energy out of them than it was out of me.

Sure enough, as the first light of dawn started to spread across the eastern sky, the two pirates became weaker and weaker. Realizing that they had lost the ability to control the situation, they ceased attacking me. Unable to escape the crystal and tourmaline barrier, and unable to return to their coffins, they had no choice but to move on. I returned with Natalia to the crypt, where we purified the atmosphere with some pungent local sage. I then called on the spirit guides to come forward and help the unruly pirate souls to pass over.

After that we didn't see the ghost of our 'crying lady' again. I realize now that as long as the pirates were haunting her they would have prohibited any spirit guide from releasing her soul. But once they themselves had been defeated, the path would have been opened for a spirit guide to release her – and who knows, it could even have been her father, the admiral.

We returned after several months to check that everything had returned to the quiet paradise it once was. The family had managed to settle a few problems that they had been having with the estate, there had been no more manifestations, the crops were growing again and the grapes and figs were in abundance. The business, which had been very affected by all this chaos, had slowly recovered and the health of the mother had returned to normal. After the cleansing of the site, they had had yet another flood in the crypt, which immediately suggested that the cleansing had happened and the release of those spirits had been successful.

It is as important to rescue discarnate spirits as it is to rid their victims of phenomena. In most cases, the spirits are in great pain, lonely and filled with fear, unable to move away from where they once lived or died. Often it is helpful to call upon their ancestors to help them come and make them feel safe. These earthbound spirits are in limbo with no purpose and need to continue the journey towards their future destiny.

UNDERTAKING SOUL RESCUE

Although effecting an exorcism can be a blessed relief for the person concerned, the aftermath for me was traumatic. When I was alone again, I could feel my whole body trembling, and I felt as though I had lost every ounce of energy. I could not sleep and could only digest liquids. I prayed that it would never happen again, but of course it did.

Betty Shine

Conducting soul rescue work requires experience and protection. The soul rescuer needs to know their own boundaries and what kind of spirits they are dealing with.

Soul rescue is a profession or pastime with no basic rules. It can be frightening! A person who becomes involved in rescuing spirits, whether voluntarily or innocently, should carefully examine both the territory itself and their own qualifications for dealing with it. A practitioner should not only have psychic vision, but also understand the complexity of the art of healing a person or land.

Soul rescuers have to be pure and connected with their God because the evil will invariably attack the healer. Just as psychiatrists should undergo analysis, so soul rescuers have often been possessed themselves. They have to go through the purification of their own corruption.

They also need to connect with spirit guides whose responsibility is to rescue the earthbound and encourage them to go into the light. The guides are very important once the earthbound spirits have recognized their condition and are willing to communicate with a higher spirit who knows how to move them from the physical levels into the spirit realms. Without these spirit helpers, we are unable to release the earthbound spirit.

The soul rescuer, having made their diagnosis and being ready to proceed to the handling of the victim's case, has to achieve three things: repair the victim's aura, clear the atmosphere of the victim's environment, their home or land, and break their contact with the forces causing the trouble. These three things are interdependent, not one of them is first or last. It is impossible to heal a damaged aura if you do not clear the atmosphere first, nor will the atmosphere remain clear if the connections with the negative earthbound or evil contacts are still being made. These can come in the form of objects, a haunted room, an earthbound spirit or from within the victim themselves by some contact with a dubious situation from the past.

A ghosthunter or soul rescuer needs to assume the passive guise of a tracker or sleuth, examining the evidence and using their intuitive skills to discover what type of spirit is causing the psychic phenomena and whether it is malevolent or harmless. The only simple ground rule is to never go into a haunted house alone and most definitely never issue challenges to that which cannot be seen, as you never know what is in there and whether your challenge would be taken as a threat. The other thing to remember is that whatever type of spirit is being confronted it will have its own set of rules and be very aware of its own ground. In addition you may not be able to see it or communicate with it unless you are a trained psychic; this puts you into a dangerous and weak position. If the force is malevolent it will use the fear and weakness in your personality against you, and this may cause psychological and physical problems in the aftermath of the ghosthunting expedition.

AN UNQUALIFIED SOUL RESCUER

Soul rescue is not for everyone. I once had a close friend called Mike who trained with me in the arts of spirit communication and rescue work. Mike had no interest in either the great light or dark but he enjoyed a challenge. He was not a serious occultist but rather an esoteric flower child from the late sixties generation, one of the 'beautiful people', all beads and patchouli oil.

Having agreed to expel a ghost that was haunting a family, he went to the house, held a night vigil and attempted to rescue the soul. The morning after, he came over to see me. When I opened the door he had a grin on his face. 'I had a great night,' he told me. 'I was prepared for the worst. I didn't stop praying all night.'

In a lively and enthusiastic voice he explained how for psychic protection he had used no fewer than six Bibles, four various religious talismans, all blessed by the sundry gurus that he had met during his journeys in India, and enough incense, if lit, to asphyxiate the Devil himself. It became very clear to me that fear had become Mike's exhilaration, an adrenaline high known to those who enjoy living on the edge. He admitted that he had seen a ghost and it had terrified him.

Mike had gone into the haunted house oblivious of any facts, with no experience in ghosthunting and unable to evaluate the spirit that was haunting the property. I found out much later that he had been unable to rescue the ghost, even with all his psychic protection. He decided to discontinue his work in rescuing spirits as a result of his fearful experience. This taught me that not everyone is capable of practising the craft of soul rescue and it is important to recognize one's own boundaries and abilities with regards to spiritual or psychic gifts.

PSYCHIC PROTECTION

There are many tried and tested techniques which the trained soul rescuer can employ as defences against an assault from a disembodied spirit. These methods will work only if what is being investigated is daunted by the power and faith of the soul rescuer and all the protection in the world will not stop the essence of evil itself. That can only be achieved by a master or someone who intimately understands its dark legacy. But protection will usually work on other types of psychic phenomena.

The most common methods are prayer to connect with higher spiritual powers, based on an act of faith and a belief in God, and the invocation of mystical powers known to a magician or sorcerer. These methods constitute a serious approach, to which may be added the wearing of amulets, the use of talismans, carefully placed lit candles, stones and crystals, the use of garlic, the burning of sage and other similar herbs, the sprinkling of salt, the ringing of bells, the beating of drums or even the repetition of the Lord's Prayer.

After clearing a person or a site, there may be a residue of the spirit's negative energy. Practical measures can be taken to break this down. Simple exercises such as stretching, yoga, walking in parks or woods in any natural setting are helpful in calming a person down. The ancient Chinese forms of exercise such as qigong and tai chi are also useful to help the body disperse a negative influence. If the effect was more on the emotions, then massage, breathing, spiritual healing, acupuncture and a positive mental attitude will help. If a place has been cleared of negative spirits it is beneficial to smudge the property with burning incense, to spring clean, open windows and let the light in, move furniture around and play loud music. These simple tools all help to break down negative energy.

My belief is that there are some people incarnated to be of service by helping the souls of the dead to find the light. It is not uncommon, particularly around battlefields for instance, for these people to incarnate in order to live close to places where the dead need help. Even if they are consciously aware of it, once they begin to delve into their dreams they often find images of helping people find the light. For some it is their life's contract to be in service in this way.

Some people do the calling to the earthbound spirits during their night hours and one of the things which I suggest is that if you feel a calling to do this work, when you go to bed close your eyes and say: 'God, help me be of service to others during my night hours in whatever way is best for me and for others for the highest good.'

People who are doing this subconsciously during their night hours are none the less having a powerful impact on others and it does not always seem to be associated with a locale, it seems to be more of an energy connection. Sometimes the person you are helping may be thousands of miles away, but a particular energy which you share connects you to each other.

Denise Linn

QUALIFICATIONS

There are four levels of professional status which may be achieved in soul rescue work: the student, the initiate, the adept and the master.

The skills and experience of a soul rescuer determine their qualifications. Each person must learn to recognize their limitations in investigating hauntings or encounters with spirits, as not all psychics can heal or rescue spirits, just as not all shamans can reverse curses or psychic attack and only a suitably trained priest can exorcize evil.

Before calling in a soul rescuer the client should have satisfied themselves that they have sought to solve their problem by practical means, leaving no doubt in their mind that the problem is of a paranormal nature. Then a soul rescuer may be enlisted to investigate the disturbance. Also bear in mind just as a doctor must refer cases to a consultant, equally a dowser who divines water is not an expert in ghosts and psychics are not skilled in soul rescue. Therefore the more information that is known and documented, the more time will be saved in calling the right person to do the job, at least in most cases.

It is essential for a client to know that if a qualified soul rescuer is treating a problem that the soul rescuer follows steps to remedy the condition permanently.

The aim of this chapter is to offer an understanding of what soul rescuers do, leaving no reason for this information to be shrouded in mystery or glamour. It is no longer necessary to join a secret organization in order to learn these skills. Soul rescuers are born to do this work and guided by spirit.

In the modern world, knowledge of spirits and the paranormal is more accessible than ever, though historically secret societies taught these skills and techniques and not so long ago people were burnt at the stake for even talking about spirits. Thankfully since then the world has changed and is still changing and whether it is the result of human evolution or part of the Great Cosmic Plan, this once hidden knowledge is now being considered with a more open mind.

As peacemakers and wisdom keepers, there is a calling for soul rescuers to be recruited world-wide. If you have the calling, *please listen*.

INTO THE LIGHT

CHAPTER SIX

The soul of man is the sun by which his body is illumined, and from which it draweth its sustenance ... Baha'u'lla'h.

Artemus Lamb, *The Odyssey of the Soul* (George Ronald, Oxford)

We live in extraordinary times when many people refuse to believe in God, the spirit worlds, spirit beings and the souls of the dead who wander amongst us. This total disregard for these subtle realities makes it very hard for those in the spirit realms as well as those in the human condition.

Not only this, but in our society we fear death so terribly that we cannot bear to discuss it. Yet if a person is really prepared for death and not afraid of it, that is true power. Preparation for death and rebirth in the spirit world are essential for living fully and joyously in this world. And if we are to enjoy our lives we will be able to enjoy our journey through the gateway of death into the kingdom of the spirit realms.

The acceptance of reincarnation brings a very different view of the death of the physical body. Instead of seeming to be the 'gate of no return', death can be seen as an incident, a recurring event in a long life-cycle of birth, death and rebirth.

In many cultures there is the belief that the individual soul has three parts: the self, the earth and the spirit. In the Western world it is believed that there is only one aspect, the soul as the individual self. But as long as we are aware that there *is* a soul part to us then the experience of death will be a simple transition from the physical reality into a spiritual reality.

Soul Rescuers

The understanding that the physical death of the body does not mean the annihilation of the soul stretches across all cultures at all times. The immortal soul leaves the mortal body and the dark mystery of eternity draws the spirit away. When families and friends are grieving the spirit wants to call the life back, even just for a second, but the ancestors will summon the soul away from the clamour of grief. Ultimately consciousness chooses for itself which way it will go: back to the physical ways of human desire or on into the clarity of the spirit realms on the journey into divinity.

THE GATEWAY

The physical element relinquishes its hold reluctantly upon the body, so that the body sometimes struggles for breath. The dying person is unconscious of that struggle and feels only the wonderful lightness, relief and freedom from the heavy burden of the flesh.

Tibetans describe the process of death as a reversal of conception, when the essences of the father and mother are united by the sperm and ovum. As the foetus grows in the womb, the male essence finds its place at the top of the head, the crown chakra, while the female essence rests in the chakra below the navel. As death approaches, the white essence of the father travels down the central nervous system into the heart while the red consciousness, the female essence, travels upwards from the base of the spine. Their meeting in heart, with consciousness enclosed within them, is the point of death. It is at this moment that it is said that immediate enlightenment is possible, for as the essences meet the light of grand luminosity dawns and if we are able, we can direct our consciousness toward that light and merge with it. Unfortunately most of us will pass out and miss the moment. Then, according to Buddhist teachings, our consciousness will wander in the bardo of becoming, awaiting rebirth.

The bardo of becoming is held to have an average duration of 49

This process of transition from one world to another is in no sense painful; we should dismiss from our minds all thought of suffering in connection with death. There may indeed be suffering before death, on account of disease or accident, but the actual process of death is not only painless, but also usually full of joy and peace...

C. W. Leadbeater, *The Other Side of Death*

days, the most important time being the first 21 days, when the soul still has a strong impression of the previous life and can be helped by the living. It is the realm of the soul mind, where reality is dependent on the visions of the mind. It is one of many realms in which the soul may find itself after death.

As the soul slowly comes to terms with its death, the family and friends begin their rites in dealing with the physical body. The tender and sacred care of the physical body after death reaches across most cultures with rites which have been passed down from generation to generation. Traditionally preparing the corpse is part of the care owed by the living to the dead and is the first act of separation from the physical body and the honouring of the spirit of the deceased.

THE SEPARATION

When the ego leaves the body at the moment of death, it leaves behind it the lower principles and passes onward to states which are the spiritual realms. Mind, body and soul separate and the individual becomes a disembodied soul.

C. W. Leadbeater, *The Other Side of Death*

THE FIRST INSIGHT

Birth is death and death is birth. Learn, therefore, to look down upon your dead bodies to galvanise them with your life, but do not make the mistake of living in them.

Dion Fortune

When we are born into the human world we are born into a dream, a lifetime of limited scope to achieve our destiny. At the point of death the question comes: did we fulfil our heart's desire? Did we achieve all our dreams? A lifetime of achievement, whatever that maybe for each individual, gives consciousness an elevation into a joyous state, while our failure to achieve our ambitions weighs heavy on the heart and mind of the soul and results in a fall or drop in consciousness. The consciousness, if satisfied, lightens the soul and if haunted by failure, fear or regret is drawn into the shadow of those memories, remaining unable to release

Soul Rescuers

those memories until there is a point of recognition within the soul.

Shortly after death, the major events of this lifetime on Earth flash with lightning rapidity through the consciousness of the ego. In that instantaneous review man sees his life as a whole. He realizes what was intended for him to do in life. He knows how far he has or has not taken his opportunities to fulfil his destiny. He distinguishes clearly for the first time the success and failures, the victories and the defeats, the wisdom or poor judgement of all that he has said and done. This is the origin of the mythological judgement after death. It is none other than our own spirit selves who see our lives and judge them. This is when we need to exercise compassion and forgiveness for ourselves, if we are not to let our minds become attached to desire, regret, guilt and pain.

THE JOURNEY TO THE SPIRIT REALMS

As the soul comes to terms with its death, it reorientates its newly disembodied self in the spirit world, where suddenly there are no boundaries. Where there is no physical world, there is no hunger, taste, warmth or cold. In one way there is nothing to fear, because there is no physical pain, no sickness and no more death. The mind, however, does not always find it so easy to be in a place where there are no sure boundaries, no duality between light and dark. The mind does not easily let go; it usually clings to the past sensations of the body in order to feel safe. It can also still feel connected to many desires of the physical world. These can be virtually anything at all. It is naturally difficult to leave a partner behind, but even the joy of an early morning sunrise, a favourite record collection or just walking the dogs across muddy heathland can be hard to part with.

In the book *The Return of Arthur Conan Doyle* (The White Eagle Publishing Trust, 1963) the deceased author of the Sherlock Holmes novels describes his visions of life after death. He had promised to return after his death to explain what it is like in the otherworld. After death he found that every soul passed through a period which he believed might be long or short, depending on their mental attitude when they left their body: 'It is to do with escaping from the physical attachments.' Many souls found it difficult to let go.

To ensure a safe passage to the otherworld, the soul seeks a connection. In the myths of Greece and ancient Rome it was the ferryman or guardian of the dead who guided souls across the river Styx. Upon reaching the distant shore, or underworld, the soul was guided to the god Mercury, who in astrological terms demonstrates an understanding of mind or consciousness. Before the soul could travel on from the underworld it had to drink of the water of Lethe or forgetfulness. This enabled it to forget its pain and sorrow, the scars borne from war, hatred and death.

For most souls journeying into the spirit realms the first thing that happens is they meet a spirit. This may be a family member, a friend, an ancient ancestor, an angel or spirit guide. It is just as if one is being met at the airport after a journey.

There is an abundance of spirit allies and helpers within the realms who help us with our journey to eternity. Many of them come to us whilst we are alive and help us through their love, encouragement, inspiration and guidance. They are with us in times of need and at the birth or death of loved ones. Whether we recognize that they are there to help us is another thing; often we ignore them.

Each person has a main spirit helper who is classified as their best friend within the spirit world; this could be a relative, a friend or a spirit guide. Then there is a wider circle of spirits who come and help each individual and the ancestral family groups who help the collective family.

However, a person who has died not knowing what to expect in death can become somewhat confused when passing over to the other side. They may fail to recognize the spirit who has come to help them pass them over, ignore them or just not see them. They find themselves with all the same mental faculties and attitudes that they had when alive, yet they realize that they can no longer communicate with the living and soon discover that they cannot be seen by them. For a person with no belief in life after death, this experience can be shattering. Yet those who are aware that there is a soul will simply move forward into the spirit realms.

Robert, a Christian lay preacher from America, explains:

Everyone should be entitled to a spiritual dimension and this is something which has to be taught. We have to learn it as children because if you are not taught some kind of spirituality as a child, it is hard to make it become second nature, so death is death. Many of us are not prepared for it and it comes like a thief in the night. And this is how people can become earthbound, unable to move into the Kingdom of God.

Those who do become earthbound must learn to shift for themselves or they will continually wait for someone to come and rescue them. They may take any of several courses of action, the most typical being that they stay in their home, or take up residence in their favourite bar, or move in with living family or friends. At worst they may remain in the hospital where they died or in the cemetery where they were buried.

What can you do to avoid becoming earthbound?

1   Have a spiritual belief with a theme of transcendence threaded through it, the belief in religious archetypes such as Buddha, Jesus Christ, Krishna and the various saints, martyrs, angels, gods and goddesses.
2   Be open minded about the spirit world and spirit beings that might be met at the point of death.
3   Have given some thought to what happened to your ancestors and which one may be taking care of your welfare.
4   Notice the light which shines momentarily, calling the spirit home at the point of death.

5   Recognize yourself as a soul in the physical death state.

6   Notice the sadness and grief of loved ones pained by your departure, letting their tears release you from the attachment of being alive.

7   Observe the ancestors calling, 'Come with us now' from the graveside after the rituals of funeral and burial.

8   Just believe that there is a life after death.

THE SPIRIT REALMS

FIRST DEATH – THE AWAKENING

When the ego leaves the body at the moment of death, it leaves behind it the lower principles and passes onward to the spiritual realms. Mind, body and soul separate and the person becomes a disembodied soul, awaiting a further separation of the sheath or skin which held the spirit bodies and the physical body together. Gradually this takes place and the inner self is housed in the astral body. Most people at this point are taken into the astral realm, some to the lower astral and others towards the higher astral worlds such as in the 'Summerland' or the celestial spheres.

The astral body is the exact counterpart of the physical body but is composed of a finer quality of matter. It is invisible to the ordinary vision, but may be seen by a clairvoyant or psychic. Many psychics describe the astral as rising from the physical like a cloud of thin luminous vapour, which remains connected to the physical body by a slender, silken, vaporous cord. The cord becomes thinner and thinner until it becomes invisible even to the psychic or clairvoyant. In death it breaks entirely from the physical body. The astral body exists in this form for some time and under certain circumstances it becomes visible to the living as a ghost or earthbound spirit.

Now the soul goes through an experience like a death. This is the 'insight', when it sees its entire life pass before it in a mental hologram image. The memory gives up its secrets and picture after picture passes before the mind. Many things are made clear to the departed soul. It has to see the meaning behind its life and how it has experienced all of it.

The soul may then hear a peculiar noise, after which it finds itself moving through a long dark passage. This is the labyrinth of network roadways leading from one realm to another. The speed may be fast or slow, but the soul does not touch the passage walls and is not afraid of falling. As it emerges from the tunnel it may see a brilliantly lit place of exquisite beauty where it may meet and talk with friends and relatives who have died. This place is called the Summerland. The soul may then be interviewed by a being of light or a being of darkness. There is no judgement as such, but an opportunity for the soul to see and feel how its life has been.

In death we go where our spirit takes us; we are carried by whatever is within our hearts to the realms where we are most at home.

THE REALMS

The spirit world is divided into spheres or realms. These are arranged into a series of bands, forming a number of concentric circles around the Earth. These circles reach out into the infinity of space and are invisibly linked with the Earth.

The Earth world lies approximately at the centre of the realms, with the spheres subdivided laterally to correspond broadly with the various nations of the Earth. Each of the national subdivisions of the spirit realms bears the characteristics of its earthly counterpart. So a soul from Iceland would expect to see a world of lava and ice while a rainforest Indian would experience a rainforest environment.

The realms begin at the heart of the Earth, within the centre or core, with a place we in the Christian world refer to as hell, because of its connotations of fire, burning and darkness. They reach into the highest celestial realm, which is located closest to the sun, a place of light and

There is a light that shines beyond all things on Earth, beyond us all, beyond the heavens, beyond the highest, the very highest heavens; this is the light that shines in our heart.

Chandogya Upanishad

peace. Life on the lower realms is very similar to Earth life, while the higher realms are more ethereal. The low realms of darkness are situated close to the Earth plane and it is through these that many souls pass by when they die. Many believe that they are led past these places with their eyes shut so they do not have to see the hideousness that the human world has cast into these dark realms. They are believed to be filled with the corruption, pain and the emotions of all the peoples of the Earth.

The realms are encompassed by the cosmic web. This connects all life. It is like an electrical grid – each part is alive with power and life. Whenever disconnections and blockages occur, the power cannot flow.

Many indigenous people see the interrelationship of the cosmic web and the inner worlds as complex and various. In contrast our perception of the spirit kingdoms is very simple: up for heaven, down for hell and in between purgatory. We see this idea reflected in Dante's *The Divine Comedy*, where Dante is accompanied by the classical poet Virgil on a tour of a Lowerworld, defined as hell, and a Middleworld, defined as purgatory, before being led by Beatrice into an Upperworld, defined as paradise.

The veil that separates the commonwealth of spirits from the human condition is very thin. It is a latticed tapestry in appearance similar to a gigantic spider's web. This invisible meshwork is marked by frontiers between dominions of each realm.

The kingdoms in general are split into seven categories from the bottom to the top, from hell to heaven/celestial kingdom:

The Celestial Realm

The Causal Realm

The Summerland

The Astral World

The Lower Astral

The Sub Astral

Hell

They are similar to countries, with frontiers and their own laws. Each realm has its own resident ruler who belongs to a higher sphere than that over which they preside. Only those who have had long residence in the spirit world hold the office. Many of them have been there for thousands of years. A great spirituality or understanding of the light is not enough to rule the realms, particularly the ones closest to the Earth itself. The rulers must possess a great deal of knowledge and experience of humanity and the nature kingdoms, and in addition they must always be able to exercise wise discretion in dealing with the various matters that come up in those realms, to be able to create a realm that functions within the laws of creation.

Each sphere or realm is completely invisible to the inhabitants of the spheres below it and in this respect at least it provides its own boundary. In journeying to a lower realm one sees the terrain gradually degenerating. As we draw towards the higher realms just the opposite happens: the land becomes more ethereal, more refined. This forms a natural barrier to those who have not yet progressed sufficiently to become inhabitants of that realm.

When a human soul attempts to journey from one realm to another, particularly when they are not ready, they encounter a natural barrier. This helps the soul to know its own journey. The journey may take a very long time for some, whilst others are able to surrender themselves to the higher levels very quickly.

To pass from this realm where I live to the next higher, I shall find myself walking along gently rising ground. As I proceed I shall see all the unmistakable signs, and feel them, of a realm of greater spiritual refinement. There will eventually come a point in my walking when I can go no further because I shall feel most uncomfortable spiritually. If I should be foolish enough to try to defy these feelings, I should, at length, find that I was completely unable to venture a foot forward without undergoing sensations which I could not possibly bear. I should not be able to see anything before me, only that which lay behind me. But whether we are standing at one of the boundaries, or whether we are well within the confines of our own realm, there comes a certain line in the bridge between the realm where the higher realm becomes invisible. Each realm possesses a higher vibrational rate than that below it, and is therefore invisible and inaudible to those who live below it. It is a natural law that operates for the good of the souls who live within each realm.

Anthony Borgia, *Life in the World Unseen* (M.a.p. Inc., 1993)

To enter a higher level the soul must experience a death, in this case a death of the self. It must let go and surrender to the higher good or God. The only other time when a soul may enter a higher level is when it is invited by the spirits from a higher level to enter into their realm. This happens more frequently in the darker realms where the soul may feel captive and need to be released.

THE JOURNEY THROUGH THE REALMS

THE ASTRAL PLANES

The astral world in which man awakens after death may be described as an inner or finer world. This world is not far away 'above the bright blue sky' but in a subtle way interpenetrates the physical world while remaining invisible because it vibrates at a higher rate.

The astral realms range from a dark sordid replica of the coarsest and crudest Earth conditions to a place of breathtaking beauty, known as the Summerland, filled with buildings, homes, schools, universities and temples of learning or wisdom.

In the astral realms, the soul awakens to surroundings which reflect its habitual thought life. If this thought life has been stormy, bitter, angry or resentful, the conditions in the astral world will closely reflect it. The lower astral realms are filled with souls of an undeveloped mind who live

Death is not an end; it is a stage in the cycle that leads onto rebirth. After death, the human soul is said to rest in 'Summerland' the land of eternal youth, where it is refreshed, grows young, and is made ready to be born again.

Starhawk, *The Spiral Dance* (HarperSanFrancisco, 1979)

Soul Rescuers

very similar lives to those lived on Earth. They are so closely connected with the world that many are unable to let it go and some are earthbound spirits, hanging around the old scenes of their earthly lives. These spirits can haunt the homes of people and masquerade at séances, often claiming to be some well known and celebrated person. They play silly pranks and use the living to satisfy their own desires.

If on the other hand, the soul habitually delights in all that is good and true and compassionate, it then awakens to the Summerland, a world rich in beauty. The Summerland can be acknowledged as a step up from this physical world of conflict as well as a rise in consciousness away from the denser astral worlds. It is in this realm that the place of the ancestors exists and it is from here that all the beloved family and friends communicate with the living.

In the realms there is an organized system of natural and universal law, which controls the spirits; all births, deaths, and rebirths. There is a policing system which includes the judges and lords of death who ensure the protection of those who are innocent and the discipline of those who choose evil or negative acts as their path.

In the book *The Autobiography of a Yogi* the Hindu saint and master Sri Yukteswar returns from the astral realms to describe them to his pupil Pahramansa Yogananda. He says they are made up of many, many worlds populated by astral beings who can dematerialize or materialize their form at will and travel using astral planes or light faster than electricity:

The ordinary astral universes are peopled with millions of astral beings who have come, more or less recently, from the Earth and also with myriads of spirits all residing on different astral planes in accordance with karmic qualifications. Various spheric mansions or vibratory regions are provided for good and evil spirits. Good ones can travel freely, but the evil spirits are confined to limited zones.

I am so pleased that I had even a little knowledge of the higher life for when I reached there, my spiritual eyes were open and I could see and realize the beauties of the spirit world. I have met many of my dear friends on the spirit side of life, many of whom I knew are still in darkness, and I have tried to help them understand their transition. If I could only express the conditions on the spirit side of life so that you would get the full meaning! There is such beauty, such harmony!

Anna Wickland, quoted in Dr Wickland, *Thirty Years among the Dead* (The Spiritualist Press, 1952)

Emma Restall Orr believes that:

The dead go through layers of energetic reality and those layers become increasingly detached from manifest reality, from matter. You may be only just over the edge, still be attached to the physical form, usually through trauma. Then you get further out and you still hold a memory of your lives and you can go backwards and forwards between each realm. Then you go beyond this and you lose the ability to return, except by choice when you want to reincarnate. As you get further and further out your choices get wider and wider – you become more spirit and less soul.

THE SECOND DEATH – THE AWAKENING

The soul will shuttle between the Earth plane and the astral plane until there is no more earthly karma to perform. Then it is able to move on. It may remain in the astral for thousands of years before it is ready or willing to undergo the death of its astral self, but finally, feeling the urge to seek deeper understanding, it will see a light on the distant mountains and be drawn towards it. So it will continue its journey through to eternity.

This 'second death', when the soul moves on from the astral is called the Great Awakening. The astral body, or 'astral shell' is discarded. It is nothing more than a corpse of finer material, with no life or intelligence without the soul mind or self, so when it is left behind, sometimes it becomes a spectre or floating form which people sometimes see as a ghost. Gradually this breaks down.

When the last possible remnant of the lower mentality has dropped away from the soul it awakens to a higher mental and spiritual state. It will stay in a dream-like state for a short time whilst it is casting off sheaths like the petals of a rose, one after the other, from the outer to the inner, then, when it wakes, it sees truth revealed and for a moment it gains a spiritual vision. This is an important evolutionary point for the soul as it begins to realize who it is and becomes aware of the order of the universe. The first level is the intellectual realization of eternity, then there is the intuitional realization and finally the place of peace before the light pulls the soul away from the mind into the inner core of peace and wisdom, the first level of the higher realms.

This is like the splitting through the skin of the self-protective veil which houses the full content of the human experience, its lessons and their memories. This final separation of the mental body from the astral is not painful. In fact it is a gentle way of shaking free from the past and the heaviness of human life.

For the advanced soul, this letting go or separation from the conscious awareness of human life is easy, due to its ability to let go of personal issues and ascend. Less evolved souls, beholden to personal experience, will seek to dwell in the arena of earthly lifestyle in order to complete or solve the mystery of unfinished business. In this way a soul becomes embroiled in the problems of the world and moving on out of it becomes less important. After a time the opportunity to move out of a limbo state into an altered consciousness causes the soul to realize that it is able to move on from the first frontier.

The first level of understanding is in the causal realm, the realm of the mind.

THE CAUSAL REALM

The mental or causal realm is called the Devachan, 'Shining Land' by the Theosophists. It is also termed Devasthan, 'Land of the Gods' in Sanskrit. It is the Svarga of the Hindus and the heaven of the Zoroastrians. It has been called the nirvana of the common people. In its true form it is the world of thought.

This is the realm from which all sorrow and evil are excluded by the great spiritual beings that guide and protect human evolution. It is a blissful resting-place where souls can assimilate the fruits of their physical lives and purify their visions and mental ambitions. Buddhists and

Here is where much important work is done to spread spiritual influence and higher knowledge in the human world. In addition they have a great field of work in connection with those whom we call dead.

A. E. Powell, *The Mental Body* (The Theosophical Publishing House, 1967)

Hindu seers speak of trees of gold and silver with jewelled fruits and the Jews describe it as a golden Jerusalem with streets paved with gold; this is how the mental realm appears to the soul, the first vision of heaven.

Here the soul develops the mind and grows beyond it to the point of great wisdom and understanding. Here artists indulge their love for their art, intellectuals pursue their studies, and so on. There is the opportunity to gain knowledge. Yet finally this is the place of having no more to learn, of learning how to be in a state of bliss. This is the essence of life in this higher realm. It is a place where the soul can dream.

THE CELESTIAL REALMS – THE HEAVENS

The causal realm is the first of the heavenly realms, but there are others higher still, places of unparalleled beauty and peace, reaching finally into the celestial kingdom or the place of the gods. To enter into the heavenly spheres, the soul must be developed to the point of purity and love, drawing the soul into the light.

Thine own consciousness shining, void, and inseparable from the great body of radiance, hath no birth or death.

The Tibetan Book of the Dead

In the Hebrew tradition, the word for 'heaven' is often used in the plural, Shemaim. The Muslims believe that there are seven levels in heaven and that the soul slowly and gradually moves through these levels until it reaches eternity. In the Koran each heaven is presided over by a prophet of the past and has a planet assigned to it. The lowest heavenly level is governed by the moon whilst the upper heaven, the seventh heaven, is governed by Saturn. This is very similar to the Hindu chakra system, with each one representing a realm or plane which is governed by a planet and has its own vibration, colour, master and power.

In the New Testament heaven becomes a place where the good souls will live after death as a reward, but the judgement of individual souls is not as heavily emphasized as it is in Judaism and Islam. In the Hindu system it is believed that the good soul waits for her divine Lord to arrive before dawn. He knocks on the door of the heart and when he is inside,

Soul Rescuers

peace and joy reign. So heaven is in the heart.

The spirit beings who reside in these realms are keepers of wisdom, peace and love. They are principally concerned with the evolution of creation and many return to work within the lower kingdoms and the Earth to support the journey of other souls.

In the majority in this kingdom are the angels, great light beings who offer an enormous amount of encouragement and safety within the physical world as well as the guidance in the spirit realms. Some serve as messengers or carry the dead into the heavenly worlds. There are also angelic beings who return to help those who need to be rescued. These spirits are called the watchers.

In the Book of Enoch in the Old Testament, Enoch was a patriarch who was 365 years old when God decided to bring him to heaven to be a scribe. One day when Enoch was sleeping two angels appeared in the form of huge radiant beings with brilliant golden wings. They shone like the sun and had burning bright eyes and lips of fire. They awakened him and took him off to heaven on their wings. The mysteries of creation were then revealed to Enoch; he was shown seven heavens and seven corresponding Earths, all united to each other by hooks (these are the realms). Beyond the seventh heaven were three more heavens. Each heaven was ruled by an angel and was a discrete domain.

The first heaven was ruled by the archangel Gabriel and was closest to Earth. It related also to the elements, so there were angels there who were astronomers and ruled the stars and heavenly bodies as well as angels who were guardians of ice, flowers, dew and stone.

The second heaven was ruled by Raphael and was a dark penal area in which fallen angels awaited judgement.

The third heaven was ruled by Anahel. It was a land of contrasts – one part hellish and filled with torturing angels who punished the evil souls who resided there and the rest an Eden, a garden where the souls of the righteous and compassionate resided, watched over by the angels of light. This third heaven resembles the astral world – one half in the Summerland and governed by light, the other in the lower astral and filled with shadows and pain.

The fourth heaven, according to Enoch, was governed by Michael. It contained Holy Jerusalem and its Temple, all made of gold and surrounded by rivers of milk and honey. The Tree of Life was believed to be here as well as the sun and moon.

The fifth heaven was another prison, a fiery ravine where the angelic watchers or Grigori were imprisoned. These angels were charged with watching the world, but descended from heaven to marry mortal women, thus incurring God's wrath.

In reality the watchers are important angels who work for the order of good, justice and universal law, and the evolution of man on Earth. They are light beings, junior angels, who come and go in the spirit realm, walking among the spirits of the dead in disguise, waiting for the moment when the disembodied soul is ready to recognize a greater purpose. Their light will illuminate those souls that are ready to be drawn into their greater purpose and make headway in their journey towards eternity. The watchers can be found in all dark corners of the world where there is war, death, disease and suffering. This work is very dangerous because where there are watchers from the light there are also dark spirits who enjoy tempting the souls of the dead away from the light so they fall to even greater depths of the lower realms, remaining trapped there and hoping for a chance to buy their way out by serving in the ranks of the darker angels and demons. There is a battleground within the world of shadow, as it is a place of neither light nor complete darkness; it is the barren ground of the sub astral realm where the desire of the self is greater than the surrender to the light.

We have met these watchers and they have come to us. You can feel them when they come, they lock in the base of the spine, drawing themselves into the physical world. When they get close you can feel the pain and suffering they are carrying for the human souls they have rescued.

They can offload their raiment in the physical world, it looks like a thick dark shadow and it falls to the ground when they release it. Then you can see their true form as angels of light. You can often see that they have been injured by the blows of the dark spirits. These compassionate beings are like spies who when they need to escape from the darkness always return to the light in the celestial kingdoms.

The sixth heaven is full of scholarly angels, studying science, nature, astronomy, music, art and humanity. This place is like the mental realm where the power of the mind and its higher knowledge is developed. Here are the archangels as well as angels who rule over nature and angels who record all the lives and deeds of every human soul. This is the place where the akashic records are kept, the library holding information on every individual soul who has ever existed on Earth.

In the seventh heaven, Enoch found the higher angels such as the thrones, cherubim, seraphim and dominions of angels. This is a place of innocence and light, where the mind is surrendered to become one with the heart.

Then Gabriel took Enoch to the eighth and ninth heavens. In the eight he saw the changer of the seasons and of the natural elements, and in the ninth, he saw the heavenly home of the 12 signs of the zodiac. The archangel Michael took him to the tenth heaven where he beheld the face of God, which burns like fire and throws off sparks of light. Enoch found the experience awesome and terrible! He eventually was summoned by the Lord to write the creation story and he became a heavenly scribe.

The story of Enoch was probably written by numerous anonymous authors in the first and second centuries AD. Although the Book of Enoch was declared apocryphal and fell into obscurity for 1,000 years it was rediscovered and is now looked upon as an important visionary experience describing the heavens and the influences of the angelic beings.

Many angels come to assist us in our journey in the otherworld. They have been present throughout history and have frequently been seen by mystics, masters and saints from all races. As well the odd visitation to the ordinary person in times of need, angels are messengers of God who inspire those who have been in contact with them. They have been seen by people both in dreams and visions and in particular during near death experiences. They have brought the miracles of healing and many times been seen by soldiers on battlefields. In all probability the survivors of battles have seen the angels come for their comrades lost in the cause of war. The angel of mercy or death has been evident in rescuing the souls of the dead.

REBIRTH

When I was brought down to Earth, I did not enter a woman's womb but I was taken into a room. There I remained, conscious at all times. One day I heard the noise of little children outside and some other sounds, so I thought I would go outside. Then it seemed to me that I went through a door, but I was really being born again from a woman's womb. As I walked out I was struck by the sudden rush of cold air and I began to cry.

A Winnebago shaman describes his birth

Some souls choose to reincarnate to undertake more karmic lessons or to help those who are still alive. Death and birth are both doorways between the spirit and the physical worlds. In some traditions, birth is actually considered more traumatic for the soul than dying. The knowledge of life in eternity is already within the spirit of each individual, but we forget it as we come into physical life, so we can learn who we are and what is within our hearts while being alive before returning and taking the long journey home.

Very few people can remember their previous lives, but the sages can recognize a person who has an 'old soul' by their noble conduct and kindness, a higher way of being. A divine spirit may also be born as a child, but such a child will always know its divine nature.

Shamans, priests and mystics have to go into their own experience of death and resurrection to know their own spirit and then learn how to communicate and heal with the power of the spirit world. They understand that to know their own soul is to be in touch with immortality. The soul is an essence that animates life. It is the non-material entity inside each individual. The soul is individual; the spirit is of the cosmos.

While the soul undertakes the journey from the physical state of death, through birth, life, death and then rebirth, it gradually increases its conscious awareness. It reaches a point of safety, peace and recognition where there is no fear, no guilt and no remorse for any of its actions. There is the 'knowing'. This is how the soul matures; it has found the key to its survival on its long journey home. When the recognition does not happen, then the cycle of life will draw the soul back to the lesson that stopped its progress. Life is a cycle. It has movement and flow, like a river snaking its way through the land back to the sea. The individual is never really prevented from journeying home; some souls just take longer than others, that is all.

There are places of healing to restore the damaged soul and enable its journey to continue, expanding and growing by every step and every moment of contemplation and healing.

Many people who have completed their journey choose to return and help those on their way home. We call them mystics, leaders, prophets and visionaries.

Then Aslan turned to them and said: 'You do not yet look so happy as I mean you to be.'

Lucy said, 'We're so afraid of being sent away, Aslan. And you have sent us back into our own world so often.'

'No fear of that,' said Aslan. 'Have you not guessed?'

Their hearts leaped and a wild hope rose within them.

'There was a real railway accident,' said Aslan softly. 'Your father and mother and all of you are – as you used to call it in the Shadowlands – dead. The term is ended: the holidays have begun. The dream is ended: this is the morning.'

And as he spoke He no longer looked to them like a lion; but the things that began to happen after that were so great and beautiful that I cannot write them. And for us this is the end of all the stories, and we can most truly say that they all lived happily ever after. But for them it was only the beginning of the real story. All their life in this world and all their adventures in Narnia had only been the cover and the title page: now at last they were beginning Chapter One of the Great Story which no one on earth has read: which goes on forever: in which every chapter is better than the one before.

C. S. Lewis, *The Last Battle*

RESOURCES

There is no official body to co-ordinate the work of soul rescuers, neither nationally nor internationally. If anyone is interested in setting up such an organization, or if there are practitioners of soul rescue who are able and willing to respond to overseas enquiries, please contact Terry and Natalia O'Sullivan at their publishers, Thorsons.

BIBLIOGRAPHY

Joseph Campbell with Bill Moyers, *The Power of Myth*, Mainstreet Books/Doubleday

Denise and John Carmody, *Shamans, Prophets and Sages*, Wadsworth, 1985

Hereward Carrington and Nandor Fodor, *The Story of the Poltergeist*, Rider & Co., 1953

Ivan Cooke, *The Heavens Are Ringing*, White Eagle Publishing Trust, 1966

Marian Roalfe Cox, *An Introduction to Folklore*, David Nutt, 1904

The Dalai Lama, *The Joy of Living and Dying in Peace*, Thorsons, 1998

Paul Devereux and Ian Thompson, *The Ley Hunter's Companion*, Thames and Hudson, 1979

Arthur Findlay, *The Way of Life*, Psychic Press Ltd, 1956

Arthur Findlay, *On the Edge of the Etheric*, Psychic Press Ltd, 1977

Folklore Myths and Legends of Britain, Readers Digest, 1973

J. G. Frazier, *The Golden Bough*, Macmillan Press Ltd, 1976

Funk and Wagnell, *Folklore Mythology and Legend*,
    HarperCollins*Publishers*, 1984

Stewart Gordon, *The Paranormal World*, Headline, 1992

Tom Graves, *The Elements of Pendulum Dowsing*, Element Books, 1997

Eric Maple Hale, *Supernatural England*, 1988 edition

Marie de Hennezel, *Intimate Death*, Little, Brown and Company, 1998

Lobzang Jivaka, *The Life of Milarepa*, John Murray, 1962

Elisabeth Kübler-Ross, *The Wheel of Life*, Bantam Books

Elisabeth Kübler-Ross, *On Death and Dying*, Routledge, 1970

Maurice Lamm, *The Jewish Way in Death and Mourning*, Johnathan
    David, New York, 1969

The Larousse Dictionary of World Folklore, Larousse, 1996

Timothy Leary with R. U. Sirius, *Design for Dying*, Thorsons, 1997

C. S. Lewis, *The Screwtape Letters*, The Centenary Press, 1942

C. S. Lewis, *The Last Battle*, Lions/HarperCollins*Publishers*, 1990
    edition

Dr Kenneth McCall, *Healing the Family Tree*, 1982

Reverend Eugene Maorey, *Exorcism*, Whitford Press, 1998

Malachi Martin, *Hostage to the Devil*, Arrow, 1988 edition

David Humphreys Miller, *Ghost Dance*, Bison Books, 1985

Raymond Moody, *Life after Life*, Bantam Books, 1975

Vusumazulu Credo Mutwa, *Song of the Stars*, Station Hill Openings,
    South Africa, 1996

Alexandra David Neal, *Magic and Mystery in Tibet*, Thorsons, 1997

James H. Neal, *Jungle Magic*, Four Square, 1967

The New Natural Death Handbook, eds Nicholas Albery, Gil Eliot and
    Joseph Eliot of the Natural Death Centre, Rider, 1997

Elliot O'Donnell, *Ghosts Helpful and Harmful*, William Rider, 1924

Elliot O'Donnell, *Haunted People*, Rider and Co., 1955

A. E. Powell, *The Etheric Double*, Theosophical Publishing House, 1979

Dr Maurice Rawlings, *Beyond Death's Door*, Sheldon Press, 1979

The Return of Arthur Conan Doyle, ed. Ivan Cooke, White Eagle
Publishing Trust, 1980

Soygal Rinpoche, *The Tibetan Book of Living and Dying*, Rider

Malidoma Patrice Somé, *Of Water and the Spirit*, G. P. Putnam, New
York, 1994

Malidoma Patrice Somé, *The Healing Wisdom of Africa*, Thorsons,
1999

Lewis Spence, *An Introduction to Mythology*, G. C. Harral, 1921

Rodney Smith, *Lessons from the Dying*, Wisdom, 1998

The Tibetan Book of the Dead, trans. Robert Thurman, Thorsons, 1998

Guy Underwood, *The Pattern of the Past*, Pitman, 1969

Peter Underwood, *The Ghost Hunters*, Hale, 1985

L. A. Waddell, *Lamaism*, Heffer, 1894, reprinted 1959

C. A. Wickland, *Thirty Years Among the Dead*, Spiritualist Press, 1952

Parahhansa Yogananda, *Autobiography of a Yogi*

Thorsons

Directions for life